# Evidence for Hope: The search for sustainable development

## The story of the International Institute for Environment and Development

*Edited by*

*Nigel Cross*

Earthscan Publications Ltd
London • Sterling, VA

First published in the UK and USA in 2003 by Earthscan Publications Ltd

'The duty to hope: A tribute to Barbara Ward' Copyright © *Brian Johnson*
'Earthscan–Panos: favourite son, via cuckoo-in-the-nest, to friendly rival'
Copyright © *Jon Tinker*
'Globalization, civil society and governance: Challenges for the 21st century'
*Anil Agarwal* Copyright © Centre for Science and Environment
All other material Copyright © IIED 2003

ISBN:    1 85383 855 1 paperback
         1 85383 854 3 hardback

Typesetting by MapSet Ltd, Gateshead, UK
Printed and bound in Great Britain by Biddles Ltd, www.biddles.co.uk
Cover design by Danny Gillespie
Copy edited by Nina Behrman

For a full list of publications please contact:

Earthscan Publications Ltd
120 Pentonville Road, London, N1 9JN, UK
Tel: +44 (0)20 7278 0433
Fax: +44 (0)20 7278 1142
Email: earthinfo@earthscan.co.uk
Web: **www.earthscan.co.uk**

22883 Quicksilver Drive, Sterling, VA 20166-2012, USA

Earthscan is an editorially independent subsidiary of Kogan Page Ltd and
publishes in association with WWF-UK and the International Institute for
Environment and Development

A catalogue record for this book is available from the British Library

Library of Congress Cataloging-in-Publication Data

Evidence for hope : the search for sustainable development : the story of
the International Institute for Environment and Development, 1972–2002 /
edited by Nigel Cross.
        p. cm.
    Includes bibliographical references (p.   ) and index.
    ISBN 1-85383-855-1 (paperback) — ISBN 1-85383-854-3 (hardback)
    1.  International Institute for Environment and Development—History.
    2.  Sustainable development—History. I. Cross, Nigel, 1953–

HC79.E5 E95 2002
338.9'27—dc21

                                                    2002151418

This book is printed on elemental chlorine-free paper

# Contents

About the authors *v*
Chronology of key events *viii*
Acknowledgements *x*

Introduction *Nigel Cross* *xi*

## PART I BEGINNING WITH HOPE

1 Only one Earth, Stockholm 1972 *Barbara Ward* 3
2 The duty to hope: A tribute to Barbara Ward *Brian Johnson* 10
3 Stockholm: The founding of IIED *Maurice Strong* 19

## PART II THREE DECADES OF CHANGE AND DEVELOPMENT

4 Time for change: IIED 1984–1990 *Brian W Walker* 31
5 Earthscan–Panos: Favourite son, via cuckoo-in-the-nest, to friendly rival *Jon Tinker* 40
6 Change that works, sometimes *Richard Sandbrook* 60

## PART III IIED PROGRAMMES

7 Forestry and land use *Duncan Poore and Stephen Bass* 77
8 The energy programme *Gerald Leach* 96
9 Sustainable agriculture *Gordon Conway* 108
10 Setting an urban agenda: Human settlements and IIED-América Latina *David Satterthwaite* 122
11 Drylands: A history of networks *Camilla Toulmin* 147
12 Economics of environment and development *David Pearce and Ed Barbier* 172

13   Strategies, plans, impacts and people: IIED's role in
     changing the world of planning and environmental
     assessment *Barry Dalal-Clayton*                              189
14   Profit in need? Business and sustainable development
     *Nick Robins*                                                 204

## PART IV ENDPIECE

15   Globalization, civil society and governance: Challenges
     for the 21st century *Anil Agarwal*                           223

*Index of people*                                                  235

# About the authors

**Anil Agarwal**, the Director of the Centre for Science and Environment in India, died on 2 January 2002. One of the world's most inspiring and innovative environment and development specialists, he spent two years at IIED, helping to develop its information and media service Earthscan, before returning to India to set up the Centre for Science and Environment in Delhi in 1981.

**Edward Barbier** is currently a professor of economics at the University of Wyoming. He joined IIED in 1996, has been Director of the London Environmental Economics Centre, and has served as a consultant for a variety of national, international and non-governmental agencies, including many UN organizations and the World Bank.

**Stephen Bass** is an environmental planner and forester, and has worked in Western Asia, the Caribbean and Southern Africa. He joined IIED in 1990, specializing in the assessment, formulation and monitoring of participatory natural resource and forest policy. As IIED's Director of Programmes he is responsible for overall strategic programme development, research planning and quality control.

**Gordon Conway** is President of The Rockefeller Foundation in New York City. An agricultural ecologist with over 30 years of experience in development programmes in Asia and Africa, he was a pioneer of Integrated Pest Management in the 1960s and developed the concept of sustainable agriculture in the late 1970s. He joined IIED as Director of the Sustainable Agriculture Programme in 1986.

**Nigel Cross** is Executive Director of the International Institute for Environment and Development. A journalist and historian, specializing in development, he was the first director of the development agency SOS Sahel UK working in dryland Africa, and was Executive Director of the Panos Institute from 1995–1999.

**Barry Dalal-Clayton** is currently Director for Strategies, Planning and Assessment at IIED, London. In his 14 years to date at IIED, he has been a consultant to numerous aid agencies and UN organizations and has been an environmental adviser to the UK Department for International Development.

**Brian Johnson** has written and lectured extensively on developmental and environmental issues, both in Europe and in the United States. He is the former director of the Ecological Foundation, London, and of the Institute for the Study of International Organisations at the University of Sussex.

**Gerald Leach** joined IIED in 1974, after a first career as a science writer, editor and broadcaster. He ran the energy programme at IIED until early 1989. Since then he has been a senior research fellow of the Stockholm Environment Institute. During 1994–1996 he was an adviser to the World Bank on rural energy and is a long-time member of the UK government's Renewable Energy Advisory Committee.

**David Pearce** has since 1983 been Professor of Environmental Economics at University College London; from 1991 to date he has also been Director and then Associate Director of the Centre for Social and Economic Research on the Global Environment (CSERGE) at University College London and the University of East Anglia. He is the author and co-author of some 50 books, including *Blueprint for a Green Economy*.

**Duncan Poore** is a classicist turned scientist. He has worked at the interface between environment and economic land use in Europe, the Middle East, Malaysia, as Director of the Nature Conservancy (Great Britain) and as Professor of Forest Science in Oxford. In 1983, he set up the Forestry and Land Use Programme in IIED. He now works closely with the International Tropical Timber Organization.

**Nick Robins** is Head of Research in the Socially Responsible Investment team at Henderson Global Investors in London. He worked at IIED from 1993 to 2000 on European policy and trade as Director of the Sustainable Markets Group. He has advised the UK Departments for the Environment and International Development, the Norwegian Ministry of the Environment, the OECD's Environment Directorate, UNEP and UNIDO.

**Richard Sandbrook** joined IIED in 1976 following the Stockholm conference on the Human Environment as Vice President for Policy

(1983), Executive Director for Europe (1986), and Executive Director overall (1989–1999). He has extensive experience in the politics of international development and the environment. He is project coordinator of the Mining Minerals and Sustainable Development project for the World Business Council for Sustainable Development.

**David Satterthwaite**, in addition to his role as Director of the Human Settlements Programme at IIED, where he has worked since 1974, is Editor of the international journal *Environment and Urbanization*. He also teaches at the University of London and the London School of Economics, and has advised on urban environmental issues for the Brundtland Commission, WHO, UNICEF, UNCHS, DfID and SIDA.

**Maurice Strong** has had a long and distinguished career in international governance. He is special adviser to the United Nations Secretary-General and is Rector of the UN University for Peace. He has served as Executive Director for UNEP and was Secretary General of the UN Conference on Environment and Development in Rio in 1992.

**Jon Tinker** joined IIED in 1974, as director of Earthscan. In 1986 he established the Panos Institutes, through which much of the early philosophy of IIED continues to be manifested. He is presently a Senior Associate at the Sustainable Development Research Institute, University of British Columbia.

**Camilla Toulmin**, an economist by training, has worked mainly in francophone West Africa, on agricultural, pastoral and tenure issues. She joined IIED in 1987, to set up the Drylands Programme, having worked formerly for ILRI and ODI. She was a member of the International Expert Panel supporting the preparation of the Convention to Combat Desertification.

**Brian W Walker** is a consultant in ecology and development. He was Director-General of Oxfam, President of IIED and Executive Director of Earthwatch Europe.

**Barbara Ward**, co-founder and President of IIED was a pioneer in the field of sustainable development, a concept she did much to articulate and tirelessly promote. She was an author, scholar, a friend and adviser of the world's decision-makers, and one of the 20th century's most persuasive voices calling for a rational sharing of resources between rich and poor nations and peoples.

# Chronology of key events

1971 Founding of International Institute for Environmental Affairs (IIEA), Aspen, Chairman Robert Anderson, President Jack Raymond (1971–1973)

1972 Publication of *Only One Earth*, by Barbara Ward and René Dubos

1972 United Nations Conference on the Human Environment, Stockholm, June

1973 International Institute for Environment and Development (IIED) established, London and Washington DC (formerly the IIEA, Aspen), Chairman Robert Anderson, President Barbara Ward (1973–1980)

1974 Gerald Leach establishes IIED's Energy Programme

1976 Earthscan established within IIED as an independent news and information service

1976 HABITAT, the first UN Conference on Human Settlements, Vancouver

1977 Jorge Hardoy establishes the IIED Human Settlements Programme, formed by a network of Southern institutions

1979 IIED opens an office in Buenos Aires, which later becomes IIED Latin America, an independent non-profit organization

1980 William Clark becomes President of IIED (1980–1984)

1983 Forestry and Land Use Programme of IIED established by Duncan Poore

1985 Brian W Walker becomes President of IIED (1985–1989)

1986 The IIED Sustainable Agriculture Programme established by Gordon Conway

1986 Earthscan Director Jon Tinker leaves IIED and establishes the Panos Institutes

1987 IIED Drylands Programme established by Camilla Toulmin

1988 IIED's Washington office merges with the World Resources Institute

1989 Richard Sandbrook becomes Executive Director of IIED (1989–1999)

1989 IIED establishes what becomes the Environmental Economics Programme

1992 IIED plays a key role in preparations for the Earth Summit in Rio de Janeiro

1999 Nigel Cross becomes Executive Director of IIED

2000 IIED launches the Minerals, Mining and Sustainable Development Project

2001 IIED celebrates its 30th anniversary with an international workshop and conference entitled 'Equity for a small planet'

# Acknowledgements

Without the cooperation and forbearance of the contributors, this book would not have been possible. Individuals have responded to my queries and editorial comments with great patience. Not everyone who was invited to contribute accepted, and some who agreed to contribute were, for one reason or another, unable to do so. This led to some unavoidable delays.

The past is not a firm place, and I have allowed conflicting memories to coexist. All contributors give a vivid and textured account of their time at IIED. We are still around, and 30 years or so from now there will be a second edition. I owe a special debt to David Satterthwaite, David Runnalls and Richard Sandbrook, who have always been ready with anecdotes and advice on the history of this unique institution. Above all, I must thank Liz Aspden, who has been the link between the chapter authors and has been ever hopeful that we would make it into print.

*Nigel Cross*
*November 2002*

# Introduction

## EVIDENCE FOR HOPE

*Sustainable development is development that meets the needs of the present without compromising the ability of future generations to meet their own needs.* The World Commission on Environment and Development, *Our Common Future*, 1987.

The first of the international development and environment summits was held at Stockholm in 1972 – the UN Conference on the Human Environment – bringing together different disciplines in a common cause. Twenty years later Stockholm was followed by the Rio Earth Summit and ten years after that by the World Summit on Sustainable Development at Johannesburg. Such international events have fuelled a major debate about the impacts of consumption and growth on our social, economic and natural environments. Some fear the world is on a binge that will lead to unimaginable disaster and conflict, others argue that we cannot afford a clean and peaceful planet without rising incomes and a strong commitment to market-based policies.

Each summit is a milestone. It is difficult to make sense of the everyday mass of opinion, opinion dressed as fact, and naked fact. Who has the answers – the skeptical environmentalists and economists who say the world is better place, that growth works, or the campaigners who see a distressed planet and over-consumption? Summitry, for all its flaws and hot air, offers a rare opportunity to catch up on controversy, debate and dialogue, which with luck and resolve might lead to a measure of international consensus on the state of the world and its imperatives.

# HISTORY

*Evidence for Hope* traces the ideas and ideals of sustainable development through the International Institute for Environment and Development (IIED).

Institutional history can be dull. This book is not framed around committee minutes, nor even around internal events – though these surface from time to time. Instead, a number of people associated with IIED were invited to describe their experiences and their ideas and relate these to today's issues. Thirty years is not a long time in the evolution of policy and global politics. In 1972 the Cold War and the Vietnam War were of paramount concern to the public, North and South, just as the global campaign for security is now. The environment and development concerns of 1972 – pressure on the global commons, the problems of food security, the impact of pollution, of desertification – are still with us today. Understanding the past is an obligation. The authors of the following chapters chart a history of sustainable development from Stockholm at the height of the Cold War, to Johannesburg in the age of globalization and ever more complex security concerns.

So why *Evidence for Hope*? It sounds a little like an evangelical tract – which to some extent it is. The goals of sustainable development are in part revealed religion (as many of the contributors make clear) and in part hard graft, using scientific methods to test hypotheses and establish verifiable conclusions. Hope is where we feel we must start from – indeed we wouldn't start without it. When IIED's President, Barbara Ward, died in 1981, a book called *A Bias for Hope* (1971) by Albert Hirschman, Professor of Political Economy at Harvard, was found on her shelves. Hirschman believed that the condition of the world, from economic, social and scientific perspectives pointed to a human ingenuity and creativity that had the power to shape a better planet for us all. Where Hirschman had the bias, Barbara, biased herself, recognized the importance of establishing the evidence, and saw IIED as a principal and principled investigator of the scientific, economic and social conditions necessary for sustainable development.

## BARBARA WARD AND THE FOUNDING OF IIED

IIED was born in the boardroom of a US oil company in 1971– an unlikely provenance for an agency committed to sustainable development, but then Robert O Anderson, CEO of Atlantic Richfield, was an unusual oilman. Chairman of the Aspen Institute and purchaser of the troubled *Observer* newspaper, he wanted to understand how his industry affected the planet, so he founded the Institute of International Environmental Affairs (IIEA) in New York, placing a *New York Times* journalist, Jack Raymond, at its helm. From the beginning the Institute was as much about information and communication as about research and policy.

IIEA's first task, commissioned by Maurice Strong, was to marshal the agenda for the Stockholm Conference on the Human Environment. A star speaker at Stockholm was Barbara Ward, Professor of International Economic Development at Columbia University. She was also one of the British great and good; a governor of the BBC, a former foreign editor of *The Economist*, a socialist and prominent Catholic, an adviser to presidents, prime ministers and the Pope.

For her, the recent moon landings and views of a blue planet Earth from space served to underline our vulnerability. She worried about a planet increasingly unfit for life, polluted rivers and oceans, unsustainable consumption, inequitable distribution: 'Stockholm has come at one of those moments when people are radically beginning to reconsider how they view their life on earth. It is only when people shake loose from their preconceptions that we get that sense of opening, of vision, of new directions that our planet most desperately needs. Nobody knows what the limits to growth are, but what is absolutely certain is that we cannot manage our future if two-thirds of us stay poor, so that one-third can stay rich' (Stockholm speech Chapter 1).

Anderson saw Barbara Ward as the ideal leader of his fledgling institute and she was persuaded to become President (an executive position) in 1973 in succession to Jack Raymond. She agreed on the condition that development as well as environment agendas would be integral to its mission. So IIEA became IIED with London headquarters – perhaps rather a grand word for its first address, the flat of David Runnalls, Barbara's research assistant and the second employee of the new IIED.

In the trajectory of organizations, there is nearly always a golden age, emerging from obscurity into the light of success, influence and approbation. Then things settle down into steady competence and delivery, or a more turbulent period of highs and lows. In the judgement of most IIED insiders – however much a tribute to Barbara Ward's vision the existing IIED may be – the most exciting times, when IIED was almost alone in its field, were the 1970s. As David Runnalls has pointed out, 'Barbara moved in the kind of circles and had the kind of access to world leaders that nobody has had since in the environment world.' She wrote briefings for Harold Wilson and Lyndon Johnson, speeches for Robert McNamara, Lester B Pearson and David Rockefeller. She also wrote a small library for sustainable development, beginning with *Only One Earth* prepared for the Stockholm Conference and ending with the hopeful title *Progress for a Small Planet*.

Barbara Ward (or Baroness Jackson as she had become) died in 1981. *Progress for a Small Planet* had on its cover the astronaut's view of Earth. One of the world's great forward thinkers, even Barbara Ward could not anticipate the strides we would take in damaging our ecosystem: the depletion of the ozone layer; Chernobyl spreading nuclear contamination for thousands of miles; human-made climate change leading to predicted temperature increases of between 1.5 and 6°C in the next few decades with a consequent exponential growth in natural disasters, flooding and environmental health hazards; and conflict over natural resources, not least oil and water.

In the 1970s IIED had been Barbara's organization. Not that she was an egoist; she was an unbeatable writer and thinker of great humility. (In this she resembles another posthumous contributor to this book, Anil Agarwal, the founder of the Centre for Science and the Environment in India, and an early associate of IIED.) Her legacy was a functioning and influential organization, staffed by her trusted lieutenants, including David Runnalls, Richard Sandbrook and David Satterthwaite.

## THE NEXT 20 YEARS

It was in the 1980s, under the leadership of first William Clark, a friend of Barbara's and a former vice-president of the World Bank, and then Brian W Walker, former head of Oxfam, succeeded by Richard Sandbrook, a founder of Friends of the Earth (UK), that IIED responded to the increasing complexity surrounding sustainable development. The clear message of Stockholm (which had led to the establishment of the United Nations Environment Programme) was the need to integrate environment and development. So many development problems and challenges could be traced to environmental causes. Energy, agriculture, drylands, human settlements, forestry, environmental economics – all were, and still are, key areas for IIED research. IIED built up a series of programmes to tackle such issues and was fortunate in attracting star-quality researchers.

It was also in the 1980s that IIED sorted out its working methods – collaborative research, participatory learning, and the combining of empirical research with policy analysis. In many ways IIED became what we would now call a 'virtual' organization. For everyone working out of London, there were dozens of collaborators around the world. Many organizations, particularly those based in the South, forged strong links with the institute, enabling it properly to refer to itself as international. Most important of all have been the hundreds of individual collaborators, scientists and social scientists, ecologists, economists, journalists and academics, who have worked with and through IIED and have contributed immeasurably to the ideal of sustainable development.

All this work was recognized in 1992 by the award of the first Blue Planet Prize for significant contributions to environmental policy and action. The citation noted IIED's 'outstanding achievement in establishing and implementing environmental policies, and realizing widely applicable research and development results'.

The 1990s also saw the beginning of IIED's engagement with the private sector. The development triad – government, business and civil society – had been around for a long time (think of the East India Company), but the creeping realities of globalization dawned on us only in the 1980s. IIED's first mature engagement with the private sector was a study of the paper industry, followed by research into an even tougher sector – mining. A consequence for IIED and the business sector has been a focus on corporate social responsibility. How can international business play a constructive role in sustainable development? This is now a major area for IIED research.

For IIED and the whole of the development community – in the fifth development decade since 1945, 30 years since Stockholm, 20 years since the Brandt Commission reported to a World Summit in Cancun, after the Live Aid/Band Aid mobilization of the public in the wake of the Ethiopian and Sahelian drought and famine in 1984/85 – the 1990s had to be a decade for delivery. After 20 years of research, analysis and practice, what could we conclude – what worked in development, what didn't? This became the focus of IIED's work, beginning with editorial and research support to the Brundtland Commission's, *Our Common Future*, which was to lead to the Rio Earth Summit in 1992.

Behind the summitry was the engagement (a key word for IIED) with the reality of life and agendas of the world's poorest and most marginalized citizens, many of whom feel they do not even have the basic rights normally accorded to citizen status – pastoralists, landless farmers, migrants, slum dwellers, indigenous peoples. At another level are the unempowered civil servants, locally and nationally, who are supposed to apply national and international rules, and to act as enforcers and regulators with pitiful resources and training. As Richard Sandbrook writes of IIED's brokerage role (see Chapter 6), 'We have to understand the bottom-up reality, life on the ground for hard-pressed communities, and connect their needs with the top-down processes that are trying to meet those needs. Applying oneself as the trusted intermediary between needs and sources of supply is not such a bad place to be in such an iniquitous and disconnected world.'

Readers of this book will see that IIED is not a perfect organization. Its work has always been financed through projects, and it has never enjoyed, save at the outset, any core funding or endowments, which has led to its various presidents and executive directors spending a lot of time with cap in hand. There has always been an element of creative anarchy, of opportunistic decision-making rather than strategic planning, and even, it has to be admitted, of arrogance (sometimes justified, sometimes not) – common to many organizations but which also contributes to the driving force and staff loyalty. As programmes developed their reputations, competition set in; by the 1990s IIED had become a house full of strong independent programmes, which occasionally collaborated, and occasionally battled with each other. But in recent years, the Institute has reasserted itself, thanks to the thinking time it has been able to achieve with support from the Swedish International Development Agency (Sida) and from the aid arm of the Royal Danish Ministry of Foreign Affairs. There is now very productive cross-cutting work between programmes and we are near to achieving Barbara Ward's vision – 30 years later – of being genuinely interdisciplinary. But we need to tell our story more loudly.

It will also be obvious from the list of contributors to this book that, for the last 30 years, we have been largely white, Northern and male. In this we are rather like our donors, though they would not all choose to admit it. But here is a challenge for the future: clearly debates about development cannot be set or managed, in the age of globalization, by middle-aged Northern men. The 2001 meeting of the

World Trade Organization (WTO) in Doha, illustrates the point – the environment and development agenda means different things to different societies and genders – and we have to reach accommodation if we are to agree global rules. If IIED is to play a new brokerage role, which requires trust, it has to realize the 'International' in its title. In the last few years we have internationalized our Board, and tried hard to recruit from all over the world. This is not simply political correctness, it is about recognizing the benefits of mixing cultures, and believing that we learn best by listening to and learning from one another. We do not claim the lion's share of the work as our own; we are facilitators and collaborators, not owners of research and analysis.

This book is intentionally anecdotal and people-centred: it is people who make institutions such as IIED work. For my own part, I first encountered IIED in 1983, making use of Alan Grainger's Earthscan report *Desertification* (1984), to understand the enormity of the challenge confronting the newly-minted NGO, SOS Sahel UK which I directed and which specialized in social forestry and natural resource management in the Sahel and Horn of Africa. We subsequently used Gerry Foley's and Geoff Barnard's *Farm and Community Forestry* (Earthscan 1984) as a handbook for our forestry extension staff in Sudan, Mali, Niger and Ethiopia. At around the same time IIED's President Brian Walker became chairman of the SOS Sahel board, joined by Ed Barbier who helped us to understand environmental costs.

When Camilla Toulmin joined IIED to set up the Drylands Programme in 1987, she held regular meetings for drylands and Sahelian buffs which were of great value in establishing a network for information sharing (and IIED has only very recently completed a joint project with SOS Sahel, learning from its experience in community management of natural resources). For SOS Sahel, an operational development agency working at the height of famine, drought and insecurity in the 1980s, IIED's work, its clear thinking and its myth-busting (perhaps most beautifully expressed in *Stoves and Trees* (Earthscan 1984) subtitled *How Much Wood would a Woodstove Save if a Woodstove could Save Wood?*) made it invaluable, a first port of call and a unique bridge between thinking and doing.

By coincidence, I followed in Jon Tinker's footsteps as Executive Director of the Panos Institute London (formerly Earthscan at IIED). My chairman this time round was Gerry Foley, no longer at IIED though IIED's assistant director Koy Thompson was a Panos board member. I finally had the privilege of joining IIED as Executive

Director in succession to Richard Sandbrook in 1999, some 15 years after I had first decided that this was a most peculiar, and most interesting organization. These apparent trails of coincidence are not, of course, so coincidental. It should come as no surprise that the acolytes of sustainable development should form a close, but not a closed, community.

Thirty years on from Stockholm is not such a long time, surely too short a time to allow cynicism to set in. We have achieved a lot, but not yet enough. The World Summit for Sustainable Development in Johannesburg was a chance for a generation to take stock, and leave a better legacy to the next generation; just as the Marshall Plan was the bequest of our grandparents' generation. As this book makes clear, it is now our time and our turn.

# PART I
# BEGINNING WITH HOPE

## 1

# Only one Earth, Stockholm 1972

## *Barbara Ward*

Are we present at one of those turning points when the human race begins to see itself and its concerns from a new angle of vision and, as a result, finds new openings for action, for courage and for hope?

When we were asked to prepare a conceptual framework for the Stockholm Conference, we didn't get a conceptual framework. What we got was something like standing under Niagra. This is a time when people's ideas about the planet they live in, about the way they have to live, about the way they can live, are changing in an absolutely monumental fashion. When we'd read through all the advice from experts from around the world, we noticed that not only the range of ideas and concepts, but also the ways in which even familiar ideas were framed, were new.

Stockholm has come at one of the moments when people are radically beginning to reconsider how they have to view their life on Earth, and what sense their existence makes to them. It is only when people begin to shake loose from their preconceptions and from the ideas that have dominated them, that you begin to get that sense of new directions which I think we would all agree our poor old planet most desperately needs.

Over two millennia ago, intellectual ferment accompanied the end of China's feudal war and the establishment of the first great centralized Han dynasty. In more recent times, people had almost to

---

This chapter is based on the transcript of Barbara Ward's speech at the 1972 Stockholm Conference on the Human Environment.

stand on their heads to realize that the Sun did not go round the Earth, but the reverse. This 'Copernican Revolution' is the archetype of fundamental change by which people learn to rethink, totally, their place in the scheme of things.

Our own epoch is, I believe, such an age again. We belong to the generation that has used radio telescopes to uncover 100,000 million other galaxies each with 100,000 million other suns. We belong to the generation that has brought nuclear energy to Earth. Computers have made possible the simulation, acceleration and forward projection of infinitely complicated human activities, and instantaneous worldwide and interplanetary visible and audible communication has opened new horizons.

Above all, we are the generation to see through the eyes of the astronauts the astonishing 'earthrise' of our small and beautiful planet above the barren horizons of the moon, Indeed, this generation would be some kind of psychological monstrosity if this were not an age of intense, passionate, committed debate and search.

So vast is the scale of change through which we live that there must be an equally vast range of competitors for first place as agents of upheaval. I want to suggest three areas in which, it seems to me, the concepts being virtually forced upon us offer a startling break from past patterns of thought and accepted wisdom.

## A PLANET UNFIT FOR LIFE

The first is the possibility of making the planet unfit for life. Hitherto, people have known that they could do local damage. They could farm carelessly and lose topsoil or deforest or overgraze or mine out a mineral. They also contrived to live through major natural disasters – earthquakes, tornadoes, ice ages. But nobody thought that the planet itself could be at risk.

Today our experts know something new. They know that air, soil and water form a totally interdependent worldwide system or biosphere sustaining all life, transmitting all energy and, in spite of its rugged powers of survival, full of immensely delicate and vulnerable mechanisms, leaves, bacteria, plankton, catalysts, levels of dissolved oxygen, thermal balances – which alone permit the Sun's searing energies to be transmuted and life to carry on.

Our experts also tell us what we do not know. Given our suddenly and vastly increasing numbers, our enormous rise in the use of energy, including nuclear energy, and our fabulous mastery of molecular chemistry, we impinge on the fine balances and mechanisms of the total system in ways and with consequences that we too often are in no position to judge.

For example, our traditional vision of the oceans is that they are boundless. But we have no idea of their capacity to absorb – as they ultimately must – virtually all the planet's wastes. In the last two or three decades, to give only one instance, a high percentage of the long-lived chlorinated hydrocarbons – including DDT – appears to have been absorbed into natural 'sinks' in the biosphere. Recent sample-taking suggests an unexpectedly high dosage appearing in the oceans.

Does this mean that natural storage systems are filling up? Will further effluents reinforce irreversible damage to marine species known to be susceptible to such substances as DDT?

Is this part of a deeper risk of deterioration from a steadily widening range of chemical wastes? We do not know. Rivers and lakes teach us that there are limits to water's self-cleansing properties. Ultimately the oceans are one vast cistern with no outlet. This image is a safer one, perhaps, than that of Keats' infinite and 'moving waters at their priestlike task of pure ablution round earth's human shores'.

## GROWTH IS NOT A SOLUTION

This concept of newly understood limits is relevant to the second reversal of earlier concepts whose implications I would judge to be most revolutionary for the present age. For over a century now, and with increasing enthusiasm in the last 25 years, we have seen in economic growth, measured by the satisfaction of both ordinary and induced material needs, a prime aim of national policy and a powerful solvent of social conflict. Inside the nation, as output and incomes rise, the flow of goods will be great enough to reward effort and enterprise and provide on an upward scale for the needs of the mass of the people. In the world economy, international trade and investment will pull the developing peoples up in the wake of the already developed nations.

But this implicit assumption of unending expansion has two self-reinforcing flaws. Even within the wealthiest states, even with all the transfers of resources from richer to poorer citizens secured by tax and welfare and social insurance, 'trickle down' economics do not ensure the ending of poverty at the base of society. The lowest 20 per cent can have as little as 5 per cent of national income; the top 20 per cent as much as 40.

In the world at large, where no systematic social transfers occur, the richer states are pulling away from the less developed ones. Even if $10,000 a year per capita is a reasonable likelihood for developed societies by the year 2000, for two-thirds of humankind, $400 a year looks like being the utmost reach of optimism. For perhaps a third, malnutrition, illiteracy, shanty-town dwelling and unemployment – in other words, the worst of all human environments – could be the most likely fate.

But now we must add another constraint. Even if we assume unlimited resources with which to develop, development is, as we have seen, grossly uneven. But suppose there are indeed strict physical 'limits to growth'? Suppose that these delicate mechanisms and balances in the biosphere that make life possible cannot sustain 10 billion people all aiming to produce and consume and discard and pollute according to present developed standards?

Here, admittedly, the range of debate is very wide. Some experts believe that 20 billion people can live at America's present standards simply on the products of atomic energy, water and the minerals in common rock. Others postulate irretrievable damage in terms of exhausted resources, thermal pollution, and environmental disruption if even half that number secure the current standards of the rich. We are at the beginning of this debate. But one point is surely clear. There are limits. The biosphere is not infinite. Populations must become stable. So must the demands they make.

But in that case, whose upward aspirations must first be checked? Given *finite* resources, we cannot evade this basic social issue. Where are the restraints to be put? What is to be reduced, the luxuries of the rich or the necessities of the poor? What are the priorities – a decent human environment for the whole human species or riches for some and squalor for the majority? We can slide over this fundamental issue of environmental quality only if 'trickle down' economics work within a context of unlimited resources. Neither assumption is correct. So, as nations, as a planet, we are compelled to confront the fundamental issues of choice and justice.

We have got to learn to live with a more modest use of resources and we cannot cheat by simply saying that we're going to carry on with the same division as we have now. If two-thirds of us stay poor so that one-third can stay rich, they won't do it. It is as simple as that.

## NATIONS ACTING TOGETHER TO AVERT DISASTER

But at this point we encounter a third basic challenge to our habits of thinking. Our effective instruments of judgement, decision and action are separate national governments. The nations give our planet its colour, its variety, its richness of life and experience. For those to whom full nationhood has come only in the last quarter of a century, it expresses the essence of their being and their hopes. None of this can be doubted. Yet it is also true that the cumulative effect of the separate actions of separate sovereign governments can, over time, injure the basic national needs of all of them.

If our airs and oceans can stand only so much strain before they lose their capacity for self-purification, it will help no government to say that others were responsible. The most flagrant case is clearly the risk of nuclear conflict and planetary nuclear pollution. (We may rejoice that a number of intergovernmental agreements now limit atomic testing in the air, keep nuclear weapons from the seabed, outer space and Antarctica. We can welcome, too, the agreements between the USA and the Soviet Union to check the arms race and hope that such agreements may signal the beginning of a joint effort to wind it down.)

But we could collectively pollute the planet not 'with a bang but a whimper' – by the small, steady accumulation of long-lasting poisons and pesticides, of chemicals and tailings, of eroded soil and detritus – and reach, almost inadvertantly, a creeping planetary disaster to which all have separately made their cumulative contribution. No single nation can avert this risk as numbers and activities rise. Its control will be achieved by nations acting together – or not at all.

This raises by another route the issue of planetary justice – which equally cannot be solved by nations acting alone. How do we ensure that the need to check pollution does not become an inhibition on the desperate need of two-thirds of humanity for development? This is an area about which we do not know too much. It is certainly not clear that all non-pollutive technologies are more expensive. It is also possible that in opting straight away for pollution control, developing states could take full advantage of the greatest asset of latecomers – to learn from other peoples' mistakes. Equally it is possible that to control wastes and effluents at an early stage of modernization would greatly add to costs and strains.

Should poorer countries then accept added costs for development or even their own modernization because developed nations have already, as it were, pre-empted so much of the biosphere's costless capacities for self-cleansing? We do not know the answers. But we do know that the relentless pursuit of separate national interest by rich and poor alike can, in a totally interdependent biosphere, produce global disasters of irreversible environmental damage.

## A DESPERATE WRENCH FROM ACCEPTED THINKING

There are then, I suggest, three vital ways in which the reality we are beginning to perceive diverges from our habitual thinking. We normally consider nature as a whole, the entire biosphere, to be safe from man, even if we can chip away at little bits of it. We have been taught to believe, with increasing intensity in recent decades, that we can modernize all our economies and settle most issues of distribution by our unlimited command of rising energy, technology and resources, and by our millennial history we have been taught to expect final decisions to be taken by separate sovereign states. It requires a desperate wrench from accepted thinking, a profound leap, a Copernican leap of the imagination, to begin to see that in stark physical and scientific reality none of these pre-suppositions are any longer true. We can damage the entire biosphere. Resources are not unlimited. States acting separately can produce planetary disaster.

We all know enough of history to realize how uncertain it is whether this change in the direction of our thinking will be made in time. Custom and habit hold us to the traditional themes. The sheer momentum of our present activities could well be enough to drive us on for another four or five decades on our present path. This is a possible 'scenario'. Realists might even call it the most likely one. But I want to give three reasons why I feel it is legitimate to entertain, shall we say, a modest hope?

The first is the United Nations Conference on the Human Environment in Stockholm. Once environmental concern moves nearer to the centre of the nations' attention, I do not doubt that its fuller implications will inevitably unfold. Its whole message is that separate drives, ambitions and policies have to be made compatible with the continuing common life of our single, shared planetary system.

My second reason is the scientific imperative. We can cheat on morals. We can cheat on politics. We can deceive ourselves with dreams and myths. But there is no monkeying about with DNA or photosynthesis or eutrophication or nuclear fusion or the impact on all living things of excessive radiation – from the Sun or the hydrogen bomb.

To act without rapacity, to use knowledge with wisdom, to respect interdependence, to operate without hubris and greed are not simply moral imperatives. They are an accurate scientific description of the means of survival. This compelling force of fact may, I think, control our separatist ambitions before they have overturned our planetary life.

But man does not live by fact alone. Our *human* environment has within it our perpetual striving to make it humane as well. In the past, historians tell us, there have been profound revulsions against the aggression, pride and rapacity of human systems. The great ethical systems of mankind – in India, in China, in the Middle East, from the benign wisdom of Confucius to the passionate social protest of the Hebrew prophets – all sought to express an underlying moral reality: we live by moderation, by compassion, by justice; we die by aggression, by pride, by rapacity and greed.

Now in these latter days, the planet itself in its underlying physical reality repeats the witness of the sages and the prophets. Our collective greeds can degrade and destroy our basic sources of life in air and soil and water. Our collective injustice can continue to create an intolerable imbalance between rich and poor. Envy and fear can unleash the nuclear holocaust.

Here I will admit to what I would call a modest hope: I would say that it is possible that our science and our wisdom are coming together and our faith and our reality are beginning to coincide. If Stockholm is a place where that begins, well, let us all thank God that we were here when it started.

# 2

# The duty to hope:
# A tribute to Barbara Ward

*Brian Johnson*

The quiet musical voice was speaking of Carlos Romulo. 'He saw', she said, 'that what makes our time unique in modem history is that the immediate questions and ultimate questions are again bound up together.' She was walking in her garden at Lodsworth on a dappled summer's day. Although I was there often, and in all seasons, I suppose that it was the gentleness of her wit, her archness in irony and the recurrent bubbling of her laughter that makes me remember this renowned thinker and moralist in a summer frock and in her garden. 'When I am old and retired', she would say gaily (she was never either, despite the awful depredations of her long illness), 'I shall play the Edwardian lady in my shawl and bonnet, snip-snipping away dead-heading my roses, pruning my vines.' Barbara Ward knew about gardening and loved her flowers.

It was typical of her to qualify the insight of Romulo, to put it into historical context. Barbara had read Modern Greats at Oxford, but she had emerged with a depth of historical perspective that enabled her to see the changes and chances of our kaleidoscopic times in a context. She looked beyond the more extravagant claims and wilder alarums of many environmental writers. The immediate questions and the ultimate questions. Their juxtaposition absorbed most of her waking hours and it was the synthesis of their increasing convergence which made up her life's work.

This chapter was first published in the *Environmentalist* 1 (1981, pp95–99).

Barbara Ward is celebrated here as a champion of the environment. Her contribution to environmental care and conservation was the more effective because she came to the environment, as it were, from economics. Indeed, she was generally described as Barbara Ward, the economist, and, as in the *Times* obituary, 'an outstanding contributor to economic thought'.

Her contribution to economics evolved in the tough school of journalism. Working with Geoffrey Crowther on *The Economist*, this young political and economic commentator soon found herself writing the weekly leader of the paper, as its foreign editor. Her speed as an assimilator who could write rapidly and almost without correction from the briefest of notes never left her, even in her long battle with pain and illness when she continued to focus ideas for the international community with *The Home of Man* (written for the United Nations Habitat Conference of 1976) and her final testament, *Progress for a Small Planet*, published in 1979.

Supreme skill with the written and the spoken word are rarely mastered by a single brain. But starting with an evangelical message of Fabian socialism – she first impressed the economist, Hans Singer, when he heard this ethereal girl speaking from a Catholic pulpit in Manchester in 1939 – Barbara's verbal powers were soon to be enlisted by the Ministry of Information to carry the message of British resolution on hazardous journeys across the North Sea and German-occupied Norway, and across the Atlantic to the USA.

These were the first of many speaking engagements in the USA. She talked then of England at war and of the British people 'with a pulse like a cannon'. Already she was amassing that following of US admirers, who stayed with her for the rest of her life, and who stirred her always in her unrelenting struggle with illness. In recent years, with the British economy almost prostrate, beset with troubles, this time of its own making, she recalled those phrases and searched for a returning glimmer of this island's solidarity and spirit.

Barbara blossomed early. By the end of World War II she was a nationally known figure, a favourite member of the BBC's Brains' Trust, on which she could match the wide knowledge and wit of the redoubtable Professor Joad. By her early thirties, she was already a Governor of the Sadler's Wells Ballet, of the Old Vic and of the BBC.

## A SECOND MARSHALL PLAN?

In the hungry, coal-short winter of 1947, that dark time when the USA had withdrawn again across the seas and renewed world war or Communist take-over were daily fears, she wrote *The West at Bay*. Barbara's theme of that time remained the theme of her life: cooperation across seas, across frontiers and across cultures – cooperation for human renewal and development. Her writing and speaking inspired that small missionary group, led by Paul Hoffman and Oliver Franks, who administered, in Churchill's phrase, 'the most unsordid act in human history'. The Marshall Plan offered a $13 billion carrot in return for a restoration of multilateralism in European trade and payments. The carrot was skilfully used: in less than four years, prosperity was returning, thanks to the economic cooperation which had replaced bankrupt Europe's resort to siege economics and barter.

As Europe returned to prosperity again, Barbara Ward's voice was among the first proclaiming the responsibilities of the reconstructed West towards the emerging post-colonial world. William Clark, Barbara Ward's successor as President of the International Institute for Environment and Development, remembers talking to her in 1950, when he was about to set out to cover the first Commonwealth Finance Ministers' meeting to be held in Asia, at Colombo: 'We must always remember', she said, 'that we in Europe and the old Commonwealth are the fortunate minority. We dare not forget the really poor, who are the great majority because prosperity, like peace, is indivisible.'

For the rest of her life, Barbara Ward wanted to repeat the Marshall Plan, the working example of how rich and poor could cooperate for the betterment of both. Only last October, she called again for a second Marshall Plan to help the poorest developing nations.

This belief that the success of the Marshall Plan – the impact of massive funds producing relatively rapid results – could be repeated in poor countries was perhaps Barbara's most widely criticized tenet. Indeed, in many circles of development thinking, it is seen as discredited today. Propositions can, of course, become discredited without ever being tried. But for Barbara, the Marshall aid parallel was never meant to be close. It was not a three-to-five- or even ten-year push that she had in mind. It was a sustained massive financial, social and intellectual drive to remove the abject poverty which, she said, 'we know we can banish from the world if we have a mind to do so'.

Throughout her life of thinking, writing and speaking, Barbara never lost the sense of outrage at people moaning amid their affluence; of Western nations shrinking from the challenge of healing other lives in the course of widening international prosperity. This moral passion which suffused her life has been seen by some to have blinded her to the myriad pitfalls and sidetracks which face the campaign against poverty: the law's delay, the insolence and corruption of office, the oppressor's wrong, the proud man's contumely being only a few. We hear as much today of the problems inherent in the transfer of culture and technology – apparently inseparable from one another. Could a massive transfer of resources also be a sophisticated transfer? Could it avoid the pitfalls of only benefiting elites or lining official pockets or encouraging short-cuts which waste and deplete vital resources? More fundamentally, there is the political problem of dependency: Could independent, sustaining development occur under the thrust of a Marshall-aid scale of Western involvement?

## THE 1960S: DEVELOPMENT AND POPULATION

Book by book, Barbara Ward addressed all these problems. She had gained first-hand experience of developing countries with her Australian husband, Robert Jackson. Together they worked for six years in Ghana, where he advised Nkrumah on the Volta River project, in India and in Pakistan. When, from 1957, she began to teach at Harvard, she produced a succession of books which refined her thinking and her prescriptions. *India and the West* in 1961 had marked Barbara Ward as a leading promoter of the concept of the 1960s as 'a decade of development'. *Nationalism and Ideology* and *Rich Nations and Poor Nations* – probably her most influential book – explained the problems of underdevelopment and charted the pitfalls and possibilities of economic assistance programmes. In each case she set her analysis in an historical context and drew on her great range and depth of knowledge for contrast and comparison.

Barbara 's influence at this time, as later, was felt in many quarters and at many levels. It was particularly strong in the USA where she was teaching and lecturing. As a regular participant at Robert Kennedy's Hickory Hill seminars, she met and made a disciple of Robert McNamara who, as President of the World Bank, turned frequently to her for encouragement, inspiration and a deepening friendship.

The evolution of Barbara's ideas in these years was inseparable too from her deeply held religious beliefs. As a Catholic, she was often accused of soft-pedalling on the issue of population control. Indeed, the director of one major US foundation told me once that she was irresponsible in her neglect of this crucial question. But population was another example of how Barbara worked at many levels and always insisted on the wider context. She loathed the prejudice against the poor and despised racial fears which, she believed, motivated many of those that pressed for population control as the unique priority. Her message on population was simple and tirelessly expressed: better living standards and hope in life are the only possible replacement for the welfare state of the large family. Short of compulsion, population control would only be acceptable alongside a rise in family standards of nutrition and health and a consequent fall in infant mortality. 'This is the vital prerequisite to persuade them to use the contraceptive', she said. 'We must help them to lengthen each baby's life.' Thus Barbara made her counsel clear as a mainstay of the Vatican Pontifical Commission on Justice and Peace while encouraging Robert McNamara to commit the World Bank further to programmes of contraception as a part of mother-and-child welfare.

Barbara was painfully aware of the strain that a world population now double what it was 35 years ago was placing on the world's natural systems. She spoke and wrote of the ecological pressures to come with six, seven, and eight billion people – as she put it, 'another world on this'. It seems, indeed, that it was partly at least her comprehension of the time that demographic transition must take, even with comprehensive family-planning programmes installed, which moved Barbara to concentrate more and more in the late 1960s on the problems of conserving resources and the ecosystems that support all life. By 1971, a decade after the publication of *India and the West*, she was at work on her grandest theme: development cooperation that would involve changes in lifestyle and expectation for all people and all nations – the vital changes necessary for 'the care and maintenance of a small planet'.

## THE 1970s: FOCUS ON ENVIRONMENT

The theme and the message of *Only one Earth* were very much Barbara Ward's own, a logical projection of earlier work. The presentation of the work as 'the book of the Stockholm Environment

Conference' and its co-authorship with the eminent biologist, René
Dubos, combining the insights and prestige of luminaries in the social
and the natural sciences, was the idea of a new friend, Maurice
Strong, the Canadian Secretary General of 'The First World
Conference on Everything'.

The Stockholm Human Environment Conference provided the
intellectual framework and the stage which launched Barbara Ward
into the final phase of her career. The idea of a popular book which
could set forth in vivid language the intricacies of Stockholm's all-
embracing theme was a new one to the United Nations' system. It
was one of Strong's most effective devices for raising the level of
participation and popular interest above what could be induced by
the documentary word-mills that traditionally supplied United
Nations conferences with their facts.

Ward and Dubos embarked upon *Only One Earth* with Barbara
recovering from a major operation for her already familiar enemy,
cancer. Then Dubos himself fell ill and Barbara faced the whole
burden of producing the manuscript by an ineluctable deadline with
translators in three countries poised for their breakneck dash for
multiple language editions by the time of the Conference. The strain
was extreme, even for someone of Barbara's fortitude. It was here
that her training as a journalist proved invaluable. At the Stockholm
Conference itself, Barbara added her extraordinary gift as a speaker
to a series of lectures by 'distinguished persons' and at several of the
other less formal and, at times, impromptu events which made up
that intellectual carnival in a Swedish midsummer.

## THE BIRTH OF THE INTERNATIONAL INSTITUTE FOR ENVIRONMENT AND DEVELOPMENT

Barbara's writing of *Only One Earth* had been supported by members
of a small secretariat which formed the staff of a newly founded and
US-based institute: the International Institute for Environmental
Affairs. They, together with her tiny group at Columbia, which she
nicknamed 'the frog pond', saw the manuscript through to its comple-
tion. This was no mean task. Maurice Strong had arranged that this
'unofficial report' to the Conference should be read and vetted by a
152-member 'committee of correspondents' (the phrase was
Barbara's, mindful of Diderot) who wrote from 58 countries with
400 pages of criticisms and suggestions. Then, when the Conference
was over, Robert O Anderson, President of the Atlantic Richfield oil

company, and the Founder of IIEA, asked Barbara Ward if she would take on the Institute's Presidency. She demurred. Would she have adequate financial backing over a reasonable time so that she could launch her own purpose-built vehicle, as it were, to convey her ideas at the level at which she could operate? Anderson told her she would. Could she change the style and title of the Institute? She could not head an institute that did not include development in its purpose. For environment alone would have little meaning to two-thirds of humanity if they could not acquire the means to improve their lives and so be able to look beyond today in managing their surroundings. She could. Her final condition, after two decades of sojourn in other lands, was that she could bring the re-founded institute home to Europe, though spanning the Atlantic with a base in both Washington DC and London.

So the International Institute for Environment and Development was born in 1973. It became, in the words of her former colleague, Roland Bird, 'perhaps her first secular interest'. In the seven years from 1973 to her retirement from the Institute's Presidency in 1980, Barbara built upon the Stockholm formula. Surrounded by a small and increasingly international staff, she was able to convene leaders of widely different – and, indeed, opposed – interests and ideas. As their rapporteur, she steered and presented their conclusions, several steps, as usual, ahead of what governments would countenance at the World Food Conference in Rome (1974) and at the Habitat Conference in Vancouver in 1976.

In the meantime, she launched her staff, chairing groups, gathering facts and statistics, drawing up statements, spurring, enthusing, phrase-making, provoking and counselling at other world conferences and on other topics: the Law of the Sea, the First World Water Conference, the World Conference on Desertification and one on the hazards and potentials of science and technology. The formula was simple: to follow and to build upon the international conference agenda, writing and speaking always with down-to-earth humour and simplicity.

At the same time, Barbara worked to shape the Institute so that it might survive her to continue her work as a technically solid centre for policy analysis and influence. In all of this, she retained the support of Anderson and gathered that of others, not least the institutional child of Stockholm: the UN Environment Programme that sponsored her books and other aspects of the Institute's work as well.

This support enabled her to use the transatlantic reach of the Institute to link and cross-fertilize not only ideas – this was happening anyway through the media and travel – but also the confidence and friendships that precipitate action. To mention even a few such linkages would turn this celebration into a catalogue. A long one too, for pretty soon the links were becoming a network – Barbara was adept at institutional crochet – that spread to many parts of the world. In all these activities of the 1970s there was constant expansion and growth, and at a time when Keynesian assumptions were under challenge and the liberal credo that Barbara had espoused was under attack in the centres from which she and her Bloomsbury and Fabian foundations had drawn their support.

What then of her own political development in a time of conservative challenge and reappraisal? Politics inevitably tend to pigeon-hole people; even people like Barbara who avoid direct party involvement and in whom analysis and idealism form heady compounds. All her urgings inevitably held clear political implications and any celebration of her contribution cannot avoid some account of her political progress, especially in today's divisive climate.

In 1945 Barbara was asked to stand in Britain for Labour. She would not do so. But in those days she spoke for Labour. Her espousal of bold government intervention, as with the Marshall Plan, and her link not only with British Fabian socialism, but with US liberalism – what Donald Tyerman called 'a freer, Chester Bowles, Adlai Stevenson sort of world' – was never diverted but steadily modified by experience. It was modified a long way from the hopes and claims of the Atlee era. In 1972 she ended a speech in London to the Conservation Society with a quotation from William James:

> *I am done with great things and big things, great institutions and big success and I am for those tiny invisible molecular moral forces that work from individual to individual, creeping through the crannies of the world like so many rootlets, or like the capillary oozing with water, yet which, if you give them time, will rend the hardest monuments of men's pride.*

In her last book, *Progress for a Small Planet*, she wrote of 'private socialism'; of the use made by both the Japanese and French governments of indicative planning and of the Yugoslav experiment. She talked of 'the dispersion of wealth through the community and the involving of all in their factories and offices – an involvement which, more than anything else, can dissolve, perhaps, the worst aspects of traditional industrialism, the alienation of the mass of workers from their community of work'.

Politically and intellectually, Barbara offered a brilliant counterpart to the propositions of EF Schumacher, to most of which she lent her warm support. She complemented his new analysis of the problem of production, bringing the worldly shrewdness of mainstream politics to the 'alternative' and the insights of the alternative to the mainstream. Never afraid to be counted in the political fray, in the last months of her life she threw her support to the nascent Social Democrats in Britain, but her prescription would never necessarily follow the format of a party platform.

In the end, Barbara returned to her message of 'only one earth'. The beloved planet was the only political unit she could happily espouse. 'In short', as she wrote in concluding her last book:

> no problem is insoluble in the creation of a balanced and conserving planet save humanity itself. Can it reach in time the vision of joint survival? Can its inescapable physical interdependence – the chief new insight of our century – induce that vision? We do not know. We have the duty to hope.

# 3

# Stockholm: The founding of IIED

## *Maurice Strong*

## THE INTERNATIONAL INSTITUTE FOR ENVIRONMENTAL AFFAIRS

IIED began as the International Institute for Environmental Affairs, established on the initiative of Robert O Anderson who was its Chairman and principal source of funding. 'Bob' Anderson was a prominent figure in the oil and gas industry, and his company was involved in the extraction of oil from Alaska's Prudhoe Bay. The construction of the pipeline from Prudhoe Bay was much delayed, and made more costly, by the controversy surrounding environmental impacts on the sensitive Arctic terrain and wildlife. This experience impressed Anderson with the emerging importance of the environment and its impact on resource development, and his company began to accommodate environmental concerns in development plans.

Bob Anderson had long been interested in broader issues of public policy, and led the development of the Aspen Institute for Humanistic Studies. This became an influential cultural and policy forum, attracting thinkers and artists from around the world. After the controversy of the Alaska pipeline, Anderson began to incorporate environmental issues into the programme of the Aspen institute, and invited environmentalists to engage in dialogue with policy-makers and business leaders. This led to Anderson's decision to establish the International Institute for Environmental Affairs (IIEA), as an affiliate of the Aspen Institute, to focus specifically on international environmental issues.

In this interest, as otherwise, Bob Anderson was ahead of his time; many of his contemporaries viewed his interest in the environment as either a response to a business imperative, or simply eccentric.

He recruited as President, Jack Raymond, an experienced *New York Times* journalist and public-relations expert with a real interest in environment but no professional background in the field. When I was appointed Secretary General of the UN Conference on the Human Environment in late 1970, Bob Anderson offered to put the IIEA at my service to assist in preparations for the Conference. I welcomed the assistance, and the Institute convened a number of sessions in New York, Washington and at Aspen which helped to build a constituency for the Conference in some influential circles in the business, policy and non-governmental communities in the USA.

## LINKING ENVIRONMENT AND DEVELOPMENT

I met Barbara Ward (Lady Jackson) when she visited Ottawa in 1971 to see Prime Minister Lester Pearson whose Chief of Staff, Tom Kent was a friend of Barbara's and had worked with her at *The Economist*. At that time, Barbara was known as the world's most articulate and influential advocate for support of the developing world and relief from the poverty that afflicted the majority of its people. When I first met her in the living room of Tom Kent's home in Ottawa, I had just agreed to take on responsibility for managing preparations for the United Nations Conference on the Human Environment and was eager to have her advice. At that time, developing countries were deeply suspicious of the emerging environment issue as a 'disease of the rich' which could impose new constraints on their central priority of economic development. Indeed there was even a move on the part of developing countries at the United Nations to boycott the forth-coming Conference in Stockholm.

Although it was clear from my discussions with Barbara that she had not really focused a lot of her own attention on environmental issues, she was clearly aware of the developing-country concerns and very much shared them. We agreed that the agenda for the Conference as it had been initially formulated focused primarily on issues of concern to the more industrialized countries – air and water pollution, urban blight and despoliation of natural resources and recreational areas. Though the developing countries were also experi-encing similar problems, they regarded them as marginal to their main preoccupation with economic development, and some said that they would welcome more pollution if it meant more development.

Barbara's immediate understanding and brilliant analysis of developing-country concerns impressed me immensely. I was completely captivated by the combination of her amazing intellectual energy with her personal charm, and before the end of our meeting asked her if she would be prepared to help and advise me in preparing for the Conference. To my great delight she accepted and thus began one of the most important relationships and valued friendships I have ever been privileged to enjoy. It was also key to the success of the Stockholm Conference.

When I took up my UN appointment full-time at the beginning of 1971, I moved to the temporary offices that had already been established for our Secretariat at UN Headquarters in New York. Barbara was at Columbia University and we began to see quite a bit of each other. At each meeting, I could see that both her knowledge of the issues and her interest in them had progressed amazingly to the point where she rapidly became our principal source of advice and inspiration. I thoroughly enjoyed our planning sessions, usually over dinner and a glass of the champagne she enjoyed so much. I always came away from these meetings thoroughly stimulated by new insights and ideas.

My first priority was to address the concerns of developing countries and I asked Barbara if she could help me to convene a small group of leading development experts to help us think through how the Conference process and agenda could be re-cast to accommodate developing country concerns. Of course she knew all the leading people in the field and none could say no to her. We met at my UN office with a small core group of those who were closest at hand – including Sri Lanka's Gamani Corea, Pakistan's Mahbub ul Haq, Uruguay's Enrique Iglesias and Colombia's Rodrigo Botero. After I explained the situation to them, Mahbub ul Haq launched a scathing attack on both the purposes and the agenda of the Conference, articulating brilliantly and caustically the position of developing countries that the environment was a problem for the rich and a threat to developing countries.

In responding, I said that, with my own deep commitment to development, I believed that the environment issue in which there was strong and growing interest in industrialized countries could provide a new rationale for increasing their support of developing countries because the state of their environment is critical to the health of the entire global environment. I suggested that we really did not have enough reliable knowledge and analysis to make the case and that if I was wrong in my premise then I had made a mistake in taking on this assignment. I invited him and the other participants to join in a rigorous process of examining this question which was so essential to the entire purpose and prospects of the Conference. Barbara, with her irresistible powers of persuasion, weighed in with strong support of my invitation and to my great relief Mahbub ul Haq joined with the others in accepting the challenge. He and Gamini Corea agreed to join Barbara Ward in leading the process and were soon joined by another eminent and creative guru, Ignacy Sachs, a noted Polish economist at the Sorbonne in Paris.

In subsequent meetings, we recruited other key people, including a young Australian investment banker, Jim Wolfenson, who had showed a real interest in the subject. We decided to organize a meeting of some 30 leading experts representative both of the major regions of the world and of the diversity of views which were emerging on the subject. Again it was Barbara's knowledge of and influence with these normally hard-to-get experts that enabled us to put together a stellar group for a meeting at a small motel in the village of Founex just outside Geneva to which, by that time, our Secretariat Headquarters had moved. Barbara Ward led and guided the preparations for this meeting to which a number of the main participants made important and in some cases highly provocative inputs.

The meeting itself was one of the best that I have ever experienced in terms of spirited intellectual discussion and creative interchange. The report of the meeting, prepared by Mahbub ul Haq and Gamani Corea with Barbara's oversight, articulated the main message resulting from the meeting that environment and development are indeed inextricably linked, and made specific proposals on how developing countries might best avoid the risks and realize the new opportunities that this could produce for them. Fundamental to its message was that the more industrialized countries bore principal responsibility for the damage done and the risks that had arisen to the Earth's environment, that they had been and are the main beneficiaries of the economic growth that had produced these problems, and had an obligation to bear the costs of dealing with them. This translated into the need for the more industrialized countries to provide 'new and additional' resources to developing countries to enable the latter to incorporate care for the environment into their development and to participate fully in global efforts to protect and improve the environment. This support was not to come from existing development assistance funds but advocated to be 'new and additional'.

The Founex Report provided the basis for the proposals I made to our preparatory committee of governments to revamp the agenda for the Conference to address the issues of particular concern to developing countries, and explicitly recognize the relationship between environment and development. Although for the most part the more developed countries did not initially buy into the substantive basis for this change they accepted the broadened agenda as the political price of satisfying developing-country demands and ensuring their engagement in the process. And engage they did. Led by Brazil and India, developing countries built a strong case for acceptance by the more developed countries of primary responsibility for environmental deterioration and for meeting the costs of rectifying it – the theme which was to dominate the negotiations in Stockholm and in the many other international fora that followed.

## *ONLY ONE EARTH*: EXTENDING THE RANGE OF INFLUENCE

Barbara Ward made these issues the focal point of her own speeches and writings. With her unsurpassed genius for articulating them persuasively, she presented them to our audiences within the larger context of the need to establish a much more fair, viable and secure world community in which the poor would share equitably and participate fully. Her messages were so central to the theme of our preparations for Stockholm, and she was so clearly its most powerful and influential messenger, that I asked her if she would write a book for the Conference. Its purpose would be to get this message out to the wider public whose interest we sought to engage and whose influence on political leaders would have a positive effect on the position they took at the Conference. Barbara was very open to the idea, despite her many other obligations.

She recognized that although she herself was from the 'North' she was widely seen as a champion of developing-country interest and we agreed that it might be useful to have as a co-author a scientist with impeccable credentials in areas related to the environment who would reinforce the credibility of the book with the public, professionals and politicians. I had been most impressed with a book I had read by a French Scientist, René Dubos, then at Rockefeller

University in New York. After some enquiries, I arranged to meet with him in a small office adjoining his laboratory. He immediately impressed me with his quiet dignity and the penetrating quality of the questions he raised. When I told him why I had come to see him, he expressed genuine surprise at the proposal I was raising with him but by the end of our conversation expressed a clear, but non-committal interest. Most importantly, he agreed to meet with Barbara Ward to discuss the matter.

I was sure he was the right person, but apprehensive about the personal chemistry between these two very different but strong personalities. To my great relief their first meeting could not have gone better. Both reported to me separately with a very positive impression each had of the other and their willingness to proceed with the project. This uniquely creative partnership produced the book *Only One Earth*, which, together with the Founex Report provided the intellectual underpinning for the Stockholm Conference and, indeed, remains one of the seminal books on the environment and its relationships to development. The contents and the credibility of the book were tested and enhanced by the participation of a galaxy of leading experts and policy-makers in reviewing drafts and making valuable suggestions. But final approval of the manuscript was the sole responsibility of Barbara Ward and René Dubos, and the book is an enduring tribute to their remarkable partnership.

## The 'voice of the people' at Stockholm, 1972

When the Conference opened in Stockholm on the beautiful summer morning of 5 June 1972, Barbara Ward was by my side as my Senior Adviser. She occupied a small suite next to that which had been given to my wife and me in the Grand Hotel in Stockholm and we were able to consult constantly on the multiplicity of issues that arose continually. Although the protocol of the Conference would not enable her to sit on the podium with me, her presence and her influence were pervasive. She was especially active in inspiring and bringing a sense of focus and coherence into the activities of the motley assortment of representatives of non-governmental organizations (NGOs) and citizen groups who for the first time at a United Nations Conference had been encouraged to participate. Their activities and demonstrations enlivened the streets of Stockholm and the corridors of the Conference chambers. But the greatest concentration of activities, a mixture of serious dialogue with a variety of folk music, dances and rituals by indigenous people and demonstrations of various kinds, took place at the 'Hog Farm' on the outskirts of Stockholm which had been provided by the Swedes for that purpose. I took time out from the official Conference to visit it and this was for me one of the real highlights of the Stockholm experience.

This 'people power' had a major influence on both the spirit of the Conference and its results. It provided the basis for much of the extensive media coverage the Conference proceedings received, and clearly influenced the official delegates to take more positive positions on key issues than they had come prepared for. But it was Barbara Ward who was able to draw on this somewhat disorganized and disparate agglomeration of ideas and energies to articulate their central message in a way which both reflected the main concerns of the non-governmental community and spoke persuasively to the official delegations and the media. As it was then counter to United Nations rules to permit anyone not an official delegate to speak at the Plenary Session of the Conference, we contrived an arrangement which enabled her to do so through the simple act of suspending the official proceedings while she spoke and then resuming them. Her speech encapsulated brilliantly and cogently the case for bringing developing countries into a new and equitable environment and development partnership to build a more secure and sustainable future for the entire human community. While other delegates necessarily spoke from the positions of the governments they represented, Barbara was the authentic voice of the people. Her message clearly got to the delegates and had a major effect in elevating prospects for success in the difficult negotiations that followed.

Particularly fascinating was the synergy between Barbara and the other main star of the Conference, also a great lady, Prime Minister Indira Gandhi of India. Her official statement to the Conference which included the memorable assertion that 'poverty is the greatest polluter', complemented and reinforced Barbara's contribution. I was delighted but not at all surprised to find that they had a very high regard for each other. I could not help but remark in reflecting on Stockholm that how in this great intergovernmental event dominated by men, these two extraordinary women were the main stars.

The Stockholm Conference has to be seen as a major milestone, not because its results met all of our hopes and aspirations, but because it was able to surmount the many divisions and controversies to produce a broad consensus which put the environmental issue firmly on the international agenda. Following Stockholm there was a proliferation of activities by governments, multilateral institutions and NGOs.

## THE ESTABLISHMENT OF IIED

Shortly after the Conference I met with Bob Anderson in New York and he asked my advice about the future of the International Institute of Environmental Affairs. As he had given me notice of this question prior to the Conference, I had given it some thought. My response was that of course it could make an important contribution as a organization that had good sponsorship in the USA and had already established a positive reputation there. At the same time, I suggested that if he wanted it to be truly international, it should become a champion of the synergistic link between environment and development which had been affirmed at Stockholm. In the meantime, Barbara Ward had informed me that she was considering a move back to the UK but had not yet taken steps to explore any of the many opportunities that would await her there. Without having raised the matter with Barbara, I asked Bob Anderson if he might be interested in having Barbara Ward head the Institute, giving it a new name and mission to embrace the environment-development nexus and move the headquarters to London. He was not one to ponder his decisions for long and he acted with immediate enthusiasm to this prospect, asking me to sound out Barbara. She was clearly interested, as this would provide her with an institutional base from which to continue the leadership of the environment–development movement, a leadership she found universally acknowledged on her emergence from the Stockholm Conference.

At that time Bob and Barbara did not know each other and I arranged for the two of them to meet alone in New York. Bob, always quick to strike a deal when he knew it was good, met all Barbara's requirements. As a result, the International Institute of Environmental Affairs (IIEA) was reconstituted as the International Institute for Environment and Development (IIED), its headquarters moved to London with Barbara as its President and Bob as Chairman. I became an active member of the Board and was delighted but not at all surprised as Barbara put together a superb team of exceptional young people who, with her leadership, made IIED into one of the most effective and influential organizations in the field.

Barbara had a great talent for spotting and recruiting the best and brightest young people, among them some of the contributors to this book. Her star student at Columbia was a young Canadian, David Runnalls, in whom she had great confidence, a confidence that was fully justified by his subsequent contributions to the movement on environment and sustainable development. As I got to know David, it became clear that he had in important influence on Barbara's own thinking while at the same time subjecting her views to the kind of penetrating challenge that any genius needs but many find difficult to accept. I developed an immense respect for David and a close friend-ship which has continued as he has moved progressively into more important positions of policy influence and practical leadership in the movement.

I continued my own close relationship with the IIED throughout those early years and my friendship with Barbara became even closer as I spent precious time with her both in London and then at her country home. Her spirit and creative intellect continued to inspire all who worked with her even as her physical health deteriorated. Right to the last she was constantly preoccupied with how IIED could help to bring about the better world to which her own life had been so totally committed. After her death, IIED continued to be driven by her vision and the foundations she had laid for its work in leading the evolution of the environment–development movement to the broader concept of sustainable development. I leave it to other contributors to this book to chronicle the rest of this remarkable story. I can only say at this point that Barbara would be proud and pleased at how the IIED which in its present form is truly her creation has continued to work and build on her legacy.

# PART II
# THREE DECADES OF CHANGE
# AND DEVELOPMENT

# 4

# Time for change: IIED 1984–1990

## *Brian W Walker*

By the mid-1980s, I had known William Clark (then President of IIED) for some years, and Barbara Ward, his predecessor, for even longer. Indeed, Barbara had been a powerful supporter of Oxfam both before and during my time as its Director General.

Ten years earlier, by one of those strange quirks of fate, IIED had arranged a conference on 'The Exploding Cities', in Oxford, starting on 1 April 1974. By chance this was my first day in Oxfam as 'Director Designate'. Leslie Kirkley, from whom I was taking over, said that I'd better go down to the Ashmolean to represent Oxfam, but to be sure to introduce myself to Barbara who was to give the keynote address. She was a powerful ally in the battle against world poverty, he explained, and our paths would cross frequently. Also, *The Times*, sponsor of the conference, had asked me to review the book recording the main papers. So there had been something of a pre-life for me in IIED.

But, moving forward again to the mid-1980s, it was William, who by this time knew that he had terminal cancer, who rang me in Geneva one day, in 1985, to say, 'Would you consider throwing your hat in the ring because I'm stepping down as the IIED President?' We both knew the awful truth, for I had been a frequent visitor to William's home after his retirement from the World Bank. We used to sit after lunch, by the window, looking onto the stream which flowed below us forming the south boundary of his property, drinking coffee and solving the world's problems. He had long since explained that despite its policy potential, funding was a difficult problem for

IIED. Its product wasn't 'sexy' enough for the donors, he explained. He didn't think he could do much on a part-time basis. A full-time president and executive director was needed.

## QUESTIONS OF FUNDING AND STATUS

If, as the former Vice-President of the World Bank, William Clark had been unable to attract funding, what hope had I? William was at once bullish and somewhat evasive. The world needed IIED, he said, especially the donor governments for whom the environment was a bit of a mystery. We had many friends in high places and our time would come, and quickly at that. Everything was pointing in our direction and there were few competitors. Lots of campaigners, many evangelists, but few scientists had the ears of governments or of the multilateral agencies. Certainly, Barbara Ward and her pals had caused UNEP to be set up, but it had never commanded the interest of the key donor governments as had UNDP or UNICEF. In any case, an essential ingredient of that particular strategy was to have an international NGO – IIED – to be free to act for the environment without the strictures laid on the UN and its donor governments.

I was unhappy in Geneva, where I had been working for a year or so for the Independent Commission on International Humanitarian Issues, so I said that I would give it a try. I would start early in 1986, travelling daily from Oxford where Nancy and I had kept our house. I would do a term of five years, before moving on. The Board agreed, but said it wanted me to work at least four months a year in the USA to try to get our US funding up to scratch. Then there was the Buenos Aires (Human Settlements) Office. The Board wasn't sure of its status. Barbara Ward had set it up to give the excellent, world authority, Jorge Hardoy, a secure base. But who owned it? How was it funded? Did it contribute, or was it a permanent drain on our slim cash resources? 'Oh, and by the way,' said Bob Anderson our Chairman, echoed by Sir Arthur Norman his Deputy, 'The Board is not sure either of the status and role of Earthscan IIED's information division. It has high visibility, and some people in the non-industrialized countries swear by it. It is creative and on the whole is saying the right things, but what does it really cost, and is it the natural bedfellow of the rigorous, scientific work our researchers want to do?' There were ominous rumours of a house divided against itself.

Gradually, other questions emerged about the lease and location of our new London offices. These had been voted through without too much Board involvement. The Board itself had 16 high-powered members, but only 3 lived in the UK. It also boasted 23 Council members, most of whom were distinguished and powerful people, but only 4 of whom lived in the UK. What were they all doing? What did consultation with them cost? Were they contributing to the real needs of the Institute? Their commitment and personal support were unquestioned. They had all been good friends of Barbara but few now attended meetings and so re-structuring was essential.

Inevitably, these negatives set my immediate agenda. I couldn't have made any real contribution to their resolution without the support of Richard Sandbrook, IIED's Deputy Director, who really was IIED in those days, and who eventually succeeded me as Director – although he always swore he would never take on the Director's job. After all, he knew, he said, where all the bodies were!

## RECRUITING NEW STAFF MEMBERS

We decided on a dual-track policy. On the one hand were the negatives listed above. But, on the other, were the imperative nature of our science-based message, the astonishingly high professional quality of our staff, the enthusiasm and loyalty of a handful of key Board members and the sense that the tide was turning in our direction. They recognized that nationally (in the UK and in the USA) and internationally, environmentalism was detaching itself from fringe/hippy activity to soundly-based research. It was about to become central to strategic planning by governments and to the thinking of key, multilateral agencies. Goodwill abounded and so did vision.

Despite our parlous finances (technically we were probably insolvent) we agreed to recruit some of the best natural scientists in our field of endeavour to supplement the work already being done by those in place – energy (Dr Gerry Leach and his team), human settlements (Professor Jorge Hardoy and his team), forestry (Professor Duncan Poore and his team), Antarctica (Lee Kimball), and marine resources (Dr John Beddington and his team). The able Lloyd Timberlake was our resident writer. In the fullness of time, to this formidable powerhouse were added the new experts, including Professor Gordon Conway (agriculture), Professor David Pearce (sustainable economics), Walter Arensberg (environmental planning and management – based in Washington), Dr Camilla Toulmin (drylands development) and Don Hinrichsen (World Resources

Report). Each brought, or attracted, some of the best of the younger minds in the business. We followed a similar pattern in our Washington DC office under the excellent leadership of Dr David Runnalls. At the same time we tried to strengthen our administration, in terms of both personnel and systems and equipment. Because of my own 'hands-on' background I was anxious to ground our work more and more in the daily realities of the Third World. Experts in the practice of 'sustainable development' were recruited – some as Fellows, some as consultants, and others as staff members.

In the same vein, in 1987, we engaged the environmental writer, Paul Harrison, to publish a study of the successes of development in Africa, as a counter-balance to the continual drip-drip of negative stories of gloom and doom. The latter are real enough, but so were the breakthroughs and the sustainable achievements in development. Paul's *The Greening of Africa* was the first of its kind, welcomed by NGOs and the UN alike. I trudged dozens of miles in New York and Washington trying to raise a meagre £20,000 to fund it. I got it in the end – but what a struggle.

Early in 1987 a former colleague of mine from Oxfam – Robin Sharp – joined us, eventually to head a unit designed to pass on as much of our work and insights as possible to NGOs in developing countries, especially in Africa. The 'Southern Networks/NGO Programme', as it was named, was a pioneering activity. It brought southern NGOs together, and acted as a conduit from IIED and like institutions in the North to our Southern colleagues. It set up training seminars. In turn we learned greatly through the reverse flow of local knowledge and traditional wisdom.

## MILESTONES IN INFLUENCING: WORLD BANK TO BAND AID

Investment in these kinds of enterprises was a high-risk policy for development agencies, which had become set in their ways and had not fully accepted the message of sustainability. But it paid off on the whole. Some of it was exciting and highly creative. At one period, in 1987/88 Richard and I were meeting with Rt Hon Chris Patten to feed ideas and IIED papers directly into the Thatcher cabinet as, gradually, Prime Minister Thatcher began to realize that environmentalists were not all hairy anarchists. This reflected the pioneering work of David Pearce and his team who had agreed to set up in University College, London an IIED team of young economists to argue out and define the true economic costs of development in terms of sustainability.

That same year we hosted a conference with the World Bank at Cumberland Lodge in Great Windsor Park. Twenty-five participants of leading institutions interested in sustainability examined the Bank's agenda and how we could help the Bank to improve underwriting of sustainability. It was a first-off. The proceedings were published internationally. We also contributed through discussions with Bank officials, principally led by our Washington Director, Dr Dave Runnalls, but supported by Richard Sandbrook and myself, to the shift in Bank policy towards listening to those of their own members, like Bob Goodland, who were researching the nature of sustainability, and pointing to the danger of dependency, the role of women in development and the value of NGOs both donor and recipient to the process of development. We were able to extend our lobbying to the African, Asian and Latin American Banks, in the process. Our low public-campaigning profile was a significant asset in this exercise.

Similarly, Lloyd Timberlake and Richard Sandbrook headed the liaison team advising Prime Minister Brundtland and her Commissioners as they produced their epoch-making report, *Our Common Future*, in 1987. It was not a perfect report: we were still in the days of Cold War politics and so the pivotal challenge of sustainable energy was ducked. Our key Board members – Sonny Ramphal, Maurice Strong, Emil Salim and Jim MacNeill, sat on her Commission – and I had the privilege of chairing the initial presentation of its findings, by Prime Minister Brundtland, to the world media, in London. *Our Common Future* was judged a triumph for IIED. It set our own agenda for years to come, in agriculture, forestry, economics and human settlements. In a way it represented the flowering of the seeds planted by IIED from Barbara Ward and her colleagues onwards to my own time.

A parallel development was the birth of the influential *World Resources Report* – the first issue of which was researched and written in our London office by the clever and knowledgeable Don Hinrichsen. Our partner was the World Resources Institute (WRI) in Washington DC. The WRI made an essential financial contribution but it was the bravery, energy and creativity of IIED, which gave birth to what was originally an annual report based on the best available research, which outshone all its international competitors. It was also unique. Two years later, however, our lack of core funds made our annual financial subvention to the project unsustainable. We sold off our holdings and our debts to the affluent WRI, which had been set up with millions of dollars by the Macarthur Foundation for just this kind of activity. WRI also agreed to take on board our now redundant staff colleagues in Washington. I continued to serve on the editorial committee for a number of years after leaving IIED and feel proud of the initiative set in motion by IIED and which became such an outstanding success by any measure.

In 1986, when wandering round the back of the IIED offices to find a café for lunch, I stumbled on the newly opened HQ of the pop star, Bob Geldof. It was a single warehouse, with a small office, opening onto the street. There I met Penny Jenden, the executive director, and we discussed Band Aid's needs and strategy over a cup of coffee. A little later I was asked to join the team on a voluntary basis to chair the 'projects committee'. Lloyd Timberlake worked closely with Band Aid, Richard Sandbrook gave encouragement and despite all the calls on our skills and time IIED staff acted as reviewers for proposals.

We were not to know that for the next four years we would sit, twice a month, in a central London office lent to Geldof, sifting through hundreds of project proposals, and recommending which Geldof and his team should support. In all those years only one of our recommendations was rejected! I also checked all those projects rejected on first sight by the staff, to make sure that nothing worthy of support slipped by. Lloyd and I won the support of the four or five 'experts' from academia, who joined us in this work, insisting that the whole programme of Band Aid should be independently assessed at the end of the four-year period, and that its results should be published internationally.

While Band Aid/Live Aid undoubtedly achieved a number of successes in the field – some innovatory – its principal achievement was to introduce the issues of hunger, malnutrition and sustainable development to a new generation of young people, largely untouched by the UK development agencies. Its capture of the world media and all the associated exposure allowed the development issue to be debated publicly, not least within the UN agencies with renewed vigour.

## FUNDRAISING FROM PRIVATE AND PUBLIC SOURCES

Fundraising for IIED was a high priority for me in my role as president. The corporate sector, just coming on-stream, was an obvious target, so were the Nordic governments and other EC countries like The Netherlands, as well as wealthy individuals and corporate trusts. We also secured contracts with the World Bank and the UN specialized agencies including the UN Environment Programme (UNEP) and the UN Development Programme (UNDP). Inevitably, and certainly in the case of the Nordic governments, there was enthusiasm for buying into IIED's ideas as central to their own policy-making processes. Corporate trusts in the oil business, banking and manufacturing were also genuinely interested in discovering from IIED's fairly dispassionate and rigorous analysis of issues where to find best practice, and what lessons could be learned from it by corporate donors.

My biggest success here was a gift of a million dollars from our chairman, Robert O Anderson, then Chairman of Atlantic Richfield. We had many meetings and became good friends. When I asked him one day why he had given me a million dollars when he had refused most other IIED entreaties, this elicited the straight-faced reply – 'Brian, I just liked your face.' I'm still trying to work that one out.

Another great supporter was the Chairman of the De La Rue Company, which prints most of the world's paper money, Sir Arthur (Gerry) Norman. Gerry was committed to IIED and chaired our Executive. He saw his role as one of introducing me to potential corporate donors through the simple expedient of inviting such guests to lunch in his boardroom, with me as the 'speaker'. Six or eight corporate luminaries would assemble, and over dessert and coffee I would 'introduce' them to IIED. Afterwards, of course, I would have to follow up each guest individually. This process tapped a steady source of new income for the Institute, although costs were rising at the same time as interest rates moved up towards 20 per cent. It was a punishing programme. Worse, Gerry was a generous host. Week after week I returned to the office, mid-afternoon, groaning, as a consequence of the gourmet food and drink consumed – to the total disbelief of IIED's admin and secretarial staff. I still blame my extra two inches of waistline on Gerry Norman and his lunches. But we made money and received considerable support.

Another generous donor I introduced to IIED was my friend Azad Shivdasani, Chairman of Inlaks – the largest private Indian company in the world. Without his timely and generous contribution IIED would not have survived. Azad's relative youthfulness at that time, his enthusiasm and his sharp brain were a major asset for the Board. Throughout this period the Board actively encouraged corporate and private-sector fundraising, within the bounds of common sense.

Our success with governmental funding was less impressive. First, the Thatcher Government would give us nothing. This became a let-out clause for other governments seeking an excuse to do nothing. But the Scandinavians, the Dutch, the EU generally, the Canadians and the Americans were generous. I failed, however, in my personal campaign, to persuade them to alter the international rules of grant-making in order to cover core costs, which are the only costs an agency like ours must raise from 'donations'. I tried hard – almost to the point of losing their support altogether. The ground rules, laid in the years soon after World War II, were firmly entrenched and the Thatcher/Reagan administrations were solidly behind them. They could not, or would not, admit that core costs are the essential product of a research outfit, just as projects on the ground are the 'product' of Oxfam or Christian Aid. A decade on, this battle is still yet to be won.

In all of this the only sad note of substance was the need to sever the ties of the successful Earthscan operation from that of the research work of IIED. By 1985 Earthscan had virtually taken over IIED in London. Certainly it was on an upward spiral of spending without control. It had many fine qualities of creativity and entrepreneurship but its lack of rigour allied to escalating costs outside budgets led to mounting opposition from our policy researchers. It also annoyed key trustees, including our chair and vice-chair, but the matter was shared eventually by all our trustees following Board discussions at which Earthscan's director was invited to put his case. Earthscan's refusal to be part of the whole team upset especially our US and Argentinian colleagues.

I had ideas for correcting these faults but was pre-empted when Jon Tinker, Director of Earthscan, declared 'unilateral independence' in May 1986 (with some encouragement from donors), while I was busy fundraising for the Institute in the US. The only possible Board decision, which had my full support, was then severance and for IIED and Earthscan to go their separate ways. That is precisely what happened. For once, our Board was rock-solid, with Jack Raymond (a long-time American admirer of Barbara Ward and close friend of Bob Anderson), and Sir Arthur Norman to the fore.

As to the future, four points strike me: the need to push ahead with research into discovering cheap, safe, sustainable energy; promoting the translation of sustainability into the methods and practice of accountancy, at all levels of society; to position 'poverty' at the heart of sustainability, a principle that Barbara Ward understood; to tackle not least from the environmental as well as the developmental point of view, the consequences of modern war. War clearly is unsustainable in the 21st century. Its techniques and tools have evolved since 1945 to the point that war today is uncontrollable, unpredictable, and inevitably of escalating cost. In other words, war is obsolete. It cannot, by definition, achieve its objects. As such it remains the biggest threat to the sustainability of humankind. War is therefore outdated as a tool of diplomacy. Clausewitz is dead! The time is ripe for the implementation of the Hague Agenda for Peace (1999). Now there's a theme for IIED.

# 5

# Earthscan–Panos: Favourite son, via cuckoo-in-the-nest, to friendly rival

## JON TINKER

In 1974, Maurice Strong, IIED Board member, was head of the newly formed UN Environment Programme (UNEP). He concluded that though public awareness was a key element in UNEP's mandate, it was almost impossible to produce accurate and forceful information from within the UN. His ingenious solution was for UNEP to fund an independent organization to produce what UNEP could not publish itself – and for which governments could then not hold UNEP politically responsible. Strong invited IIED to examine this idea; its report somewhat predictably concluded that Strong's concept was a splendid one, and requested a year's UNEP funding to test it out.

Late in 1974, Richard Sandbrook and David Runnalls asked me to head this new global information unit. I had been the UK's first full-time environment journalist, and *New Scientist*'s environment and development editor for some years, creating a certain reputation for digging up unlikely stories. IIED's invitation intrigued me, and I accepted it. The result was Earthscan, which later morphed into Panos.

## THE DEVELOPMENT OF EARTHSCAN WITHIN IIED

From Earthscan's start in 1974, I insisted that this new component of IIED should have its own name, and that its complete editorial

I am grateful to James Deane and Gerry Foley for their careful critique of this text. But any remaining errors are mine, and memory is fickle. I deeply regret that lack of space makes it impossible to mention the invaluable contributions of so many former colleagues, who each helped build a remarkable clutch of organizations.

independence, both of its parent IIED and of its funder UNEP, be placed on its letterhead. Our initial staff team was four people: John Austin, Caryl Panman, Kath Adams and myself. Caryl left after a few years, but John and Kath were to be mainstays of Earthscan for well over a decade. We occupied one-and-a-half rooms and a magical roof garden, in IIED's small central London office.

Our initial information work was based on three principles. First, we would target only the two or three most influential media in each country. Second, we would work on only a few global issues. Third, we would not be propagandist; while we would identify and critique policy options, we would leave journalists and media outlets to draw their own conclusions.

We chose Earthscan's core issues carefully. Each issue had to be: globally and not just regionally important; neglected by the media; and one where we could envisage imaginative information activities, where we could make the issue sexy. There were always more subjects than we could cover, and our key decisions were on what issues not to adopt, for our strength was a relatively narrow subject focus.

By 1980, Earthscan subjects had included urbanization, law of the sea, desertification, primary health care, marine pollution, generic drugs, climate change, drinking water and renewable energy. Our areas were sometimes ones where IIED had significant in-house strength: David Satterthwaite and Jorge Hardoy on human settlements, Gerry Leach on energy, Barbara Mitchell on Antarctica, John Beddington on fisheries. All these IIED specialists were generous with their advice, as were Richard Sandbrook, David Runnalls and Brian Johnson.

Barbara Ward's great skill was to allow me, and IIED's other half dozen key staff, the freedom to follow our instincts. There was internal discussion and argument, of course, sometimes ferocious, and we often talked one another out of our wilder plans. But I remember no occasion when I or anyone else was ultimately over-ruled.

Within a few years, Earthscan had grown to around half the size of IIED as a whole. This duality became one of IIED's greatest strengths, and both its information and its policy research components began to refer to it as IIED-Earthscan. The dichotomy was in fact more apparent than real, for IIED then prided itself on effective and timely delivery of its policy research to decision-makers, and Earthscan's information was prepared only after detailed research.

I had many fruitful conversations with Barbara about Earthscan's philosophy and activities, for she understood instinctively our goal of factual, non-propagandistic information. Her own books had an uncanny ability to present new ideas in a commonsense way. Her readers responded with 'Yes, that's just right. It's exactly what I think.' Barbara had worked for so long in the international arena, and knew so many of the Kennedy generation who then dominated it, that in almost any field she had a personal friendship with the key players, and she was generous with her introductions.

Earthscan's first basic product was the press-briefing document: a 50-page photocopied dossier giving facts, policy options and opinions on a chosen subject. In all, we published around 50, most of which I edited, and sometimes rewrote. They were mailed to a network of about 1000 specialist journalists worldwide. In Earthscan's early days I also edited all of our features, of which we distributed about 70 a year to over 100 subscribing newspapers; many in the Third World reprinted nearly every one. Our third main activity was the press-briefing seminar, where about 30 journalists spent an intensive day listening to and debating with four speakers, deliberately selected to have conflicting views.

Within a couple of years, Earthscan's outputs had developed an international reputation for quality and independence. They were widely reported. *Natural Disasters: Acts of God or Acts of Man?*, for example, was used by over 200 media outlets; we did not employ a clippings service, so the total use must have been far higher. It had a significant policy impact, accelerating the early evolution among agencies from disaster-relief to disaster-prevention.

In 1977 Earthscan initiated a new type of briefing document, for the UN Conference on Desertification in Nairobi. As at most UN meetings, the total documentation made a stack about two metres high. Some were worthy but boring; some were rubbish; a few were excellent. I read every one, and prepared a brief summary of each, together with a *Guide Michelin* rating: five stars for 'essential reading', down to one star for 'can be missed'.

In Nairobi, although some countries and agencies whose texts we had savaged made ritual protests, most welcomed Earthscan's objectivity. Originally aimed at journalists trying to cover an unfamiliar subject, our document proved to be the main tool for delegations themselves to find their way through the paperwork, and the conference secretariat paid for an emergency reprint.

Earthscan was fun. Our press seminars were enjoyable as well as useful, which helped to attract journalists. We held them in interesting locations – Bali, Ashkhabad, Costa Rica, Khartoum, Oslo on midsummer's eve – and they always involved a good party (which we soberly called a press reception). Our first seminar on Antarctica, for example, opened with drinks at dusk on board Scott of the Antarctic's *Discovery*, then moored on the River Thames. Our seminar was held on the next day in the New Zealand High Commission, on the eve of an Antarctic Treaty meeting in London.

The British Foreign Office considered this unhelpful, preferring to sort out Antarctic policy quietly, away from the vulgar gaze of the media. So, with consummate skill, the UK mandarins arranged for the Australians to pressure New Zealand to withdraw their invitation to Earthscan. This was about as intelligent as the Americans asking the British to persuade the Irish not to do something. I asked a senior New Zealand official what their reaction had been. 'What do you think, mate?', he replied, with an evil grin.

Our second Antarctic seminar was in Washington DC, and its Earthscan press reception, well-attended by Antarctic Treaty diplomats, was just winding down when some Soviets burst out of a cab, having driven straight from the airport. As the Russian scientists and diplomats reeled round the room, one emptied a large bottle of vodka into our vast silver tureen of krill soup (krill, a planktonic shrimp, is the centre of the Antarctic food web). That was another good party.

The flavour of those early days was exciting, with a heady and partly justified feeling that we were helping to change the world. Earthscanners often worked late into the night; we usually lunched together, and developed our best ideas in the pub. But if Earthscan was fun, it was also hard work; if we were a young, boisterous and happy family, we also imposed on one another accountability, editorial quality and deadlines. I recall once having to cross-question a colleague's failure to perform. It ended with him storming out of my office with a resounding door-slam. Half an hour later, I told him that shouting at me was inappropriate behaviour. I have never forgotten my chagrin at his reply: 'Jon, you were yelling at me without even raising your voice.'

Earthscan's activities steadily expanded, as we learned the art of fundraising and broadened our donor base way beyond UNEP. Since our duplicated briefing documents soon became dog-eared and many users kept them for years, we started reprinting them as booklets and later as paperbacks, the start of the Earthscan book imprint. We soon had a respectable bookshop sale. Since NGOs as well as journalists used our feature service, we started the *Earthscan Bulletin*; soon, Earthscan was targeting NGOs as much as the media, as effective information multipliers. Some of our one-day seminars expanded into week-long field trips, and we started a radio tape service and a photo-library.

By the beginning of the 1980s we were producing nearly all our material in French and Spanish as well as English, with some in German and a couple of forays into Arabic. By 1981 we had 9 staff, on a budget of $460,000; by 1986 we had 20 staff, and a budget of $760,000. Earthscan's finances, after paying an overhead, were essentially independent of IIED's; like many NGOs dependent on project funds without any core support, we were often balanced on a knife-edge. Each year, we started a few new projects on donor promises, long before contracts were signed. If sometimes we were in deficit as a result, enough of our gambles paid off for us to remain ahead of the game.

At first, Earthscan's aim was greater public awareness. But we began to articulate a more specific vision. In 1981, I was in Indonesia, planning a journalists' workshop with Soedjatmoko, then Rector of the UN University. 'We can tell these journalists some of the answers to development problems', said one Indonesian excitedly. 'No', replied Soedjatmoko slowly, 'we don't know the answers ourselves. But if we can help them ask the right questions ...'

Earthscan started to talk about public understanding rather than public awareness; our goal was redefined as identifying solutions as much as exposing problems. We were increasingly coming to realize that Earthscan materials had most impact at second-hand. When Southern journalists and NGOs used our briefing documents to write their own materials, they were both more likely to find a receptive audience than was a Northern agency like Earthscan, and more likely to propose policies which were appropriate to national needs. To use a phrase which later became the watchword of the Panos AIDS programme: 'Trust the messenger: trust the message'.

In 1980 we developed a scheme to establish independent media units (IMUs): a mini-Earthscan for each subcontinent. But donors were never more than politely interested. It was not until the early 1990s that they backed our wish to move control of our programmes southwards. However, we did start fellowships for Southern journalists and NGO writers, and 'co-publication' of our briefing documents, whereby Southern partners adapted and re-published national editions of Earthscan papers.

In 1982 the Nordic Council published *Miljö och Bistånd*, a report which shifted Nordic aid to a sustainable development track. It also rightly argued that sustainable development could not be imposed on the South, and that long-term success depended on greater awareness within Southern societies. Earthscan used this report to justify a scheme which we sold to the four Nordic governments and to the Dutch. We called this the Focal Country Programme (FCP), for it focused on six countries in East Africa and South Asia, states which were both major recipients of Nordic and Dutch aid, and contained many Earthscan partners. There we would concentrate (though not confine) our activities, and through joint programmes with media and NGOs try to reinforce NGO and media capacities and have a more sustained public and policy impact. The highly successful FCP started in 1984, and was later expanded to the Sahel, the Caribbean, Southern Africa and the Horn of Africa.

Co-syndication was a typical FCP technique. First, we would set up a deal with a national NGO or media group to translate Earthscan features into indigenous languages, and to distribute them; then this partner would edit our features to adapt them to national readers; then they would commission features of their own, some of which were re-used in London in our international service. By 1984 there were five such services in nine Third World tongues; under Panos this grew to around 20.

The funding of the FCP marked another significant development in Earthscan: a widening of our donor base, as well as our first three-year grants. In 1984 we had an income of nearly $700,000 from 15 funders, plus nearly $60,000 from our own sales.

I cannot mention all those whose skills and personalities helped to shape Earthscan, and the following selection is hopelessly arbitrary. There was Lloyd Timberlake, a suave Georgia boy from Reuters who became editorial director and whose juggling skills were legendary; Anil Agarwal, who alternated Tiers Mondiste advocacy with obsessive one-finger pounding on a portable typewriter; Barbara Cheney, who handled our production headaches from endless retyping before photocopying, through our first noisy daisy-wheel printer in a cubicle known as the Black Hole, into the glorious freedom of computer-typeset books; and Gerry Foley, our energy guru, whose deprecating Irish humour always oiled our internal wheels.

There was also: the gentle Sumi Chauhan, whose World Water Decade skills enabled Earthscan to outgun the information budgets of WHO, UNICEF and the World Bank combined; John Austin, whose hissing indrawn breath, whenever I proposed spending money we didn't yet have, kept Earthscan just on the right side of insolvency;

Jacquie Craw, who proof-read impeccably in English, French, German and Spanish; Dominique Side, who combined a passion for Tibetan culture with a Parisian relish for hard-headed negotiation; Don de Silva, an experienced Sri Lankan who oversaw the expansion of the FCP; and Rosemarie Philips, whose quiet assurance underpinned our growing Washington operations.

Lest this account of Earthscan is sounding too self-servingly successful, I must mention two cases where events proved me resoundingly wrong. Mark Edwards, whose superb development photos we had used in Earthscan for years, proposed that we become part of a new photo agency he was planning. I helpfully told him that he didn't have enough business ability. Mark and his photos left us, and the organization he started, Still Pictures, thrives today. And when Rob Lamb, one of our editorial team, suggested we establish a TV unit with him in charge, I foolishly told him he didn't have enough experience. Soon after, Rob left us to establish the Television Trust for the Environment (TVE), which still plays a leading international role in brokering environmental programmes (see Box 5.1).

But TVE, like the Centre for Science and Environment (CSE) which Anil Agarwal founded in Delhi when his productive period with Earthscan ended, are both organizations in which much of the IIED–Earthscan ethos is clearly recognizable. Similar information-based NGOs, loosely or closely modelled on Earthscan, were established by associates in Kenya, Nepal, Indonesia and elsewhere. All these groups are in a very real sense the progeny of the early IIED.

## SEPARATION OF EARTHSCAN AND IIED

In 1980, Barbara Ward became ill, with the cancer that was to kill her. IIED had raised funds for her to write a book on the tenth anniversary of the Stockholm Conference, which it soon became clear she would not be able to do. I persuaded my friend Erik Eckholm to come to London for a year to 'co-author' it; we all knew this was a euphemism.

My last sight of Barbara was in her sickbed at her beloved country home in Sussex, discussing the book's theme with Erik. Her face was white as the finest porcelain, so translucent that one could almost see the skull beneath. But through pain and exhaustion the old fire still sparkled. I taped our conversation, and from these fragments concocted a coherent foreword which later appeared under her name as the introduction to Erik's book, *Down to Earth*.

## BOX 5.1 TVE: THE EARTHSCAN OF THE AIRWAVES

When I suggested at the end of the 1970s that television was the way to go for Earthscan/IIED, it was an idea ahead of itself. Back then, producing one or two films would have taken up Earthscan's entire budget. Entering the high-risk world of television needed a TV company to be involved. In 1984, while I was with UNEP, we succeeded with the UK company Central TV. Together the two organizations set up the independent TV Trust for the Environment (TVE). Only years later did I find out that those in the know thought that TVE would crash and burn. It didn't. But for the first few years it was touch and go. TVE was set up with the demanding brief to be a 'broker' between the worlds of donor agencies and broadcasters. We researched the idea, raised the start-up funding and then found TV stations to contribute the remaining costs.

It was a formula that worked because we learned how to walk the editorial tightrope between the needs of the two funding entities. Nearly two decades and some 800 programmes later, TVE is overseeing the production of two films a week that go out to 700 million homes via the BBC and other broadcasters. TVE has built up a network of 50 partners in the developing world, which put the programmes out on their national TV networks. Our news releases reach 900 news stations. Most encouraging is that independent evaluations have linked the broadcasts with direct action. Like Anil Agarwal or Lloyd Timberlake or James Deane, also all ex-Earthscanners, we owe a great debt to IIED: for its foresight in setting up Earthscan and in appointing Jon Tinker as its first director. We have all carried on the IIED ethos into our different fields.

Robert Lamb, TVE

Barbara had decided that she should be succeeded by William Clark, an erudite and urbane man who had just retired as a World Bank vice-president. Sadly, he too was soon to die of cancer. William at first found IIED somewhat bewildering, and never quite understood how Richard Sandbrook, David Runnalls and myself could have such furious arguments while retaining our friendship and mutual respect. Though, like Barbara, he moved sure-footedly among both the British and the international development establishments (both still somewhat exclusive in the mid–1980s), he was in many ways very different, and his camp humour was not always appreciated by some of IIED's more intense researchers.

Through William's interregnum at IIED, little changed on the surface. Like Barbara, he was a part-time president, content to

---

## Box 5.2 The Earthscan of today

The story of Earthscan doesn't end with its period as an information service. At Richard Sandbrook's instigation, it was reincarnated as a fully-fledged publishing house, to build on the reputation of the original Earthscan by continuing to provide penetrating and robust information, analyses and policy foundations, and to do so on a securely self-funding basis. This latter meant that Earthscan had to live by what it sold, initially owned by IIED, and after 1992 as a subsidiary of an independent London publisher.

The 15 years since the new Earthscan was born have seen both the consolidation of the agenda of sustainable development and its ramification into almost every area of policy for the public, the private and the third sectors. Earthscan has kept pace with this evolution, mirroring, serving and defining the informational needs of those doing the research, teaching, policy formulation and practical implementation involved. And it has succeeded, both in establishing a distinctive, if not unique position, and in the continuously demanding task of combining commercial survival and growth with fulfilling its public interest goals. Throughout, we have continued to work closely with IIED, co-publishing much of their most important and influential work, and now plan a formal joint imprint. Our overall output has risen to 50 to 60 new books each year, many with a range of other partners as well, while keeping the growing backlist of 350 titles in print for as long as possible, and distribute and sell them throughout the world. That demand for our books is growing may be a reassuring sign; that they are needed in the first place is not. But if sustainability is ever to be more than an aspiration, information will be the key.

Jonathan Sinclair-Wilson, Earthscan

---

orchestrate IIED's many prima donnas in what Richard loved to call a 'collegiate' structure and Barbara's presence outlived her. Two or three years after her death, IIED arguments could still be effectively closed when someone said: 'Barbara would never have agreed to that!'

We didn't realize it at the time, but William Clark's 1985 memorial service in St James', Piccadilly, marked the end of an era. Like the requiem mass for Barbara in Westminster Cathedral some months earlier, the service was packed with the great and the good, those whom both Barbara and William had seen as IIED's natural allies. But IIED's golden years were over.

My last few years at the Institute started with IIED–Earthscan as amicable if occasionally squabbling Siamese twins, and was to end with their forcible severance. First in tandem, and then separately, each was to make some painful transitions.

In 1985, IIED's Board, a somewhat disparate group of Barbara's friends, chose a former head of Oxfam, Brian Walker, to take over from William. Within a year, IIED had changed radically; and Panos had been born from Earthscan's ashes. But before touching on this melancholy if melodramatic denouement, I need to explain some of the underlying tensions which had been brewing long before Brian arrived.

Since Barbara's final illness started, she had played little active part in IIED, though her influence was rarely absent. IIED was already beginning to change, from Barbara's institutional persona into a coherent professional organization. But this evolution was not easy, and IIED's Washington office began to follow so many US non-profits, towards federal contract work. This made many of us in London uneasy: we were happier with independent policy research. The diarchy of David Runnalls and Richard Sandbrook was no longer close, and David moved to run IIED's Washington office, later leaving the staff for good.

At the same time, tensions were growing between Earthscan and the rest of IIED. These were more based on style than on substance, but proved corrosive none the less. Some saw Earthscan as a state-within-a-state, separately funded and with dangerously cordial donor-relations, growing faster in budget and staff than its parent. We had a clear sense of what we were, and where we were going, while the rest of IIED was still struggling to articulate a post-Barbara identity.

In those days, IIED (like most UK organizations) had a blatant class structure. There were the senior staff, researchers and administrators, who apart from Barbara were virtually all men, and there were the support staff, who were all women. That some had degrees was not seen as relevant: they had been hired as secretaries, and secretaries they remained. There was no way through this glass ceiling, for IIED had no posts which straddled the professional–secretarial divide.

In Earthscan, by contrast, two of our first four staff were women, and both gender-balance and promotion were easier since we were steadily expanding and had many functions in the grey area between professional and non-professional: media and NGO liaison, design and production, book sales, translation, etc. Just as we managed to hire staff from the Third World and from ethnic minorities in the UK, so we were determined to have gender parity. In 1985/86, for example, Earthscan's Paris and Washington offices were both headed by women, and there were twelve women to eight men on the payroll.

Moreover, through nearly 20 years of Earthscan–Panos, we held a Monday-morning meeting at which each staffer outlined his/her coming week's work. These could occasionally be an ordeal for shyer staff members, but at their best they were stimulating tutorials on sustainable development, playing a crucial part in engaging everyone in policy discussion.

Such differences in style caused some problems, with younger IIED staff sometimes feeling under-valued and with few prospects, comparing themselves with Earthscanners with their greater equality, upward mobility and esprit de corps. Unsurprisingly, some in IIED began to see Earthscan as an insubordinate cuckoo-in-the-nest, expanding at its parent's expense.

It was against this background that Brian Walker arrived in 1985. His was a full-time post, and he expected to run IIED, not chair it. His time at IIED was patently unhappy, both for him and for the Institute. His personality never gelled with our contumacious way of reaching decisions, and he was puzzled by our lack of any comprehensible management structure. He never understood why Earthscan should be editorially independent of IIED, and made little secret of his wish for greater integration.

Brian's Quaker background brought some useful ethical clarity to our work: he insisted that development was something you did *with* people, not to or for them. But he had an inflexible internal sense of what was right, which sat uneasily with IIED's pragmatism. While Brian was in fact an acute listener, he tended to take on a glazed expression in the process. I remember a fruitless argument on whether Lloyd Timberlake's award-winning and highly influential book, *Africa in Crisis*, should be published in-house by Earthscan or given to a commercial company like Penguin. I was concerned with which route would be fast and effective; Brian seemed to want to identify which would be morally correct.

Our mutual suspicions grew until finally, exasperated at spending more time on IIED politics than on running Earthscan, I wrote a somewhat inflammatory and angst-ridden memo to the IIED Board, suggesting that Earthscan's semi-autonomous status be formally recognized. This triggered a Greek tragedy in which we all played our appointed roles, and all seemed unable to avert what may have been an inevitable outcome. Richard Sandbrook was in his element, devising ever-more ingenious schemes for rapprochement. But to no avail.

The basic moves are simply told. First, Brian proposed that Earthscan should leave IIED, and pay it $100,000 a year for ten years for the use of the name Earthscan. The Earthscan team agreed to this idea, because we believed donors would later insist on it being abandoned. But the IIED Board saw the same flaw, and rejected it. Then a special Board committee proposed that Earthscan remain in IIED, with both Brian and myself reporting directly to the Board. We accepted this formula, but it was rejected by Brian, presumably because by formalizing Earthscan's autonomy it would have removed half of his institute from his control. So Brian Walker asked the Board to approve my dismissal. Despite of some opposition – one director telexed that the move would gravely damage IIED in the South – the majority backed the man it had recently appointed. As requested, I left the IIED offices on the same day, in May 1986.

## THE BIRTH AND DEVELOPMENT OF PANOS

Within Earthscan, we had for some weeks considered the possibility of this endgame, and had discussed setting up a new organization. Within a couple of days, using the six months' salary IIED had to pay me to break my contract, we had established a one-room office less than a kilometre from IIED. Within a week we had registered our new NGO, issued a prospectus, and notified our partners. Month by month, we re-started most Earthscan activities: features, briefing documents, press seminars, NGO magazine.

I urged all Earthscan staff to stay in their jobs, at least for the moment, for I had no way of paying 20 salaries. Gradually, as funds started to flow, some resigned to work with me, some initially without pay and often at considerable personal cost. Some obtained other jobs, and the remainder were eventually made redundant by IIED and joined Panos. Only one, Lloyd Timberlake, accepted a new position at IIED, and although a year later he and I twice discussed his joining Panos, this sadly never proved possible.

The nascent Panos could not legitimately claim to be Earthscan, for IIED insisted that Earthscan still existed. But we could and did say that Panos was 'founded by the former staff of Earthscan'. By late 1997, virtually all Earthscan's old donors were funding Panos, and IIED had quietly abandoned its initial claim that Earthscan was still alive. Happily, IIED maintained the name Earthscan as its in-house publishing imprint, and later sold the name to a commercial publisher. So 'Earthscan' still appears on book-covers, some of them on publications originating from IIED.

Inevitably, perhaps, Earthscan's rebirth as Panos left a legacy of bitterness. A few weeks after my departure from IIED, I was at an international conference in Ottawa, where many of our donors and partners were easily accessible. In Ottawa, too, was an IIED delegation. At the opening reception, Maurice Strong told me bluntly that while he wished me all the best personally, he had heard that I was planning to recreate Earthscan under another name, and if so would do everything in his power to destroy it. It was not until 1991, when Maurice was preparing the 1992 Earth Summit in Rio, that I decided we must bury this hatchet, and met him in Geneva.

Maurice, I discovered, had been told that while still employed by IIED I had asked donors to fund a breakaway group. I remarked that while he might consider me sufficiently unethical to do this, did he think me sufficiently stupid? If I had indeed approached donors in this way, I argued, word would rapidly have got back to IIED, killing the idea stone dead. Maurice saw the point, and I was happy to have our interrupted friendship restored.

At that same Ottawa conference, a Canadian NGO was due to present Earthscan with an award, and in order not to take sides between Panos and IIED it insisted that David Runnalls, Richard Sandbrook and myself jointly accept the trophy. All three of us trooped onto the stage – although not exactly hand-in-hand. I was grinning broadly; Dave looked thunderous; and Richard collapsed in laughter at the absurdity of it all.

Dave's lack of amusement was understandable, for IIED was going through a difficult post-Earthscan transition. It had suddenly lost half of its staff and income, and throughout 1987 I knew from my own visits to donors that Brian was working hard to finance new programmes as well as arguing that Earthscan still existed and should be re-funded as part of IIED.

Through these tense months, Richard provided continuity and stability, and eventually took over in 1989 as Executive Director. Panos–IIED relations then slowly began to thaw, and in the mid-90s Richard ensured that the institute's 25th anniversary booklet included a generous account of Earthscan. Today, hardly anyone in either organization remembers the traumatic quarrels of 1986. Only David Satterthwaite remains on the IIED staff from Earthscan days, and James Deane and Marty Radlett are the only former Earthscanners still working for Panos.

So how did we manage to recreate Earthscan? We said from the start that we would recommence all Earthscan's former activities, and we did. But we also determined on some key changes. First, we needed a new name, as Earthscan was the property of IIED. 'Earthscan' had been a great title, but when we chose it (I think it was Dave Runnalls' idea) we never considered its non-English pronunciation. Francophone tongues found the five consecutive consonants unmanageable, so we looked for a new name that had some but not too much meaning, and that would work in any language: rather as a transnational company chooses a name for a new car.

Finally, Gerry Foley proposed 'panos', a classical Greek dialect word derived from Pharos, the island with the famous lighthouse. The syllable 'pan' in Greek means universal; its Latin root is the basis of the word for bread in most Romance languages; and in Hindi 'pani' means water. That in Finnish slang the word has sexual connotations, and that Pan had been the Roman god of debauchery and chaos, we found amusing.

The Earthscan bureaux in Paris and Washington had always been seen locally as branch offices of a British organization. The second major change in forming Panos was that we were determined to establish totally autonomous Panos institutes in these cities, with the status of French and US NGOs respectively. I served as their common president, but their boards and staff were drawn from the francophone and pan-American cultures. In the longer term, I hoped that one day we could have similarly autonomous Panos institutes in the South.

The third change was the conscious increase in the Southern content of our information materials. Analysis and policies on sustainable development which are formulated within a society are both more likely to be believed, and more likely to be socially sustainable, than those suggested or imposed from outside.

NGOs are by nature fissiparous, and there have been many instances of disaffected staff leaving to form breakaway organizations. Nearly all disappear without trace. How did Panos succeed where so many others have failed? The biggest reason was the extraordinary determination, mutual loyalty and sense of outrage of the former Earthscan staff. If IIED had taken our ball away, we would damned well start a new game next door.

We received a similar commitment from our Third World partners, and many friends proved willing to join the boards of an unproven trio of new NGOs. It is impossible to mention all those who played a key role as Panos directors, but they included Andras Bíró, Bill Carmichael,

Halle Jørn Hanssen, Brad Morse, Vicente Sanchez, Kristian Sørensen and Tarzie Vittachi; many other influential friends, such as Sonny Ramphal, helped us in other ways.

Our ultimate success was heavily underwritten by two chance events: a decision of the Swedish government to examine its aid programme openly, and the early growth of the AIDS pandemic. A new international NGO needs a high-profile event to make it visible, and a major issue to make its own. Panos, by great good fortune, found both.

In summer 1986, Johan Holmberg of the Swedish government development agency, Sida told me that Sweden was to host a Nordic conference, opened by the four prime ministers, to examine the sustainability of their aid programmes. Could Panos write some project evaluations? Sure, I replied, provided you let us commission them from journalists in the recipient country. Johan was excited at this approach, and sold it to his bosses. By autumn 1986, Panos was hard at work on fourteen 10,000-word studies: development projects from the consumer's viewpoint. And we had our funding from all four Nordic aid agencies. By mid-1987, Panos had built a solid reputation, unusual when development 'experts' normally jetted in from outside, for providing authentic Southern voices on Southern issues. Many other Panos studies and books later reinforced this tradition.

Our second stroke of luck, if such an evil development can be called fortunate, was that 1986 was in the early days of AIDS. Renée Sabatier, an inspired and painstaking young Quebecker who had joined Earthscan's editorial team, moved with most of the rest of us to Panos and started studying this new disease.

I was of course aware of AIDS, even though the deaths of so many close friends were still to come. (These were to include two well-loved colleagues in Panos-Washington: director Richard Horovitz, and fundraiser Steve Lembesis.) But what had AIDS to do with development, I asked Renée? I had an institute to create and finance: don't bother me with issues I don't need to know about!

Renée took me to lunch with Dr Richard Tedder at the Middlesex Hospital Medical School, whose unpublished figures on the high incidence of HIV among prostitutes in Africa, combined with the long symptom-less incubation period before HIV infection showed itself, persuaded me that AIDS was a development disaster in the making.

Through autumn 1986, Renée worked on the first Panos dossier, *AIDS and the Third World*. Meanwhile, I sounded alarm bells among development aid agencies. AIDS was not, we argued, just a growing problem for gay men in Europe and North America, nor even just one more disease for the health divisions of aid agencies. It was an issue which would come to dominate development, and demanded a top-level strategic rethink.

These treks through the chancelleries of Europe began to have a double purpose: funds for Panos, and talking AIDS to anyone who would listen. Responses varied. Some got the point quickly, but said they had no budgets. Others simply disbelieved our data. One young high-flyer in a Nordic foreign ministry cross-questioned me closely about the incidence of HIV among East African prostitutes a few years previously. His concern, I later realized, was motivated less by development than by recollections of his own past sexual encounters in Nairobi.

We had two more lucky breaks. First, Renée put me in touch with Calle Almedal at the Norwegian Red Cross (Norcross), who became a firm friend. Norcross quickly and repeatedly helped fund our AIDS work, and when our dossier was published in November 1986 it had the Red Cross emblem on the cover, giving it crucial respectability – much to the initial rage of many national Red Cross societies, who felt that the subject was not quite nice.

Second, I happened to arrive for a meeting at the World Health Organization (WHO) on the same day that Dr Jonathan Mann took up his post as WHO's AIDS coordinator. No one at WHO was ready to talk to him, so we spent the morning having coffee in the chilly Geneva sunshine. Jon Mann was to prove another long-standing friend of Panos, privately advising on virtually all our AIDS publications, and with a shrewd political sense of what an international NGO could usefully say that WHO could not.

*AIDS and the Third World* was probably the most influential publication that Earthscan or Panos ever produced. Jon Mann later told me he had visited more than 100 countries for WHO, and in only a handful was he not shown a copy, or a dog-eared copy of a copy, of the Panos report, and told that it had been crucial in stimulating action.

'Our picture of the AIDS epidemic is a grim one', I wrote in *AIDS and the Third World*'s foreword. 'In the US, the worst-hit city so far is New York, where one in 15 people is now thought to carry the virus. But in some Central African capitals, up to one person in five is infected. Most of them are in their twenties and thirties, as many women as men. These are their nation's breadwinners, many of them educated professionals. The impact of their gathering death march will scar Africa for a generation.'

Events have since justified this gloomy rhetoric. But being prematurely right is not always prudent. To many in government, Panos was irresponsibly alarmist. We decided to convene a meeting of heads of Western development agencies. Norcross and WHO backed us, and our Washington board member Beth Kummerfeld wrote out a personal cheque.

With Halfdan Mahler and Jim Grant, the respective bosses of WHO and UNICEF, giving opening statements, the Talloires Consultation was held in spring 1987, in a restored medieval monastery in the French alps. I asked Maggie Cattley-Carlson, President of the Canadian government development agency CIDA, to chair the meeting. 'Sure,' she replied, 'but don't think I share your agenda.' She had been advised that our analysis was exaggerated, and she intended to make this clear. Her scepticism worked well for us, as by the end of the meeting she was fully persuaded, and said so.

Talloires was to prove an important turning point in the AIDS policies of many agencies and governments, and the Panos strategy in convening it was classic IIED, recalling the high-level symposia with which Barbara Ward preceded several UN conferences of the late 1970s. Renée Sabatier, together with Martin Foreman and Marty Radlett, brought out half a dozen more important AIDS publications for Panos; Martin now has an international reputation in this field. Renée, sadly, left Panos, and later died while working on AIDS in Zimbabwe. Jon Mann was tragically killed in a plane crash.

## PANOS AND IIED TODAY

This chapter is not a history of Panos, and having described how we survived our separation from IIED I shall say little more. It is unfair to single anyone out, but once again I can't resist a few names, quite arbitrarily selected: Geoff Barnard, whose nose for a bargain located Panos-London's two successive offices, orchestrated our increasing computerization and oversaw our finances and administration for years; Liz Carlile, who hard-headedly ran Panos Books; Nigel Twose, who became director of Panos-London, bringing better management and a sharp political nose; Nigel Cross, who took London through a difficult period of retrenchment, established a decentralized Panos programme in South Asian and East and Southern Africa, and laid the groundwork for current success; Patricia Ardila, a US-Colombian who delighted in the *Star Trek* implications of her US identity card headed 'resident alien'; Aida Opoku-Mensah and Carmen Miranda, who skilfully developed our work in Southern Africa and South Asia respectively; Robert Walgate and Benjie Pogrund, two superb writers and editors; Charles Condamines, Diana Senghor and Francoise Havelange who brilliantly ran our work in Paris and the Sahel; James Deane, whose sure-footed sense of direction underlies the present growth of Panos in the South. Throughout Earthscan and Panos, one of my joys was watching previously hidden talents bloom, as so many of my colleagues grew far beyond their initial roles.

By 1993, I had been running Earthscan and then Panos for nearly 20 years. It was still fun – but not as much as it had been. In the early 1990s Panos had become highly regarded in the development world, with a staff of about 50 (of 20 nationalities) in three offices, and an annual budget which in 1990 reached \$3.5 million. I decided that enough was enough, and moved to Canada. There, I joined the Sustainable Development Research Institute (SDRI) at the University of British Columbia, and work as a consultant and writer.

Of Panos since 1993, I want to make only one point. There are now Panos institutes, autonomous or on the way to becoming so, in Washington DC, Haiti, Dakar, Lusaka, Kampala, London, Paris and Kathmandu, as well as offices in other locations. There are other links, too: Panos Pictures has been spun off into an independent profit-making company, under its shrewd manager Adrian Evans; and the highly regarded Gemini News has merged into Panos-London.

The inheritors of Barbara Ward's IIED are now to be found on four continents. It is a measure of the parallel paths which Panos and IIED now follow that while former Earthscanner James Deane heads Panos-London, former Panos-London director Nigel Cross now runs IIED.

As IIED enters its fourth decade, and Panos celebrates its 15th birthday, the two have evolved distinctly different personalities. But they share some strong common strands: a sometimes pedantic resolve to get things right; an instinct for pragmatism over theory; a neither-fish-nor-fowl identity somewhere between research and activism; a liking for influencing the levers of power, perhaps at the risk of elitism; an understanding of Brian Walker's dictum that development is with people, not for or to them; some of Barbara Ward's humane Catholicism, and her sense of moral outrage; an echo, perhaps, of the Kennedy generation which saw the world as it might be, and asked 'Why not?'; the belief, with Soedjatmoko, that you can help people ask the right questions, but that they must find their own answers.

In Earthscan's first few brochures, we quoted Barbara Ward: 'The chief environmental insight is that everything interconnects. But if

everything connects, where are the threads through the maze?'
Earthscan-IIED provided some of those guiding threads.

Thirty years on, this need is as acute as it was at the time of
Stockholm. The Internet gives access to vast banks of information
(for those on-line at least, which excludes most of the South). But
where are the threads through today's cyber-maze? The signal-to-
noise ratio is far lower than it was then, and the Web provides as
many opportunities for delusion as it does for enlightenment.
Consider the cost in human misery of South African President
Mbeki's view, gleaned from the Internet and imposed on his country's
public health system, that AIDS is not caused by HIV.

If it can afford a satellite phone, the remotest community can
now choke itself on information. But there is today an even more
urgent development need for evaluated and critiqued information,
that helps others ask the right questions without manipulating them
into accepting the answers and values of the webmasters, most of
whom accept the predominant global consumerist ideology.

*Connecting with the World*, a 1996 report to the Canadian government from a task force headed by Maurice Strong, argued that the
Internet is central to development, and Canada's IISD, now headed
by David Runnalls, has played a pioneering role in this field. It is
perhaps no coincidence that both people were for many years closely
associated with IIED and Earthscan.

IIED and Panos have historically shared a commitment to creating and disseminating timely, sharp, policy-relevant information, with
the specific goal of shifting public policy. As we move nearer to
Rio + 10, we should perhaps be asking ourselves whether, and how
effectively, we are still reaching this goal.

Today, hundreds of NGOs and academic bodies work on policy
analysis. The Pollyanna belief that good policies, like good science,
will eventually drive out the bad, is appropriate for scholars and may
be enough for research institutes. But the Bush administration's
decision that climate change is not a US priority, and the pathetic
post-Kyoto record of Canada, the UK and other major states, shows
how sterile this approach can be. Competent policy studies are of
little value unless they are adopted. 'Give me a lever and I will shift
the world', said Archimedes. Barbara Ward was never satisfied with
creating the lever: she wanted to pull it as well.

I am currently working on a book that takes a new look at sustainable development, and argues that, far from our environmental and
social goals being in conflict with economic goals, the three are recon-
cilable. Humankind can design its own futures, and then go there. A

single human brain, with its billions of interconnected cells, is capable of the insights of Gandhi, Michaelangelo or Einstein. The potential of billions of human brains, if they could be effectively interconnected, is one resource that is infinitely sustainable. Only connect. But how?

Those two redoubtable *grandes dames* Barbara Ward and Margaret Mead did not always work easily together. But the many institutions which are descended from Ward's IIED underline one of Mead's favourite remarks. 'Never underestimate two or three people coming together and talking about changing the world. That's the only way the world ever is changed.'

# 6

# Change that works, sometimes

## *Richard Sandbrook*

Where to begin? The answer cannot be at the beginning for that would lead to a chronological discourse that is not intended. Rather, with an incident – for events illustrate the crazy life led by those concerned with 'change'.

The incident was in Vancouver in 1976 shortly after I had joined IIED. The institute members were there in force – all eight or nine of us to organize a 'high-level seminar' to give the UN Habitat Conference a lift. Barbara Ward was the host. She had just completed the book *The Home of Man* and was busy on a crusade for clean water for all that incidentally led to the 'international drinking water decade'. Barbara was many things including a publicist. I was asked to help to get a 'demo' – a march for water – underway, and to ensure that Margaret Trudeau (wife of the then Canadian Prime Minister) agreed to carry the statutory bucket on her head. But it was not the only demo in town. An old friend, the late David MacTaggert rang to see if I could get any of Barbara's glitterati onto the Greenpeace boat *Rainbow Warrior*; I agreed to try. One of the seminar grandees was Margaret Mead of anthropological fame. She was an enormous woman in many ways – larger than life, with a long stick that she always carried as her trademark. I spoke with her PA and it was pencilled in for the following Saturday.

On the day in question I was woken at six by the PA and asked to attend on Margaret 'at once'. There she sat on the edge of the bed – legs wide apart with stick in between. 'Who are you to put me on a boat? Barbara's boys don't run me!' On and on she went. Then came the classic line as she prodded me with the stick: 'You think I am being unreasonable don't you? Well, I have been through menopause and I don't bloody care any more!' She went on the boat just the same – always intended to, I'll bet.

Barbara could operate in the same vein when put upon: without fear or favour; blunt, yet with a sweet smile. (I recall her telling Mrs Marcos at the same event that she did not deal with cobblers much less crooks!) But between these two great women, Ward and Mead that is, was a common thread. They both firmly understood the importance of the natural resource base to livelihoods and the relief of poverty. They correctly argued that life for the poor becomes impossible without a robust system for conserving resources while using them for economic gain. Environmental stewardship and sustained livelihoods are, in all subsistence economies (and many more) the two sides of the same coin – you cannot have one without the other.

## ENVIRONMENT AND DEVELOPMENT AND IIED

From Barbara's perspective, it was an absurdity that the environment and development issues ever came to be separated, much less seen as opposing. Perhaps this view developed because so much of the environmental movement originated in North America. Here, there is so much land per head of population, such productive soils and so many areas of kind climate that the idea of wilderness areas set aside just for nature's sake becomes a possibility. But in most other parts of the globe this can never be done on an extensive basis – unless the population was to crash or the land became equitably shared across the board. Land is the key resource and its distribution the all-important issue. Few realize, for example, that the top four places in the league table for population per unit of productive land are occupied by Bangladesh, Taiwan, Holland and the UK.

Little wonder that a major part of the thinking around the global environment in The Netherlands and the UK centres on the ecological and resource footprints that they have elsewhere. For poorer countries, the preoccupation is to find ways to build a diaspora economy to relieve the pressures on the land at home; in effect to create a footprint elsewhere too. Or take Brazil, where 80 per cent of the productive land is held by a mere 3 per cent of the population – no small wonder the forests disappear. This sort of thinking led Barbara to concentrate on how to make an interdependent world

work with some semblance of social and economic justice and equity.
She could see we could never turn the clock back to autarchy – even
regional autarchy without conflict. So how to make the inevitable
work? She was a 'free' trader but also a true cynic about unregulated
markets. The tradition lives on.

I joined IIED straight from Friends of the Earth in London in
1976. I had co-founded FOE-UK after university – in many ways as
an extension of the student politics of the 1968 era. I left FOE to join
'Barbara's boys', as some called us (there were in fact three men and
three women by that stage) because I wanted to extend beyond the
shores of the UK. FOE had been active in the Stockholm Conference
in 1972 and then in the foundation of the UN Environment
Programme (UNEP). I went to UNEP for all the early meetings on
behalf of FOE. Thus I vividly recall my first visit to Kenya in 1974
with David Brower – FOE's real founder (the archdriud of the
environmental movement). It seemed to me to a heaven within a hell.
The wealth of the UN crowd, the expat Brits, some in the Asian
community, surrounded by a sea of poverty and wretchedness. How
could all this be reconciled?

However, my first job with IIED had nothing to do with any of
this. I was asked to get a 'marine programme' going because as a
marine biologist of sorts I was interested. This was at the time of the
'Law of the Sea' negotiation – the longest intergovernmental negotiating process ever known to that point, lasting a little over five years!
We set about it on two tracks. One was based in the IIED US office
in Washington DC, and the other in London. The lawyers had the
brief in the USA, and the marine scientists in London. What an
education it was – all at once I was able to appreciate the rules-based
approach of the Americans in contrast to the fudge of the Europeans
(or perhaps certain Europeans) I saw that science could be mightily
abused by all sides, and just how powerful the industrial lobby was as
it pursed deep-sea mining rights alongside distant-water fishing alongside whaling. All this was done – initially as a joint FOE/IIED venture
– as we came to grips with that perennial conference process.
Resulting publications included *Towards an Environmentally Sound
Law of the Sea* (1974) and *Critical Environmental Issues in the Law
of the Sea* (1975).

At the time IIED was still very small. It had moved from the
USA, with Barbara, to London in 1973. Initially the office was housed
in the flat of Barbara's first lieutenant David Runnalls who had been
with her since she was at Columbia University in New York. Then it

moved into Mortimer Street to enjoy the hospitality of the Margaret Pyke family planning centre. Barbara had been the star of the first UN Conference on the Human Environment, with the book *Only One Earth*, and was thus able to attract help from all manner of luminaries in the emerging world of environment and development. I was lucky indeed to be asked to join in.

In retrospect I realize how my joining IIED – and indeed my previous experience in the FOE family (that I have never really left) – was privileged. We all were and are lucky to have chanced to work in environment and development. I suspect that many who read this book will also belong to the environment and/or development crowd, and will thus appreciate the point. The 'not for profit but for change' community is a worldwide club and basically very friendly. It attracts people who are committed but also usually able to laugh at themselves and with others. They know they are lucky even if they are not as well off in financial terms as many others. But what a sacrifice – as they travel the world, attend some of the most interesting of debates and discussions, meet brave and intelligent people in the most diverse of situations. Let's hope that the multicultural and international approach long continues and that the sense of privilege never disappears either. When that happens, the interests of those less fortunate somehow get left behind in the pursuit of personal and institutional gain. It is all too easy to have an organization that trades on the back of the very people it claims to help. I mention this because IIED staff have always been more privileged than most. To understand this is essential to understanding the organization's history.

Three things explain why the place is lucky. First, it works in an area that has, from the start, been in demand not least by those with sources of funds. Initially this applied to the big and foresightful US foundations, then gradually the whole of the OECD aid community became involved. So strong and flexible has this support been that, despite some notable hard times, IIED has never had to appeal for funds from the public; not that a research institute would find much public support in competition with aid charities. It has only once ever employed a fundraiser as such. Second, the mission of IIED from the start – to promote sustainable development – has become so widely accepted as a general societal aim that it has been able to ride a wave of political and journalistic sympathy. Third, because of the 'access' that Barbara Ward gave it initially (and staff have maintained ever since), IIED is a very creative and satisfying place in which to work. The target audience is often reached at the highest level. It is no wonder that it has always attracted the very best of staff. Three stories illustrate this.

## BANKING ON THE BIOSPHERE AND AID REFORM

One of the early recruits to IIED was Brian Johnson. He was an academic from Sussex University who had begun a small institute concerned with the study of international organizations. After working on and off for IIED Brian finally joined in the fray at IIED in 1978. He and Bob Stein (who ran our tiny US office left in Washington DC when Barbara moved to London) set about examining the environmental *bona fides* of the international finance institutions, and particularly the World Bank. This was a classic study – published under the wonderful title of *Banking on the Biosphere*. Connections counted. Barbara was a guiding light to Robert McNamara who was the then head of the Bank. Because of this, Brian and Bob were given complete access to the Bank's staff and procedures, and because the Bank had (and has) pull with all of the regional development banks, the IIED researchers were allowed in there as well.

The result was a softly spoken but nevertheless damning indictment of the environmental record of the international financial institutions. This book was in a way the first of the 'bank-bashing' reports that followed from such persistent campaigners as Bruce Rich, Catherine Caufield and Jim Barnes. As a direst result of *Banking on the Biosphere*, all of the banks signed up to a declaration to do better but more significantly created the Committee for International Development Institutions and the Environment (CIDIE). This was never a very functional club as it was superseded by an OECD group with more direct access to the treasury votes – but it still exists in a revised form. It is still one of the places where the reformers meet and push matters forward. It has, along with so much more, led to change and improvement.

One can ask how important IIED was in all this – a question almost impossible to answer. But the banks were keen to claim their environmental progress publicly, and IIED encouraged them into it. With all good political change the change agents have at some point to bow out and let the powerful claim the credit. I cannot count the times I have felt 'there goes another politician claiming he has had another (IIED) idea'. (If only we were called IIDEA – the International Institute for Development and Environmental Affairs.)

This work on the international financial institutions was a new gold seam for IIED. No sooner was the study done than we worked with the bilateral aid agencies too. Sweden, Holland, the USA, the UK, Norway, Denmark, Switzerland and Germany allowed us in to 'audit' them in the same way. What followed was a bit of a race to the top as each tried to show that they cared for the environment more than the next. International competitions of this sort have always been a key campaign method of the environmental community, and this was no exception. Much of the change was procedural – concerned with environmental impact assessments and the like – and a little with systemic and strategic issues too. But we failed in those early days to get the real poverty and environmental issues onto the agenda where they mattered. The urban issue was all but ignored. 'Livelihoods thinking' was still to happen. The agenda was all too much concerned with trees and wetlands, elephants and savannahs, important as these are.

## OUR COMMON FUTURE

From their beginnings in the early 1970s, IIED had enjoyed a very special relationship with UNEP, and again Barbara was responsible here. She had been the star of the Stockholm Conference in 1972 and was closely aligned with Maurice Strong who had run the event and then founded UNEP. As a UNEP groupie, I used to attend every governing council and busy myself with NGO coalitions to push the governments forward. Out of this era came the Environment Liaison Centre (now Environment Liaison Centre International (ELCI)), and Earthscan (located in IIED) which was the 'privatized' information arm of UNEP run by Jon Tinker. Both institutions now continue to prosper – one as one of the largest activist NGO coalitions in the world, and the other as the largest publisher on environment and development.

However, by the tenth anniversary of UNEP (by then under the direction of Mostafa Tolba), all the veterans of the process were feeling that governments were going nowhere fast on living up to the wider challenges of Stockholm. Something had to be done. It was two other great Canadian friends of Dave Runnalls and IIED who really deserve the credit for what happened. Bob Munro and Jim MacNeill – with IIED – mobilized to set up a global commission to examine why the environment and development issue was so stalled in the UN. (The answers are much the same today – isolated environment ministers; a lack of joined-up UN governance; issues of genuine international inequity but used to hide downright poor government; ignorance of private flows, and so on.) UNEP was a small agency with no executive power – we used to wonder how we could possibly put the world's environment to rights when UNEP had fewer professionals than most of the larger NGOs in the business. Nevertheless, out of the UNEP tenth governing council came a resolution to establish the so-called Brundtland Commission with Jim MacNeill as its tireless secretary.

IIED could claim no less than six of the Commissioners as past or present Board members. But it was Gro Brundtland who was the star. She never met Barbara (who died in 1981) as far as I know, but they would have loved each other. Here was a new champion aided and abetted by a strong commission and an equally strong team under Jim. Needless to say he came to IIED for help. This began a fertile time for us. We had by then pioneered work on the greening of economics (of which more later), and to relate the green agenda to the social field. IIED had a stable of researchers who knew their sectors: Duncan Poore for forests, Gerry Leach for energy, Jorge Hardoy and David Satterthwaite for human settlements and cities (Camilla Toulmin, Gordon Conway and David Pearce came later).

We wrote the initial drafts of three chapters in the report *Our Common Future* and contributed to many more. Always the thesis was the same – there is no need to be negative about the world if the energy of the human spirit is realized in circumstances where the incentives to safeguard the environment are in place. Property rights, human rights, economic rights, educational rights are all precursors to the positive response and responsibilities! The Brundtland report was a spectacular success in our terms – and as they say the rest of that story is history. Somewhere in the midst of all of this, the new jargon of 'sustainable livelihoods' emerged, but it was a decade and more before this idea began to take off as a guiding idea.

As all this energy was applied to others, IIED was not so fit itself. Several things came together to cause a crisis. As Barbara was dying, William Clark had agreed to take on the IIED presidency from her in 1980. William was also a journalist at heart, having worked at the *Observer* newspaper in its Astor days, and then as McNamara's head of external affairs at the World Bank. William had no idea on joining IIED how much money we expected him to raise. But he could not do it. It was just not his forte nor his style. By now, IIED had some 30 dependants spread across its London and Washington offices. The most active and growing programme was Earthscan under Jon Tinker. It was a cuckoo's egg in the nest, for, by the time Jon left in 1986, it generated over 40 per cent of the budget. To cut a long story short, William too fell ill with cancer and in 1984 resigned.

The Board under Robert Anderson, the ever-visionary oil baron, and without any discussion, asked me in an open meeting to take over. Suffice to say I refused. It was not our style to manage in this way – Dave Runnalls was my peer and senior, Jon Tinker was special too as were all the rest of the team. The Board then (as so often happens in the charity sector where trustees do not always relate to management realities) decided to appoint on its own. Brian Walker was their choice.

Brian inherited a very demoralized staff in 1985. He joined us as the former head, of ten years' standing, of Oxfam UK. He was known for his boldness of stroke (he took Oxfam into Vietnam and Cambodia when all thought it mad) and for his management style. Not everyone at IIED got on too well under the new direction. Within months the cracks began to appear between Brian and the Washington crew under Dave Runnalls (culture across the Atlantic is different), and with Jon Tinker who was by now his own boss. What followed can be only described as a very expensive break-up of the amalgam of structures that made up IIED hitherto. Jon and his team moved out *en masse* to form Panos, taking a large measure of the European aid support with them. Dave and his team merged with the new World Resources Institute in Washington, and Brian and a much reduced team were left in London rattling in a building we had recently leased. It was not a happy time.

## THE FORMATION OF THE DAC
### ENVIRONMENT GROUP

But we were busy at what we were meant to be about too. Bob Geldof had turned to Brian and the team to help organize the spending of the Band Aid money. This was a triumph of NGO cooperation largely due to Brian and Lloyd Timberlake – the one member of Jon Tinker's team who had not changed ships. As the Brundtland report took off, so the pressure grew on IIED to promote it – eventually to the point where we needed to have an event that capitalized on it in the UN. By now the trend for celebrating the major conferences of the 1970s with repeat runs 20 years on was well established. (In fact the cycle is now down to 10 years and even 5 in some cases.) Maurice Strong and Nitin

Desai were called in to mobilize the process for what became known as the Earth Summit in Rio de Janeiro in 1992.

A little before this, a group of like-minded aid officials who variously handled the 'environment portfolio' had begun to get together to discuss a formal intergovernmental process to accelerate their work. The movers and shakers were the likes of Mats Segnestam of the Swedish International Development Cooperation Agency (Sida), Jill Hanna of UK Overseas Development Administration (ODA), Frits Schlingemann of the Dutch Ministry of Foreign Affairs (DGIS) and Hans Peter Schipulle of the Federal Ministry of Economic Cooperation and Development (BMZ) Germany. They invited Mike Cockerell of IUCN and me to join in to get the terms of reference right and to progress the whole operation within the framework of the Development Assistance Committee (DAC) of the OECD. This 'club' became one of the most creative that I have ever belonged to. It was a unique atmosphere in which formal process gave away to informal friendships and debate. It became a key part of the run up to the Earth Summit.

It was very special for IIED as an independent policy institute (which was by now doing all manner of work for the European aid frame) to be invited to join one of the key policy fora in the business. Each meeting was an exercise in controlled excitement for me and Barry Dalal-Clayton (who normally accompanied me) to cope with. With the back-up of what was by now a strong IIED home team working with all manner of partners overseas, we had a wonderful opportunity to help steer the debate in ways that were consistent with our sustainable-development objectives – provided that we never looked for funding! On one occasion the Word Wide Fund for Nature (WWF) was invited, and did just that. I recall the very excitable French delegate going apoplectic with their mistake and very nearly ending our privilege for good in the fall out.

But this was not a one-way street. We worked hard to represent opinions outside the room and to bring the NGO perspective to bear. In turn it was good to see how this group widened the perspective on the environment in the UN summit process – resulting as it did in the Agenda for the 21st century (Agenda 21) and the key conventions on Biological Diversity, Climate Change and eventually Desertification. Of course with hindsight we know that the failure of Rio was that no additional funds to speak of were delivered to pay for all the heady ideas that were agreed upon. But I suggest that was not the fault of the officials but of the economic downturn that was happening precisely as the Rio process took place (not that this is such an excuse either).

My conclusion from these three instances is that it is possible to be a radical from within just as much as radical from without! In no way is this meant to be a sideways glance at the campaigning NGOs, for without their media and hence politically motivating work very little would be possible from within at all. The wide spectrum of civil-society organizations is its innate strength. But the process of policy change is a constant back and fill – or stretch and secure. The running is made by a good media story from an NGO, the politicians take note, the officials get instructed, the policy shops fill in the details and the result is agreed. Then the process begins anew. But all this depends on some brave person starting the process of change in the beginning – and on many brave souls maintaining the momentum thereafter. It has been good to be involved with such folk.

## THE CHALLENGE OF THE INTERCONNECTED AGENDA

It would be wrong to see IIED as just a servant of intergovernmental process – important though that has been. It is also, one hopes, a pioneer and innovator. For this reason it has always had a close relationship with the academic community, indeed attracting a good many academics to join as we never had the burdens of teaching to contend with. Perhaps one of the real contributions has been in making a place for bringing diverse disciplines to bear on a common problem. There is a great difference between a multidisciplinary institution and an interdisciplinary one. IIED has always aspired to the latter but not without a deal of internal strife and tension at times.

The story of the three circles is perhaps most illustrative here. It was in 1984 that we were wrestling yet again with the idea of sustainable development. Time to have a unifying theory we all thought, and so one lunchtime four or five people turned up for one of those brown-bag affairs. I do not recall quite who started it off but onto the flipchart went three separate circles representing the economy, the environment and the social sphere. What sustainable development is all about is getting to a point where these three systems (for we were at the time deep into systems thinking) could overlap optimally. Thus, the overlapping circles were drawn. Then the next issue was how to reconcile the different language systems of the different disciplines involved. What – apart from mathematics – would do? What was the currency to be? Energy? Money? How could the trade-offs or compromises between the systems take place – what processes were needed?

None of this is exceptional to anyone who has taken part in university seminars. But what was different was that we resolved to write it up and follow through with popular promotion. That weekend, I was to address a group of Save the Children staff in York on the environment and development debate. So I tried it out on them and was somewhat taken aback by the result. Debate literally took off. We were onto something here. The idea of sustainable livelihoods happened in a similar way but was not to become a strong 'currency' until the late1990s.

Gradually it became apparent that an ingredient missing from much of our work on sustainable development was good economics. So we approached David Pearce, round the corner at University College, London University (UCL) and he, Anil Markandya (from UCL) and Ed Barbier (from IIED) joined forces to form a new operation in the middle that we called LEEC (the London Environmental Economics Centre). That was a beginning that led to a succession of papers and books and projects that considerably expanded the field and the interest in environmental economics. Sadly, that group dispersed but the three circles, as the simplest way I know to communicate sustainable development as an idea, and the fertile field of environmental economics remain. Alongside this there has been a gradual coming together in IIED of the natural, economic and social sciences but through a wealth of field experience. What also has remained central to all of this has been a process that engages the differing perspectives from all sides so that trade-offs and compromise can be reached.

## THE GROWTH OF THE DEVELOPMENT TRIAD

This talk of trade-offs does not suit the green purist. Understandably there are those who feel that a line has to be drawn, most particularly when it comes to disappearing species, ecosystems and cultures. In many circumstances one has to agree. Then the suggestion that everything can be reduced to economics is unacceptable to many, who rightly point out that it is the ethics of society that matter – indeed that was the very origin of the economics discipline. Taking this a degree or two further, one arrives at the new liberation agenda which is all about global versus local values. The principal target here is the complex and lonely superpower and all it upholds for its citizens; as the elder Bush intoned at Rio 'no environmental or developmental fad is going to interfere with the needs of the American citizen!'

How was (and is) IIED going to cope with all this growing polarization centred on that catch-all word 'globalization'? The question was made all the more poignant as the origins of IIED were in large part based on multinational leaders with Bob Anderson – of Arco oil (now a part of BP!) – Maurice Strong of, *inter alia*, Petrocan, along with Barbara Ward who was all that is Catholic and Oxford bluestocking!

It is fair to say that all through the 1970s and 1980s, IIED was quietly anti-corporate on both sides of the Atlantic. This began to change in 1987 by the time Gus Speth had taken over what remained of our Washington office and absorbed it into a corner of the World Resources Institute (WRI). In WRI and in IIED there was a gradual awakening that the private sector mattered to development outcomes, and sustainable ones to boot! We had both had to play with the timber industry, the food industry, not to mention the development industry with all its consultants and banks! To ignore the development triad – civil society, the governments and the private sector – was an incomplete answer.

Of course the difficulty is again in the differing language and values of the three sectors. IIED and WRI combined to produce the first edition of the World Resources Report but then followed separate paths. This was caused as much as anything else as by our relative poverty as an institute. WRI was born with an enormous multimillion-dollar endowment, and IIED had nothing but the annual grind of project financing. But culture too had its influence in the drift apart. It was enough having to cope with a new set of 'corporate speak' without doing it in the USA and in Europe all at the same time.

In Europe our real opportunity came in 1990 at a seminar in Lausanne. This was to address a challenge Maurice Strong had issued to get the 'business community' involved in the Earth Summit. I had arrived late at the event and was thus in the dark about who was there. In the first break I was with an old colleague – Hugh Falkener – using the wall in the manner that men do. I asked: 'And who the h..l is this Stephan Schmidheiny anyway?' My elbow was grasped and a voice said, 'I am he.' Despite the faux pas much common endeavour followed with the formation of the Business Council for Sustainable Development (BCSD, now called the [Q]WBCSD) Eventually, after a few steps in between, we lent our star journalist Lloyd Timberlake to Stephan to help write the business book of the conference, *Changing Course*. I never got him back which was indeed a real loss to us but a real gain to the BCSD. But more followed between us.

At the Rio event in 1992, I was again teasing Stephan – this time in the presence of Erling Lorentzen. He runs the largest paper-mill in the world out of Brazil. Tempted by my cynicism he said, 'Why not tell the whole paper industry how to be sustainable?' This led to a very big project for IIED that was the called 'the Sustainable Paper Cycle'. We had something to start with – an excellent forestry team under Steve Bass, economics under Josh Bishop and new 'consumerism' under Nick Robins. Together we spent a year and a bit assembling all the problems and possible ways out for this rapidly globalizing and growing industry.

In the USA the average consumption of paper per capita is over 300kg per year while in the 'poor world' it is less than 12kg – or was then. Just to be able to run an education system and the most basic of sanitary and packaging needs you need 40kg per capita per year. In effect, the poor are in a paperless world while the rest of us are drowning in it. The only way out – if the forests are to survive – are plantation and managed mixed forests. More industry, more land-take (but less forest destruction we ever hope) but more met needs and welfare. So, who can deliver this? Not NGOs, that is for sure. Not governments, from all experience to date. It will be a mix of the local, regional and multinational enterprise – hopefully one day operating to an agreed set of norms and incentives for the common good. Should all this be a globalized trade? Probably so, for the best solar collectors in the world are trees and they work best in the tropics (5cm growth per day in some circumstances!) So why not encourage a developing world economy in all this that is free to export worldwide? (The same can be said of sugar, wine, and more!)

This experience led to another alliance with the 'devil' – no fewer than 30 mining companies. We took their shilling (along with some from elsewhere) to look at the mining sector and sustainability. The Mining Minerals and Sustainable Development Project was one of the largest yet for IIED, with a combined budget at some $9 million. Again, IIED tried to do the job with independence and integrity but this time it has been far more ambitious about reaching out to the various constituencies involved by working in regionally. The dilemmas have been the same. How do we get the standards of the industry up, promote a better system of governance within which the sector works, ensure that the benefits of the sector spread, and reduce the environmental and social impacts to as low a level as we can consistent with the legitimate needs of people for mined products? An ambitious call. At the end of the day it was a decentralized (or subsidiarity) model that delivered, built around the engagement of many constituencies and groups that acted as the 'check and balance' to the corporate bottom line.

Thus IIED lives in an 'and-and' world. To be useful in resolving the dilemmas we all face it still has to find ways to address the appalling environmental changes we have alongside the ever growing needs and wants of billions of people. The agenda has not changed but the opportunities are now much more open. It has to position itself as a trusted ally – when it agrees – of the NGO community, of officials and of business folk. It has to be rigorous in analysis, open in dialogue and process, and brave in what it attempts. It certainly has to shatter myths and pursue pragmatic solutions.

But serious constraints apply now more than ever before. The capacity of all parts of the development triad to cope with what is implied in sustainable development is very limited. There are all too few in government, civil society or the corporate world who understand the constraints of the other two. Most discussion is decidedly bilateral. Very few (including IIED) can bring rigorous science and economics and social science to the table. The cultural divides between rich and poor, and the different faiths and traditions, are as marked as ever. Thus an essential brokerage function remains open for IIED and its ring of fellow institutions. We have to understand the bottom-up reality, life on the ground for hard-pressed communities, and connect their needs with the top-down processes that are trying to meet those needs. Applying oneself as the trusted intermediary between needs and sources of supply is not such a bad place to be in such an iniquitous and disconnected world.

Barbara Ward was highly prophetic. She could see the stark choices long before words such as 'globalization' had ever entered the lexicon. In 1973 she wrote:

> *But there are a number of reasons that give us greater hope. The first is that some changes in our patterns of claims and consumption are inevitable. Under no conditions can unlimited growth and the trickle down economics postpone the problems of justice and solidarity for more than a decade or so. Under no conditions can we bolster our consumption by simply continuing not to*

*pay for the pollution and waste it causes. Under no conditions can a world inhabited and carrying seven to ten billion people offer still rising standards to a minority and, at best, stagnation to everyone else. What ever we plan or think, the external realities of our limited planet are changing, and we shall meet the new restraints either with resentment, anger and revolt, or with dignity, patience and sharing.*[1]

And, as she added elsewhere, 'we all have a duty to hope'.

## NOTE

1   Ward, B. *A New Creation? Reflections on the Environmental Issue*, Pontifical Commission, Justice and Peace, Vatican City.

# PART III
# IIED PROGRAMMES

# Forestry and land use

*Duncan Poore and Stephen Bass*

## BEGINNING WORK ON SUSTAINABLE FOREST MANAGEMENT *BY DUNCAN POORE*

To me, IIED was (and is) a wonderful and exceptional organization: driven by idealism but severely practical in application; lean and unimpeded by bureaucracy; efficient and with a dedicated staff. If it had faults, they were to do with excess of its good points. It was lean because it was always short of core funding; more would have helped to give thinking time and the exploration of new avenues for work. Sometimes, firmer management would have been an advantage; I had an annual contract for a number of years – never renewed, but that never seemed to matter.

To explain why I found it wonderful I shall have to do delve back into my past. At the end of World War II I became a biologist, changing from classics. There were two reasons for this. I was passionately fond of wild country and I was inspired by reading two books about the devastation caused by soil erosion, both published in the 1930s and 1940s – *Rape of the Earth* by Jacks and Whyte, and *Road to Survival* by William Vogt. I was also influenced by the writings of Frank Fraser Darling and by Frank himself, when I had the good fortune to work with him.

I soon found that there was a conflict between the two interests of the pure pursuit of nature conservation and the pure pursuit of productive land use. Working for the then Nature Conservancy in the mid-1950s, it seemed that too little consideration was given to economic land use. Working for the land-use survey company, Hunting Technical Services, on survey for pasture improvement in Jordan and Cyprus, it appeared that the complete acceptance of recommendations for improvement would lead to the disappearance of many beautiful types of grassland, rich in plants and insects.

It became evident that biological richness and biological productivity were inversely related to one another. At that time, all systems of land classification were based on the hierarchy: irrigated agriculture had preference over dryland agriculture; pasture came next in the pecking order; then commercial forestry; and, finally, the residue was left for the conservation of biological diversity. This hierarchy was axiomatic. For me, the resolution of this conflict became an important objective: how to devise a land-use policy to make room for both production and diversity?

Change came slowly in the 1960s and 1970s. Milestones were the system of land-use planning adopted in Canada and in the book, *Ecological Principles for Economic Development*.[1] There was a ferment of new thinking in the preparations for the Stockholm Conference, which in its turn led to the foundation of IIED by Barbara Ward, and big changes in the programme of IUCN.

At that time I was working at IUCN and was able to set out the principle of planning for each use according to its individual merits in the IUCN *Ecological Guidelines for Development in Tropical Rain Forests*[2] and in guidelines for mountains and for arid lands. The *World Conservation Strategy*[3] appeared shortly afterwards, then Brundtland[4] – and this particular conceptual battle was won. But, granted the concept, its application depended upon social and economic considerations, in which IUCN was weak. Collaboration with IIED seemed the most fertile possibility. David Runnalls came to IUCN in the mid-1970s but no joint programme materialized – I do not know why.

My next contact with IIED came in 1982 when I was at Oxford. I had then become interested in the ways in which the future of a developing country's forests was affected by other aspects of that nation's policy, and by the trade and aid policies of those developed countries that dealt with them. As though in answer to a prayer, I was visited in Oxford by Brian Johnson with proposals for an IIED forestry programme in association with the Commonwealth Forestry Institute (now the Oxford Forestry Institute). At that very moment, Oxford University had decided to abolish the only undergraduate course in Britain which combined agriculture and forestry (a particularly important and topical combination). The result – I joined Brian in setting up what soon became the IIED Forestry and Land Use Programme. (Brian departed almost immediately afterwards and left me holding the baby – a baby of which I became inordinately fond. At the same time, I was joined by the economist David Burns and tall young Dutchman, Ronald van der Giessen.)

The programme that we developed together had two elements, one concerned with the tropical forestry policies and the other with the potential likely to be offered by the new International Tropical Timber Agreement. The first of these got off the ground in 1983, the second in 1985.

## Developing policy on tropical forestry

Our forest policy programme was ambitious and not all of it came to fruition. We hoped to conduct simultaneous studies both in a few tropical countries and in some of their trade and aid partners. Among the developed countries, we discussed the proposal with the UK, The Netherlands and the Federal Republic of Germany and in all instances, though in different forms, reports were produced on the effects of trade and aid – what came later to be known as 'ecological footprints'. Although these were not issued as part of a coordinated IIED programme, it would be nice to think that IIED had some influence in promoting the notion. The programme in tropical countries depended upon gaining financial support for each country study. There were finally three: Indonesia, supported by the Government of The Netherlands; Cameroon, by Canadian CIDA; and Zaire, supported by the World Bank. Indonesia was the most complete and successful.

The thinking behind our initiative was set out in a paper given to the 9th World Forest Congress in Mexico City by Mike Ross, who ran the Indonesian study, Setyono Sastrosumarto (Head of the Agency for Research and Development within the Ministry of Forestry in Jakarta) and myself[5]. Here are some extracts.

> *There is much stress in this Congress on the need to take a comprehensive, new look at the policies affecting the future of tropical forest lands … It is clear that the future of these forests and of the soils they protect is greatly influenced by the policies and actions of other arms of Government than forestry – by overall economic policy, by population policy, by employment policy, by agricul-*

*ture, public works, energy, trade, industry and transport.*

*If, therefore, these lands are to be developed effectively and used wisely, it is not enough to look at the policies of the forestry sector alone, but it is necessary to examine the ways in which these other policies affect the forest – in fact to conduct a wide-ranging policy review* **centred** *on the sustainable development of the tropical forests. The Government of Indonesia, in collaboration with the International Institute of Environment and Development (IIED) is carrying out such a review.*

*IIED's ... ultimate objective is ambitious – to influence the development and use of uncultivated lands in the tropics so that they may best contribute to the lasting benefit of the peoples there ... The way in which the Institute aims to go about it is to persuade Governments that it would be in their own interests to review their present policies; and, if they should then think it desirable, modify them or alter the priorities which they give to various aspects of them. In fact, to invest more in prevention rather than cure; the analogy of health and disease is very close.*

*There is no need to emphasize the need for change in many countries. The prevalence of erosion, floods, droughts and natural disasters speaks for itself. Yet, many Governments, for a complex of apparently very pressing social, economic and political reasons, continue to act in a way that pays scant regard to one of their greatest natural assets; and much bilateral and multilateral aid continues to abet them in short-sighted and destructive processes.*

*The review is primarily a domestic review. It is mainly carried out by Indonesia and Indonesians, and is intended to examine problems, explore possible solutions and to reach a consensus – an important part of Indonesia's policy formation – about possible alternative future policies. The role of IIED is to act as a stimulus, to provide assistance and to co-ordinate the review with those being carried out in other countries. It must be emphasized that this is* **not** *solely an evaluation carried out by a team of external consultants.*

*[Thus] the report ... will not be the only result of the review, perhaps not even the most important. The*

*Ministers concerned and IIED place the utmost importance on the effect of the **review process**. By exposing these issues to wide discussion and debate, both within and outside Government, it is hoped that a substantial change of views may be effected; and that the future of forest lands will become a central issue of Government policy, so that it may be used as one of the indicators by which satisfactory overall policies may be judged.*

*The IIED programme envisages stimulating comparable reviews in a number of tropical countries ... These would be carried out in a similar manner and, it is hoped, would lead to some generally applicable policy initiatives, particularly towards aid from donors and investment from overseas.*

The review in Indonesia was conducted by Mike Ross, an eccentric and individualistic Australian born in New Britain, assisted by Deanna Donovan whom he later married. Mike had been working in Indonesia for several years on the controversial Transmigration programme by which large numbers of people from the over-crowded islands of Java, Bali and Madura were resettled in lowland areas of Kalimantan. He had become disenchanted with this programme but remained *persona grata* with the Indonesian authorities. He was ideally suited for our work. In the course of it he obtained personal interviews with almost all the Indonesian ministers and directors of departments of government. All of these were taped, except one; and the tapes – a remarkable record of views of the time – are stored in the IIED archives.

I was with him on the occasion of the single tape that failed. We had secured a much sought-after interview with General Moerdani, at that time Minister of Defence and Commander in Chief of the Armed Forces. We set up the tape with an introduction in the taxi as we approached the ministry. The interview was most cordial and very open. Moerdani agreed to be taped; in fact there was an exchange about the great benefits of tape recorders as Mike changed to the second channel. In the taxi afterwards we replayed – nothing! The tape had been wiped clean in the security check as we left. Distinctly humbled, we reconstructed as much as we could from memory. I can remember only two remarks Moerdani made. One was that, if we wished the forests to be kept secure from illegal encroachment or logging, it would be best if this were the responsibility of the army.

The other was on the navigability of the Bornean rivers. He remarked that when he had been on active service in the mid-1960s in the 'Konfrontasi' with Malaysia, the lower reaches of the major Bornean rivers had been navigable for about nine months in the year; this was now reduced to three or four.

How effective was the Indonesian policy review? It is difficult to say. Although commissioned by the Minister for Forests, Soedjarwo, and received by him, the recommendations were never officially accepted; the report was too controversial for its time. The greatest effect, probably, was on the younger generation staff in the Ministry. Certainly, in the years that followed, the issues and conclusions of the report became more and more part of the accepted wisdom of the Ministry and gradually became incorporated in later reviews. Perhaps we were right in believing that in the long run the process was more important than the immediately resulting action.

Our ambitious programme never materialized. There were two more reviews, of Cameroon and Zaire – neither as thorough as that in Indonesia. The whole programme was unfortunately overtaken by the Tropical Forestry Action Plan, an amalgamation of work by the World Resources Institute (WRI) and the World Bank on one hand, and of FAO on the other (developed over the previous two years and launched at the 9th World Forestry Congress), and which had support and funding from UNDP and the World Bank. We were smothered by the big boys. There is, though, an ironical twist to the story. The Tropical Forestry Action Plan ran into serious criticism, and eventually had to be recast, for failing to do exactly those things which the IIED programme had insisted were essential – to look at the effects of non-forestry policies on the forest, to consult widely and to influence policy from within rather than producing a portfolio of projects for external funding. But, our effectiveness was also drastically reduced at that time by the loss of the North American part of IIED which constricted possibilities for funding and narrowed our range of contacts, especially in Latin America.

## The International Tropical Timber Agreement

The second main string to our bow was the International Tropical Timber Agreement, resulting from over seven years of negotiation under the Integrated Programme for Commodities of UNCTAD; the final text was agreed in November 1983. Its particular interest to IIED lay in the linkage it established between a flourishing timber trade and the sustainable management of the resource upon which that trade was based. It remains the only commodity agreement with an equal concern for the resource base, as illustrated especially by Article 1, paragraphs (b) and (h) of the Agreement:

> *Article 1 (b). To promote the expansion and diversification of international trade in tropical timber ... by taking into account, on the one hand, a long-term increase in consumption and continuity of supplies, and, on the other, prices which are remunerative to producers and equitable for consumers, and the improvement of market access.*

> *Article 1 (h). To encourage the development of national policies aimed at sustainable utilization and conservation of tropical forests and their genetic resources, and at maintaining the ecological balance in the regions concerned.*

Moreover, the International Tropical Timber Agreement was the only international Agreement to cover tropical forests; there might, therefore, be some hope of affecting policies under this umbrella.

By late 1984, it appeared that the Agreement was likely to lapse because of lack of signatures and ratifications. The whole forestry team in IIED, Brian Johnson, David Burns, Ronald van der Giessen and I, considered that this would be a disaster and determined to call an international seminar in the middle of March 1985, in a last-minute attempt to bring in the laggards.

The seminar was held on 8–10 March 1985. The state of the ratification was then as follows: a deadline of 31 March had to be met for the Agreement to enter provisionally into force. On the 'consumers' side, there were enough signatures but one further ratification was required. On the 'producers' side, the situation was not nearly so favourable. Ten countries holding 500 votes were required. As only 7 countries with 356 votes had signed, 3 more signatures were required and, in addition, 8 further ratifications.

The seminar attendance figures were interesting: the highest proportion came from producer countries, and interest from consumer countries was variable. The UK was represented by the Overseas Development Administration (ODA), the Forestry Commission and the Department of Trade and Industry; but the Timber Trade Federation was lukewarm about the Agreement and absent from the seminar. Canada was represented by CIDA. The USA did not come. Only France and The Netherlands sent representatives connected with the timber trade. Japan, which was making a strong and ultimately successful bid to provide the headquarters of the new organization, sent a large delegation. The members came under the firm impression that IIED was promoting London as the potential headquarters; only after we convinced them that this was not the case was their attitude transformed and they became very good friends to IIED within the Internatiolan Tropical Timber Organization ( ITTO). Of the environmental NGOs, IUCN and WWF were represented but both tended, at that stage, to be disinterested.

The debates during the seminar were interesting and constructive but most important were the conclusions and subsequent action. The final statement urges 'everyone concerned to do all in their power to see that the Agreement enters into force, as soon as possible'. Telexes were then sent to the Foreign Ministries of all countries party to the Agreement. The result was dramatic. The necessary signatures were obtained and ratifications deposited before 31 March. This was a rare example of the right initiative at the right moment, and IIED could justly be styled the midwife of the International Tropical Timber Agreement.

From that time on, for a number of years, IIED was able to exercise an influence in the development of ITTO through being an observer at meetings of the Council. Our involvement led to our being commissioned by the Organization to work on a sequence of projects which have significantly promoted the sustainable management of tropical forests. The first and most influential of these was a request from the Executive Director that IIED should coordinate a study, in all the producer nations of ITTO, of the status of the sustainable management of their forests for timber production. This was a major effort in which I was involved with the assistance of Peter Burgess (Asia), Simon Rietbergen (Africa), Timothy Synnott (Latin America) and John Palmer (for a global commentary), aimed at finding out how much tropical forest was under sustainable management 'at an operational scale', identifying the factors which led to success or failure, and recommending what might be done about it.

The results, presented in 1988, shocked the International Timber Council and the timber trade in general; you could have heard a pin drop as I presented them to the Council. Less than 1 per cent of production forest was found to be managed to a satisfactory standard. Neither the tropical countries nor the timber trade queried the findings! We found that success was guaranteed only if four conditions were met: legal security of tenure for production forests; adequate control of operations within the forest; fair distribution of benefits and costs; and sufficient information to support sustainable management. In fact, the situation was not quite so bleak as this single figure might suggest; in several areas in several countries, one or more of the conditions for success were present; it only remained to attend to the missing elements.

The IIED report was written (and eventually published by Earthscan as *No Timber Without Trees*) in a form intended to induce the Council to develop an action plan. The Action Plan duly followed and was succeeded by a sequence of *Guidelines, Criteria and Indicators* and a further study of the status of forest management in 2000. Although IIED priorities have subsequently moved in other directions, I have built on the original IIED connection and have remained closely associated with the work of ITTO; and this has proved a fruitful and satisfying association. The work for ITTO of the Forestry and Land Use Programme was complemented by Ed Barbier and his colleagues who carried out a study for ITTO on 'The Economic Linkages between the International Trade in Tropical Timber and the Sustainable Management of Tropical Forests'.

In 1985, I decided to give up any management role in the Forestry and Land Use Programme although I remained closely associated with its work. Julian Evans took over from me; and he was succeeded by Caroline Sargent and then by Steve Bass. The Programme has continued to go from strength to strength and produced some outstanding results in, for example, its integrated study of the paper cycle, its work on timber certification and, perhaps most significant of all, the series of studies on 'Policy that works for forests and for people'.

The IIED experience, both the work itself and the people with whom I worked, have left a deep mark on all that I have done since. IIED has striven to integrate the ecological, the economic and the social, and to use this insight to promote environmentally sustainable development by realistic means. I believe now that the net has to be cast even more widely if Barbara Ward's vision is fully to be realized. The book I completed recently, *Where Next? Reflections on the Human Future* is, I hope, a small step in this direction. In it, in order to benefit from a wide range of perceptions about the present human predicament, I have assembled a collection of essays by people with wide experience in philosophy, science, economics, ecology, law, sociology, entrepreneurial skills and international relations. Taken together, these give the overwhelming impression that present attitudes and institutions are still ill adapted to the nature and scale of our problems. The future is in our hands; only we can put it right. I look upon this recent work as part of my inheritance from IIED.

## POLICY THAT WORKS FOR FORESTS AND PEOPLE
### BY STEPHEN BASS

By the time Duncan had left the Forestry and Land Use Programme, foresters in dozens of countries were preoccupied with compiling encyclopaedic wish-lists. The 'Tropical Forest Action Plans' (TFAPs) of the late 1980s may have offered glimpses of a better world for forestry. They certainly conjured an illusion of progress for the bureaucrats in charge: lubricated by the aid system, promises of further funds were being stacked up fast to help developing countries realize the TFAPs' dreams.

However, it soon became clear that real strategies for change were not going to be made by filling in proforma plans handed down from FAO or the World Bank – especially if the form-filling was done by external consultants. Such proformas included far more subject lines than any local stakeholder could possibly be interested in. Even so, stakeholders often could not find space for what they believed to be the real problems. As it turned out, little real change took place, and most of the promised funds did not materialize.

IIED's research was making it increasingly clear that TFAPs were as straws in the wind compared to the underlying causes of forest problems. Deforestation and disenfranchisement of forest-dependent groups are problems of perverse policy, unfettered markets and unequal stakeholder power. Forests are destroyed whenever people find it profitable and have the resources to do so. Any policies that make food production attractive, that lower transport and labour costs, and that reduce liabilities for the use of forest land will tend to help that profitability. Such policies tend to be pronounced or protected by people in power – both for corrupt reasons and through sheer inertia or fear of change. In contrast, those with the potential to change things for the better – the 'forest stewards' in waiting, with the knowledge or the livelihood-based incentives to sustain the forest – are being excluded from both rights to forests and access to policy processes.

From 1992, IIED shifted attention from servicing international model solutions, such as the TFAP, to working with local and national processes as the framework for tackling underlying causes of forest problems. Here, the challenge was to balance our servicing of national forest authorities' immediate needs (we made the authorities the boss, not the TFAP) with exposing the authorities to other local stakeholders' analyses of problems.

So began the approach we called, bluntly, 'policy that works for forests and people'. Real progress requires changes in policy and power, otherwise all you have is the 'planners' dream'. Real progress links political will and good ideas from the top – the 'policy-holders' – with 'what works' from the bottom – the forest-dependent stakeholders.

Two IIED activities were precursors to 'policy that works'. One was our exploration of national conservation strategies and environmental action plans – early versions of what Agenda 21 had called for in 'national strategies for sustainable development' (see Chapter 14).

The second precursor was a programme in Ghana to trace and improve the incentives for sustainable forestry. James Mayers, Nii-Ashie Kotey, Eddie Prah and Michael Richards pioneered ways to identify stakeholder motivations for sustaining or degrading forests, to 'map' the policies and market signals influencing these motivations, and to get the authorities talking with local groups. It was the Forestry and Land Use Programme's baptism in participatory appraisal; and also in the risks of confusing policy-makers' *openness* with their *readiness* to change.

Many local Ghanaian stakeholders and forestry staff acclaimed our work – 'you have sowed the seeds for change'. But a letter from higher authorities to ITTO, which had commissioned the project, claimed that 'the IIED report is replete with scandalous falsehoods'. (An IIED staff member endured a long journey to Japan to report the findings, only to be ordered by the Ghanaian delegation to get right back on the return flight.) Since then, however, this work has inspired many improvements in Ghana: farmers have regained rights to trees on their land; a collaborative forest management unit has been set up; and decentralized forestry consultation and planning is routine.

We explored 'Policy that works for forests and people' in six countries – Ghana (we patched up old relations and went on to make real progress in use rights and certification), Zimbabwe, Pakistan, India, Papua New Guinea and Costa Rica.[6]

The art was to identify the 'policy-holders' (the authorities and heads of big companies and associations), the real representatives of forest-using groups (including the poor, although that was difficult), and the kinds of researchers who were both expert in forestry and institutional change, and credible to these other groups. We formed these people into national learning groups, which were spurred on by our local 'engaged' researchers.

These learning groups were charged with postulating some idea of success – what do we mean by 'working for forests' and 'working for people'? Moreover, they had to go and look for those successes on the ground. Once found, these stories had to be told in full, and correlated with policy (not just formal policy, but the intentions and norms of all groups who had some kind of authority over forests). We were aware that, unless you understand the policy conditions for something that works on the ground, you can end up replicating it where it won't work – the old 'cult of the success story'.

Finally, we needed to tease out what had produced those policies. What processes – of participation, information flow, innovation, investment, and capacity building – had led to decision-making for sustainable forestry? Where did they come from – traditional means of dealing with change, new projects, or special 'process' initiatives? These would be our elements of 'policy that works', which any national system would then need to bring together and build on – to keep sustainable forestry on the agenda and deal with change.

In practice, almost all was 'policy that partially worked'. Even in Pakistan, a country with weak relations between civil society and government, and a forest department that was a museum piece serving anomalous anti-people purposes, there was evidence of hope. Major rural development projects, such as those run by the Aga Khan Rural Support Programme, were turning first to villagers for information and skills, and were breaking down high institutional walls between government departments (even training officers and villagers together). They were forging new paths for making decisions that, later, began influencing thinking in the corridors of power.

In some countries, our work began to rehearse what was needed on a permanent basis – local and national multi-stakeholder fora, interdisciplinary research groups, or (for so many, and for the first time) a new 'big picture' and the emergence of a locally agreed vision for sustainable forestry. This is why many people did not call our work 'research'. Key people in the aid system had the vision to push IIED into this role of 'engaged research' – Bill Howard and John Hudson of DFID really stand out. The result – as the Inspector General of Pakistan expressed, 'is what the Forest Sector Master Plan [the TFAP] should have done'. Perhaps one of the most important outcomes has been the identification of the local groups that matter – the small farm forestry association in Costa Rica, for example. As Vicente Watson, our team leader in Costa Rica, put it, both he and the association 'now really understand how decisions are made, and are routinely involved in policy change'. We were subsequently invited to extend the 'policy that works' approach to Malawi, Mozambique, South Africa and Himachal Pradesh. For the first three, this was to facilitate the design of a 'national forest action plan' that would avoid all the pitfalls of the TFAP approach.

## International agreements, *lingua franca* and verification of forest sustainability

We developed a number of methods to find those local groups that matter most to forests and livelihoods. For example, Olivier Dubois tested the '4Rs' diagnostic – rights, responsibilities, rewards and relationships – with charcoal burners in Zambia and farm foresters in Uganda.[7] Now many African colleagues have used this framework for both participatory diagnosis and negotiating new roles. Generating your own information is much better when you want to strike a bargain than using other people's 'facts' and arguments.

Indeed, there is nothing more foolish to many forest stakeholders than the exhortation from northern NGOs to 'save the rainforests'. 'Save'? For whom? The real challenge is getting the forests that people want, and are prepared to pay for (including international payments where global services are being provided). Security of forest goods and services, and of the cultural and spiritual values associated with forests, is a more meaningful goal than arbitrary targets for halting deforestation or increasing the area of forests.

The search for 'forest security' seemed attractive, especially as the notion of food security had helped agriculture in earlier decades. It preoccupied me and, on the occasions we were invited to play, it anchored IIED's approach to the international forest games of the 1990s. (For example, Ola Ullsten, Chair of the World Commission on Forests and Sustainable Development, liked IIED's idea of 'forest security' and promoted the idea of a 'forest security council'.)

In 1991, we were asked by GLOBE, an impetuous group of European MPs, US senators and members of the Japanese Diet, to work with Bart Romijn, James Cameron and Farhana Yamin in constructing a model 'global forest convention'. At IIED, our hearts were not really in it, as we felt that the threat of supranational control of forests outweighed any likely willingness to pay countries for securing global forest services. Although we thought it was a useful straw man, it did not go away and we were asked to look at the case for a convention again – and again. Jag Maini, who ran the secretariat for the Intergovernmental Panel on Forests (IPF), got to know us during the work of the IPF. He is adept at explaining complex problems simply. He divided countries into four types – combinations of forest-rich/poor and income-rich/poor. His scheme helped us to explain why different countries seek different things from a global agreement – and why you can still witness amusing (or maddening) non-dialogues on forestry between trade officials from some countries and conservation officials from others.

IIED's Chairman, Sir Martin Holdgate, co-chaired the IPF, and IIED established its customary independent position on a convention. We put perhaps too much faith in delegates' desire for a logical outcome, offering them a number of decision-making guides to help them work out whether a convention was really needed. (This faith was often misplaced. I was told by one delegate that 'the need for a convention is irrelevant to whether there should be one'.) These guides were written for delegates to IPF, and subsequently to the Intergovernmental Forum on Forests (IFF, son of IPF), and may again be requested for the UN Forum on Forests (UNFF, grandson of IPF) which again will address the need for a convention. (The UNFF work programme includes a task on 'Consideration with a View to Recommending the Parameters of a Mandate for Developing a Legal Framework on All Types of Forests'. The title suggests how it may be tackled.)

IIED has been asking: 'what is it that can only be done by a global forest convention, and is there willingness and ability to pay?' We have thrown attention on to the genuinely global services from forests (notably biodiversity and carbon storage), and on global causes of forest problems (debt and trade rules, for example). We have stressed the need to exercise existing instruments, as well as to get these instruments better informed about good forestry. For example, the Kyoto Protocol is particularly ill-informed, and could end up putting the cause of sustainable forestry back decades by creating incentives for huge blocks of heavily protected simple forest, owned by just a few groups and excluding others.

If a legally binding agreement on forests was not forthcoming in the 1990s, there was no shortage of guidance to help 'bottom-up' decision-making. The Earth Summit produced a set of forest principles. The IPF crafted these into an over-rich menu of 150 'proposals for action', none of which were to be forced on any country, and the UNFF is adding more. Even the original set was so indigestible that I was volunteered to work with GTZ's energetic Chris Mersmann and the calm and ever-wise Markku Simula, chewing them for days until the early hours. The idea was to help countries work out which proposals would be most palatable to them. The answer is that few are particularly nourishing unless you have the local systems in place – the 'Policy that works' approach.

More significant than the IPF/IFF guidance were the many sets of 'principles, criteria and indicators' (PC&I) for sustainable forestry. The 1990s may go down in the history of forestry as the decade when foresters – and just about everyone else, it seemed – sought to define, or to prescribe, 'sustainable forest management'. IIED was there at the beginning of the movement with Duncan Poore's guidelines on natural forests and plantations for ITTO, which were subsequently crafted into C&I. Other country groups followed suit. The Montreal process was kicked off by Canada, which had been a strong protagonist for a convention, and which sought in PC&I a *lingua franca* to keep international debate going. The Europeans followed with a Helsinki process, the Africans with a 'Dry Zone' initiative, and the South Americans with the Tarapoto process.

Spotting a spark of genuine concern for getting to grips with the dimensions of sustainability, IIED worked up Duncan's early idea of 'Forest Resource Accounting' for ITTO. This was a simple enough national monitoring protocol to keep track of forests and their management and use, through employing such PC&I. But it proved to be an object lesson in why people do not accept an idea just because it is clever. With no real incentive to broadcast the truth about forests, and without policy processes that encourage learning, many forest authorities were not – and are still not – in the business of tracking and reporting on sustainability. They *are* in the business, however, of keeping a conversation going between very different countries (the positive view of PC&I) and of applying fig-leaves to vulnerable parts (the uncharitable view).

Where PC&I really did 'bite', however, was through certification. From humble beginnings amongst woodworkers and small NGOs in the late 1980s, the idea became a reality when the Forest Stewardship Council (FSC) was launched in 1993. Its aim is to create market-based incentives for products that can be proven to have been harvested from well-managed forests. The attraction to IIED was that this could open the doors to good forestry and close them to the asset-strippers. With Chris Upton of SGS, the internal audit company, I prepared a book on how certification could and should work, an offering that influenced most of the schemes and many of the players in the early years. IIED has since come to be known as the main independent body tracking whether certification is actually helping forests, stakeholders and trade.

We found that most certified producers are northern, industrial operations or 'boutique' tropical producers who were bankrolled by donors and patrons. They were already practising good forestry. In contrast, the valuable qualities of small, community operations in developing countries, which may have been contributing local livelihood and environmental benefits, cannot always be recognized by certification standards. Their complex land-use systems just don't follow the well-documented, 'scientific' forest management methods of industrial operations that are more evident to outsider inspectors. Certifiers have their own ideas of how the 'social' C&I should look locally, giving rise to some 'social engineering'.

This might seem to suggest that certification has failed. The truth is far from this. Certification has publicly recognized many good cases of forest management (good news, especially when contrasted to Duncan's depressing findings in 1988). More significantly, multi-stakeholder certification working groups in many countries (tasked with setting the national standard based on FSC's global principles and criteria, or with developing an alternative to FSC) have been debating: What is good forestry? How do we recognize it? How do we hold people accountable? and Are current policies and laws supportive?

This is a big leap forward for institutional change in forestry. A global forest convention may not have been agreed – for good reasons – but FSC offers a new kind of 'soft' forest agreement involving 'real' players and not just government. If national policy remains the normative statement of forestry officials, then national certification working groups and standards can be seen as a multi-stakeholder forum and set of consensus rules. Forest stakeholders are certainly paying more attention to certification than to the latest international policy initiatives from Washington or Geneva.

## Getting involved in the business of forestry

From the 1980s to Rio, it was assumed that governments would lead us on paths towards sustainability. But policy has subsequently opened out to other players with different attributes to offer. With increasing NGO and business influence in policy, ostensibly for sustainable forestry, it is no wonder that their mandates and accountability are increasingly being questioned. The late 1990s was the period when IIED decided it had to get to know the private sector better.

Erling Lorentzen, the chairman of Aracruz Celulose, a huge Brazilian paper company, had become worried by rumours of impending European legislation to make domestic paper recycling mandatory and penalize virgin fibre imports. Surely this would prejudice against sustainable land use and employment in Brazil? In any case, would recycling not entail huge energy costs in Europe? These questions made it evident that there was no good way of judging the multiple trade-offs involved in paper production and consumption.

Through the WBCSD, Erling got together with several forestry and paper companies, as well as concerned European governments, to commission an independent review of the sustainable paper cycle from IIED. Richard Sandbrook's involvement ensured a high profile, and an (at times) sweltering political climate for the project.

The result: we showed what a huge environmental clean-up had been made by the bigger players, mainly for self-interest (and the win–wins have not been exhausted); we highlighted their more significant social challenges; and we drew attention to the dangers of defining 'good practice' only in terms of what the big players can do. However, we made the mistake of not designing a change-management and monitoring programme to commit the companies to improvements. (We have learned this lesson and are applying it in the project on mining, minerals and sustainable development. )

None the less, the report remains the big milestone, the Domesday Book, the BC/AD, of the global paper industry.[7] It is frequently quoted, including by the industry. We have since gone on to review 'instruments for sustainable private sector forestry' – different forms of company–community partnership, and markets for forest environmental services, as well as certification. In five countries, we are examining policy and market signals along the commodity chain between producer and consumer, finally doing what Duncan had envisaged for the very first IIED policy reviews.

## A new focus on governance challenges

So IIED has contributed to the search for sustainable forest management, on the ground, in language, in agreements, and in forging multi-stakeholder partnerships that give all a better chance to get the forests they want. Many of the paths we blazed are now more approximately paved by others. But if we were to collect up all the 'magic bullets' fired in the international forest games of the past twenty years, by IIED and by others, they would still not offer all that is required for sustainable forestry. Present attitudes and institutions are still ill-adapted to the nature and scope of the problems, and we need a more robust governance system.

Thus two challenges now stand before IIED. They concern the difficult terrain thrown up when the 'tectonic plates' of globalization and localization collide – a landscape of both tough peaks and of fertile valleys.

First, the powerful extra-sectoral forces that cause forest problems have not really been tamed, although IIED has been in the vanguard in analysing them. They are treated as an 'act of god' by forest inhabitants and forest authorities alike. As David Kaimowitz, Director of CIFOR[8] pointed out in an IIED/CIFOR workshop on 'Policy that works for forests and people', foresters persist in formulating forestry-based solutions to what are really extra-sectoral problems, which are therefore bound to fail. I would add that the 'bigger' initiatives for sustainable development – which could possibly tame the extra-sectoral forces – are not necessarily informed by good forestry.

Second, and often at the local level, we need to redress the imbalance between those who hold the power and those who have high potential or a critical need for better forestry (who are often the weaker groups).

Both of these challenges are governance issues. (Curiously, I have seen a colourful sticker with the deeply unsexy message: 'forests are a governance issue'. While this is a step forward from 'save the rainforests', it is hardly a communications triumph.) For forestry, governance is complicated by the fact that forests do not define a 'sector' in the normal sense, with neat institutional boundaries. They are resources which other sectors and ordinary people use, and they use them in ways which reflect how society is organized, divides its wealth, produces and consumes. This reality explains why IIED's Forestry and Land Use Programme is not a separate institution. Its purpose lies within IIED, with experts and networks in economics and trade, and with leaders in local, corporate and global governance. It is from these alliances that the next generation of IIED innovations for forestry will surely spring.

## NOTES

1   Dasmann, R, Milton J and P. Freeman. (1973) *Ecological Principles for Economic Development* International Union for the Conservation of Nature and Natural Resources, Morges, Switzerland and the Conservation Foundation, Washington DC.
2   Poore, Duncan (1976) *Ecological Guidelines for Development in Tropical Rain Forests.* IUCN, Morges, Switzerland.
3   IUCN, UNEP and WWF (1980) *The World Conservation Strategy.* IUCN, Gland, Switzerland.
4   World Commission on Environment and Development. 1987. *Our Common Future.* Oxford University Press, Oxford.
5   Poore, Duncan, Ross M and Setyono S. (1985) A review of policies affecting forest lands in Indonesia. Paper delivered at the 9th World Forestry Congress, Mexico City.
6   Our overall conclusions are in James Mayers and Stephen Bass (1999) *Policy that Works for Forests and People. Series Overview.* IIED, London
7   Dubois, Olivier (1996) *The Sustainable Paper Cycle.* WBCSD, Geneva and IIED, London.
8   Centre for International Forest Research, Indonesia.

# 8

# The energy programme

## *Gerald Leach*

When IIED was born in 1973, the world energy scene was rather different from today's. A quarter century of ever-increasing global energy consumption had led to many deep problems and concerns. In the industrialized world, at least, there was much talk of an 'energy crisis': nuclear power, acid rain, oil spills and the threat of dwindling fossil fuel resources were never far from the headlines. Political recognition of the climate change problem was still two decades away in the future. Oil cost only half as much as it had 20 years previously and there was still a year of calm to go before the sudden and massive price hikes of the winter of 1973/74. The fuelwood crisis of the South had yet to be discovered by the North.

No less important was the very different perspective on energy which almost everyone adopted: politicians, researchers and the energy business itself. Decades of cheap energy and economic growth had created an almost universal belief that energy demand could rise forever in step with continued economic growth. If massive energy growth should one day run up against finite fuel resources, the resulting energy 'gaps' could be filled by nuclear power: fission reactors, fast-breeder reactors and, one day, fusion reactors. The policy and academic agendas were almost wholly concerned with the coalmines, oil and gas fields, and nuclear power stations of energy supply. There was little curiosity about the other side of the energy coin: the nature of energy demand, with its huge diversity of users, uses and consumption technologies – let alone the enormous latent potential for more efficient energy use.

The OPEC oil price rises during the winter of 1973/74 changed all this. Energy became a top political priority and a hot academic research topic. It also began to experience a profound paradigm shift as policy and intellectual interest switched increasingly from supply-side to demand-side issues. IIED was to play a leading role in this revolution.

But this would come later. When Barbara Ward and her tiny team opened the first IIED office, up near the rooftops above Mortimer Street, energy was only one among many topics on the programmatic wish list. David Runnalls kept in his head an immense database about who's who in energy – as in most other subjects. Barbara had written and spoken powerfully about energy and its importance to environment and development concerns, not least in *Only One Earth*, her book for the 1972 Stockholm Environment Conference. IIED had no staff working on energy, however, until the summer of 1974 when I started my 15 years hard, mostly enjoyable but sometimes fraught and frequently broke, labour with the Institute, running its energy programme.

*Energy and Food Production*, published in 1976[1], showed how the food chains of the industrialized world, from farm to factory, truck and supermarket, had become major users of energy, both directly and indirectly, through labour-saving mechanization and land-saving fertilizers. With a few other studies along similar lines, it provided another club, labelled 'energy profligacy', which environmentalists could (and still do) use to assault modern farming practices. However, later events should have (but mostly didn't) put an end to such attacks. Higher energy prices after 1974 stopped the most energy-extravagant practices of food production – such as growing lettuces in the British winter courtesy of oil-heated glasshouses – and led to many all-round improvements in energy efficiency. Within a few years, farming in Britain (and doubtless in other industrialized countries also) had become one of the most energy-effective sectors of production.

The years 1975 and 1976 were taken up by work on two major projects: the European Commission's 'Europe Plus 30' project, which examined the need for a European forecasting agency; and the first multi-national examination of energy demand and supply prospects – the Workshop on Alternative Energy Strategies – which was led by Professor Caroll Wilson, of the Massachusetts Institute of Technology. Political historians might like to know that this work – or, more exactly, one of the more purple passages in a draft introduction written by the IIED energy programme himself – was responsible for the gales of derision which greeted the remark by US President Jimmy Carter that 'the energy crisis is the moral equivalent of war'. Even today I wonder what on earth this phrase was supposed to mean.

## THE LOW-ENERGY STRATEGY:
### ANALYSING ENERGY USE

In early 1977 the energy programme began perhaps its most influential project: the two-year study which culminated in the publication, in January 1979, of *A Low Energy Strategy for the United Kingdom*.[2] Christopher Lewis and Frederic Romig joined IIED at the start of 1977 for this project, which also enjoyed Ford Foundation support. In early 1978 I was struck down with cancer (but continued working most of the time) and Gerald Foley nobly accepted an appeal to move down from the floor above IIED, where he directed the Architectural Association's postgraduate energy programme, to help out as unofficial co-director. He brought with him the fifth team member, Ariane van Buren.

*A Low Energy Strategy for the United Kingdom* (LES) was remarkable in being one of the first ever-detailed studies of how a nation uses energy. It broke down energy use in the UK into over 400 separate categories determined by economic sector, fuel, appliance and end use. With such a 'bottom-up' perspective it is not hard – merely time-consuming – to figure out where and how future energy growth might be constrained both by energy-efficiency measures and by natural saturation effects, such as a slowdown of the rapid growth of central heating (and, consequently, warmer offices and homes) during the 1960s and 1970s. This the LES did for 1990 and 2000 (and somewhat reluctantly, under pressure from allies in the government's Energy Technology Support Unit, who helped us with invaluable energy-use data for industry) also for 2010 and 2025.

The biggest problem with this approach was the huge amount of calculation needed. For the first year we relied on pocket calculators, but it was taking literally weeks to make substantial changes in the scenarios. We had to computerize. But in 1978 that meant big money. The only desktop computer then available was a behemoth called the Altair: a stack of three huge boxes including two 8-inch floppy disk drives, but with only 32k of available memory and BASIC as the only software. And the bill? Around £8000. Barbara Ward and Dave Runnalls, with gritted teeth, somehow raised the cash – and we launched off into a Neanderthal version of the Computer Age. Aunty Altair saved the LES but ended its days in a corner printing envelope labels for Earthscan.

This data-intensive, bottom-up approach was in stark contrast to the 'top-down' methods used by virtually all governments and economists. The UK government energy forecast at the time was based on only five sectors: iron and steel, transport, all industry (except iron and steel) lumped together as one unit, the commercial sector (consisting of offices, hospitals, schools and shops, etc also lumped together as one unit), and the average household. With the last three of these sectors, future energy use was estimated by the simplest possible linear extrapolation of past trends, with economic output or family expenditure as the only variables which determined the projections of energy consumption. Using these equations, Amory Lovins and I once calculated that in the winter of the year 2000, upper-income UK families would be sweltering indoors at an average temperature of 40°C.

Not surprisingly, the LES came out with future energy use way below the government projections. Its projection for 1990 was 224 million tons of oil equivalent (mtoe) for UK primary energy use, compared with 207 mtoe for the baseline year of 1976. The government forecast was 295 mtoe. Actual consumption was 215 mtoe, a shade below the LES projection. For the year 2000 the LES projection was almost 11 per cent below the actual figure (233 mtoe) but the government forecast was too high by 54 per cent.

The response to the LES was as varied as these projections, ranging from cheers to outrage. 'The case of the vanishing crisis' headlined the *Guardian* story. 'I've seen the future – and it's less' echoed *Energy Manager*. 'Bleak forecast for UK energy' countered the *Financial Times*. Sir Francis Tombs, chairman of the Electricity Council, accused us of showing 'lack of respect for civil liberties' by invoking government intervention to promote energy saving. Six months later the Department of Energy launched an energy conservation division to do just that. Revisiting today the many yards of reviews and commentary about the LES, the basic schism which it uncovered remains as clear as ever: the true pessimists about the energy future were not the conservationists (often written off as doom-mongers) but those with interests vested in the nuclear and other energy-supply industries. They had to believe in high-energy growth and widening supply–demand gaps to keep their costly enterprises at the forefront of policy and supportive government expenditures.

## BIOMASS, POVERTY AND DEVELOPMENT

In 1979, Richard Sandbrook wryly observed that IIED was supposed to be about development as well as environment and could we please think about projects in or for the Third World. Well, yes, we said. But how, where, what? Fortunately, President Nyerere of Tanzania had the answer. He had approached the Commonwealth Secretariat with a request for help on a long-term sustainable energy policy for his country – and IIED got the job.

Tanzania in 1980 was an inspirational shock. For me, Gerald Foley and Ariane van Buren, it was the first experience of acute underdevelopment. We worked out of the cabinet secretariat office in State House, with a flag-flying chauffeur-driven car at our disposal. But the office was allocated only three sheets of photocopy paper per month. National statistics often existed in only one copy, handwritten in pencil. The country's one coal mine was producing just 3000 tons a year, with bare-footed workers scrabbling in the dark as there was no cash for boots or lightbulbs. A US$2 million Japanese consultant's report had recently advised the government to 'do a Brazil' and launch a massive programme to convert sugar cane to fuel-alcohol. Meanwhile the country's largest sugar mill was tipping around US$700,000 worth of molasses each year out of its back door into a river for want of two rail wagons to carry the stuff to the molasses tanks on the docks of Dar es Salaam. Nearly two-thirds of the country's import bill went on oil and most energy aid went on power generation and distribution lines. Yet oil and electricity accounted for only 1 and 3 per cent respectively of national energy use. The remainder was traditional biomass fuel: firewood, charcoal and crop residues.

What could we do but recommend a cautious approach? Learn to manage better the resources one has and forget the grandiose, costly and high-risk schemes for renewable energy which Nyerere had perhaps been hoping for. But in one crucial respect, IIED did change things for the better, while learning some cardinal lessons that would infuse much of its policy research work for the next decade.

Received wisdom said that biomass fuels were in a serious supply–demand crisis. Women everywhere were allegedly walking miles to gather fuel. Forests were supposedly being devastated to provide charcoal for urban consumers. The Forest Department was trying to spread its scant resources around every village, hoping to persuade people to 'behave rationally' by planting energy woodlots and buying improved cookstoves. But the people were taking little notice. Then to his great credit, during the IIED study, Gerry Foley faced a roomful of village foresters and told them there was no fuelwood crisis in Tanzania. The immediate response was a hostile uproar. Then, gradually, over the next hour of discussion, the foresters came round to agreeing that most villages were so poor that they needed and were calling for many things: tin roofs, fresh water supplies, better access to markets, schools and health clinics, and, oh yes, as an afterthought, easier fuelwood supplies. (The same low priority given by Tanzanian villagers to fuelwood needs, despite entrenched official beliefs that the country faced acute fuelwood supply crises, was to emerge again in a 1988 survey for the Tropical Forestry Action Plan in which IIED was involved, and yet again in a 1995 survey conducted by the Stockholm Environment Institute).

The IIED solution was to propose a new structure for Forest Department assistance, whereby villages were helped with their energy problems only when they called for help because energy had become a top priority. The most lasting lesson we learned from this experience is that one must never approach rural energy issues wearing the blinkers of the energy specialist. Instead, one must place them in the much broader context of effective land management by societies who are almost wholly dependent on – and know about – a huge variety of biomass resources and management practices. Another lesson we learned was that received wisdom about a problem will continue so long as the flow of aid funds depends on the continuation of that problem, whatever facts are revealed that show it to be a myth. In a few year's time Gerry Foley would create a global uproar from NGOs working on improved biomass cookstoves by subtitling an Earthscan report which was critical of improved stove programmes: '*How Much Wood would a Woodstove Save if a Woodstove could Save Wood?*'

Biomass energy and the many fascinating hard facts, soft facts, rumours, myths and lies which surround it, were to dominate the IIED energy programme for most of the 1980s. In 1981 I had started a decade of repeated trips to Pakistan to work there on traditional biomass energy for three successive five-year plans. Despite all best efforts, it proved next to impossible to wean government officials away from a top-down, command and control view of biomass energy 'solutions'. These consisted mostly of setting targets for expanding government plantations and exhorting farmers to grow more trees. It wasn't until 1991/92, when a World Bank study revealed that Pakistani farmers were planting over 100 million trees each year, with little if any help from government programmes, that policies began to change. Meanwhile, once again, poor farmers had been demonized for not behaving 'rationally' about their energy needs.

In 1985 the World Bank, European Commission and UN Food and Agriculture Organization combined to fund a one-year study of traditional biomass energy in Bangladesh, India, Pakistan and Sri Lanka, published in 1987 as *Household Energy in South Asia*.[3] Publication led to a flurry of questions in the Indian parliament asking what an Englishman was doing dictating Indian energy policy, when in fact the policy chapter of the book had been based entirely on a workshop, organized and paid for by IIED, of household energy experts from the four countries, including some very senior Indian representatives who helped to smooth their countrymen's ruffled feathers.

Meanwhile, Gerry Foley and Geoffrey Barnard began work on their widely acclaimed and influential series of Earthscan technical reports[4] on key aspects of biomass energy supply and use in developing countries: biomass gasification (1983), improved cooking stoves (1983 and 1985), farm and community forestry (1984), agricultural residues as fuel (1985) and charcoal-making (1986).

The last major phase of IIED's energy programme began in early 1987. The Norwegian energy aid programme was spending vast sums on electric power developments but the Norwegian people were calling for a much greater focus on poverty, women and the so-called woodfuel crisis. Could IIED help? Could it accept substantial funding for the next three years to research and report on what could be done to improve the biomass energy situation in Africa. Well, yes ....

This was a wonderful chance to look, in depth and breadth, at all those facts, myths and lies that had been accreting around and concealing the realities of the woodfuel issue. Most ably assisted by a young geographer, Robin Mearns, we were able over the next two years to uncover at least some of these realities, first in an early 1988 IIED report – *Bioenergy Issues and Options for Africa*[5] – and then in late 1988 with an Earthscan book: *Beyond the Woodfuel Crisis: People, Land and Trees in Africa*.[6]

A key theme of the book was that the environmental devastation supposedly caused by woodfuel use – from deforestation to the loss of soil nutrients by burning animal wastes – was nearly everywhere being hugely exaggerated. So was the hardship imposed on women and children by the need to collect woodfuel. In some places, and some seasons, woodfuel collecting was certainly a serious burden on hard-pressed women. But over vast areas it was not, as there was plenty of biomass around, or it was only one of many physical hardships of rural poverty – and not necessarily a leading one for people to address by spending scarce resources on the woodlots and improved cookstoves which visiting energy experts proposed. In short, the biomass energy problem was not at heart a problem of energy but a manifestation of much deeper social ills and environmental constraints.

Years later, a survey[7] of the most influential forestry books of the 20th century picked out *Beyond the Woodfuel Crisis* as one of the main influences which sank that crisis: 'Eric Eckholm put the "fire wood crisis" on the policy makers' agenda in the late 1970s, while the subsequent questioning by Gerald Leach, Robin Mearns and Peter Dewees of whether such a crisis really existed helped take it off'.

But this questioning was also about to sink the IIED energy programme. Late in 1988, Richard Sandbrook, Lloyd Timberlake and I visited the Ministry of Development Cooperation in Oslo to review the Ministry–IIED relationship. Towards the end of the day, as night fell and the room darkened, energy came up on the agenda. 'We like very much your work on biomass and Africa', the energy representative said, 'and we will order several hundred copies of the book to distribute. Thank you. But what the book has taught us is that this is not an energy problem. It is more to do with agriculture and forestry. And so we will not be funding you for next year, as originally planned.'

Lloyd leaned over, through the darkening gloom, and whispered for all to hear: 'Gerry, I've never actually seen anyone shoot themselves in the foot until now!' Yes indeed: next year's funding vanished through a bureaucratic masterstroke. Deep depression and fury, until a few days later another good fairy from Scandinavia made an offer no one could refuse: join the new Stockholm Environment Institute, with ample funding to work on whatever seemed most interesting and important, from my London home. So, with many regrets after nearly 15 years with IIED, but also with excitement, the sole remaining representative of IIED's energy programme jumped ship.

## EPILOGUE: SUSTAINABLE ENERGY IN THE 21ST CENTURY?

What can one say about the future of energy in helping to make a sustainable world? The frank answer is: right now, not much. Technical progress in the areas most critically pertinent to this question is extremely rapid but the outcomes – in terms of just what, when, and at what cost – are, for the moment, extremely uncertain.

We need to backtrack a little. Few would deny that the dominant issue of global energy development is how to mitigate climate change. Energy production and consumption are by far the most important sources of rising greenhouse gas emissions which are the root cause of global warming. As many people know, global emissions must be cut by some 60–70 per cent over the next few decades if global warming is eventually to be stabilized. Even deeper cuts will be needed in the high-emission industrialized world if the developing world is to be allowed some space to increase its per capita emissions – even by only modest amounts – to fuel essential economic growth.

How to make these cuts is one of the supreme political and technical challenges of this century. Underlying this challenge is the familiar but fundamental question of how much can be done by technical fixes? Depending on this, how much belt-tightening (or life-enhancing?) changes to rich-world 'lifestyles' will be needed? The zero-emission fuel-cell car – or the bus and bicycle?

The prospects for *sufficient* lifestyle changes look increasingly hopeless. Many speak and write of them; some march and demonstrate for them; few make them. The slogans of politics – with the connivance of the vast majority of the media and public – cluster around more economic growth, better public services, or tax cuts. When the occasional tough environmental policy does emerge – such as the UK's high vehicle fuel taxes and prices during late 2000 – the ensuing rage and revolt are met with official evasions and denial. Few politicians dare stand up and emphasize long-term benefits.

So that leaves 'tech fix' to cover the failure of sufficient lifestyle change. What are the prospects here? Huge declines over the past 20 years in the energy intensity of industrialized nations (that is, in the energy use per unit of GDP) are now being followed by some developing countries, notably China in the past 4 years or so. A combination of real energy-efficiency improvements and of structural change towards less energy-intensive forms of production – notably from industry to services and from heavy to light industries – is in many places allowing economic growth alongside much slower growth – or even declines – in associated emissions of greenhouse gases.

There are huge remaining gains to be had from these emission-reducing trends – a point that environmental groups persistently underline when they object to projects designed to increase energy supplies, whether based on fossil fuels, nuclear or even many forms of renewable energy (including onshore wind, hydropower, biomass energy crops, or energy from urban waste via incineration and landfill gas). Quite right too – up to a point. More, much more, could be done by the spread of effective policies to promote energy efficiency that are now applied in a handful of countries.

But, crucially, efficiency and structural change will not be nearly sufficient on their own to effect the required cuts in greenhouse-gas emissions, even if we pursue them with increased and enduring vigour. A low-emission energy future must be based not only on lots of energy efficiency but also on the maximum feasible reliance on renewable energy sources. Insulating a home might cut its energy use in half; providing that energy from the sun and wind cuts it to nearly zero.

There is also crucial problem with most renewables: the sun goes out at night, the wind dies to a calm, and even wave energy and hydropower vary with the seasons. Energy storage to smooth out the highs and lows of these renewable energy sources, on a scale sufficient to run an industrial society, appears to be prohibitively expensive. Only two classes of renewable energy avoid this flaw – by providing stored energy, as fossil fuels do. One is 'modern' biomass: growing trees and grasses or using crop, animal and urban residues as fuel to convert into high-grade energy (as opposed to using biomass in traditional ways, such as for cooking). The other is the so-called solar-hydrogen economy: use solar cells to convert sunlight to electricity and use some of that to split water into oxygen and hydrogen. Both approaches can provide all the forms of 'modern' energy we need: electricity, liquids, gases and heat. But neither is ready yet for take-off; and no one yet knows what their potential for providing energy will be, or their costs.

Biomass is the best-established of renewable energy sources. There are working biomass energy projects and programmes right across the world, from Brazil's sugarcane-alcohol programme to innumerable village-scale biomass-electricity schemes. However, in capital-scarce developing countries, production of biomass energy is mostly un-mechanized and has to rely on large pools of very cheap labour. Typical labour productivities are about 20–40 workdays to produce an amount of energy equivalent to one tonne of crude oil. In contrast, the equivalent figure for UK opencast coal mining is less than one working hour. To keep the bioenergy competitive, developing country wage rates cannot rise above roughly US$1–2 per day. So one mechanizes to allow better wages and hold down costs? Yes, but at the end of that road lies the typical European or North American biomas-energy crop producer, mechanized up to the hilt and hostage to bank interest rates and bank managers, growing 'green energy' that costs roughly twice as much as energy from fossil fuels.

Research is underway to reduce bioenergy costs, while subsidies are fully justified in order to pay off biomass for its low to zero greenhouse-gas emissions. Much the same applies to the solar-hydrogen idea: intensive research, development and desk studies are underway to 'prove' the concept and find the best approaches to its widespread application.

It will be some time yet before we get credible answers on either of these research fronts. Meanwhile, we know remarkably little about where these two paths to a climate- and development-friendly energy future might lead us. Abundant low-cost clean energy for 10 billion people? A trickle of high-cost energy for a few? Or something in between? Much is at stake – but for a few years most of us can only wait and see what they come up with, while pressing governments and industry to do much more on research and development and to spend real money on deploying the best technologies as they become available.

## NOTES

1   Leach, Gerald (1976) *Energy and Food Production*, IPC Science & Technology Press, Guildford.
2   Leach, Gerald, Lewis, C. Romig, F. Buren, A van. Foley, G. (1979) *A Low Energy Strategy for the United Kingdom*, IIED and Science Reviews, London.
3   Leach, Gerald (1987) *Household Energy in South Asia*, Elsevier Applied Science Publishers, London.
4   Foley, Gerald and Geoffrey Bernard (1983) *Biomass Gasification in Developing Countries*, Earthscan, London.
    Foley, Gerald and P Moss (1983, revised 1985) *Improved Cooking Stoves in Developing Countries*, Earthscan, London.
    Foley, Gerald and Geoffrey Bernard (1984) *Farm and Community Forestry*, Earthscan, London.
    Barnard, Geoffrey and L Kristoferson (1985) *Agricultural Residues in the Third World*, Earthscan, London.
    Foley, Gerald (1986) *Charcoal Making in Developing Countries*, Earthscan, London.
5   Leach, Gerald and Robin Mearns (1988) *Bioenergy Issues and Options for Africa*, IIED, London.

6  Leach, Gerald and Robin Mearns (1989) *Beyond the Woodfuel Crisis: People, Land and Trees in Africa*, Earthscan, London.
7  Spilsbury, M and D Kaimowitz (1998) *The Influence of Research and Publications on Conventional Wisdom and Policies Affecting Forests*, Centre for International Forestry Research, Jakarta, Indonesia.

# 9

# Sustainable agriculture

## *Gordon Conway*

I can't remember when or where I first met Richard Sandbrook and who introduced us. It was probably at Richard Macrory's house in the early 1980s, at a gathering of environmental types, most of whom seem to have turned up on Harley Davidsons. I am probably maligning a lot of people but it was several incarnations ago for me.

What I do clearly remember is that Richard and I hit it off from the start. Both of us were passionately committed to changing the world, at least in helping to change the developing world, in a way that married development, the alleviation of poverty and environmental protection. We also both had a strong sense of humour; we were collectors of human follies, particularly the follies of development experts (of the Evelyn Waugh *Scoop* variety). We were both, under our respectable exteriors, iconoclasts unwilling to accept the conventional wisdom whether from government servants, international bureaucrats or NGO activists. Scratch the surface and you will find that neither of us have changed that much.

At the time I was Professor of Environmental Technology at Imperial College in London. I had created the multi-disciplinary Centre for Environmental Technology at 48 Princes Gardens in South Kensington in the mid-1970s and, within the centre, had formed a small team of young people, with ecology or economics backgrounds, who were working on the theory and practice of sustainable agriculture. Richard suggested we should cooperate, which we did, and then in 1986 I moved full time to IIED on a sabbatical, taking some of the team with me – Jules Pretty, Jennifer McCracken and Melanie Salter.

(If I remember correctly, Richard felt that I would benefit from the less rarified atmosphere of Bloomsbury. The downside was the Northern Line and having to find all my own money. Actually, not only my money but others' as well. I do remember Doreen Ward, IIED's accountant, catching me on the stairs and saying there was not enough to pay everyone at the end of the month and would I go over to Washington and do a job for the World Bank and come back with a fistful of dollars. I have had a healthy respect for the realities of NGO life ever since.)

Many, today, exercise proprietorial claims over the concept of sustainable agriculture. The organic farming lobby, in particular, claims it as being synonymous with organic agriculture, and the mixture of fact and myth that that entails. I usually point to Varro, the second-century-BC Roman writer and estate owner, who refers to agriculture as an 'Art and Science ... which teaches us what crops are to be planted in each kind of soil, and what operations are to be carried on, in order that the land may produce the highest yields in perpetuity.' As is common in the best of Roman writing, the definition is clear, elegant and succinct.

For me it all began in the late 1970s with the work that Ian Craig, also from Imperial, and I were doing with a remarkable team of agricultural scientists at Chiang Mai University in northern Thailand (Benjavan and Kanok Rerkasem, Manu Seetisarn, Phrek Gypmantasiri, Aree Wiboonpongse and Laxmi Ganjapan were the prime movers at the university). They were remarkable in many ways – for their intellectual skills and curiosity, their commitment to inter-disciplinarity and their ability to work as a team. They had a strong sense of humour and half of the team were women, both of which helped. I have never come across a team like it since. They are still together, with notable additions and some younger faculty, although sadly they are getting close to retirement.

What we did together has been written about elsewhere, but in essence we developed a technique called agroecosystem analysis as a tool for the holistic analysis of agricultural development. We defined agroecosystems as 'ecological and socio-economic systems, comprising domesticated plants and/or animals and the people who husband them, intended for the purpose of producing food, fibre or other agricultural products'. We maintained that such agroecosystems had four distinctive properties – productivity, stability, equity and sustainability – and, most important, that these tended to be traded off against each other. For example, an agroecosystem with high sustainability might have low productivity and vice versa. The point of this analysis, although interesting in its own right as an academic exercise, was to help identify the key questions that would help design a development pathway in which the trade-offs between the properties could be minimized. The Chiang Mai team subsequently used the analysis to identify the key questions for the Chiang Mai valley and built a research programme on this.

The technique rapidly spread to other countries in Southeast Asia and in 1984 an Indonesian sister organization called Kelompok Penelitian Agro-Ekosistem held a conference in Java entitled 'The Sustainability of Agricultural Intensification in Indonesia'. I think that can justifiably lay claim to being the first conference explicitly on sustainable agriculture.

Although agroecosystem analysis was intended as a technique for identifying key research questions, we soon found that it had other uses not least, as we learned from a colourful experience in the Philippines, in dispute resolution. The US Agency for International Development (USAID) had constructed a small dam at the outlet of Lake Buhi in Bicol Province in order to provide irrigation water for downstream rice growers. But, as so often happens in such situations, the upstreamers did not like it, in fact were hopping mad – to the extent of getting the New People's Army (NPA) to stand armed on the dam to ensure that it did not function. In 1986 USAID asked IIED for help and Richard happily volunteered me. On arrival in Manila the USAID office provided us with a bulletproof car and pointed us in the right direction. We enlisted the help of Professor Percy Sajise of the University of the Philippines whose team was by this time expert in agroecosystem analysis. A week of mapping, diagram-making and interviewing provided a wealth of material that we then used for a workshop in a local hotel. The villagers, upstream and downstream, showed up, as did officials from the relevant Manila government agencies and also some representatives of the NPA. After three days of intensive argument around the maps and seasonal diagrams we had a resolution – involving staggered releases of the water – which seemed to leave everyone happy.

## THE BREAKTHROUGH: PARTICIPATORY APPRAISAL

But it was two years later when we had moved to IIED that the breakthrough came. Like most breakthroughs, although it seemed revolutionary at the time, none of us could figure out why we had not thought of it before. The Swedish Red Cross, acting on behalf of the

Ethiopian Red Cross, asked us to go to Wollo Province in Ethiopia to help them plan development priorities for the region which only four years before had suffered from a massive famine, killing nearly half the inhabitants. Jenny McCracken and I went, and with us, at the suggestion of the Swedish Red Cross, Robert Chambers of the Institute for Development Studies at Sussex.

Robert and I had known each other for some time but had never worked together. We started off with a degree of mutual suspicion and a major disagreement over who should use the single electric outlet in the room in Wollo we had been allocated. I wanted it to plug in my computer; Robert insisted that the priority was for his kettle to brew tea. We managed, with Jenny's help, to get that sorted out and then began to tackle the seemingly more difficult task of reconciling our agroecosystem analysis with Robert's skills in semi-structured interviewing. I was wedded to the discipline of maps and diagrams; Robert was insistent that it was only through free-flowing questions that one got at the truth. Of course, as was soon obvious, these approaches complemented one another and the workshop began in this way, with teams from the Red Cross and government agencies walking though the villages interviewing farmers and, at Robert's insistence, climbing to the tops of the hills to construct transects (it was one such climb that uncovered the existence of cultivated gully plugs, crucial to the agriculture yet ignored in the government's push to resettle everyone in the new villages in the valley bottoms).

The workshop was going well, apart from one day when Robert kept his team out way beyond curfew and we had to do some political smoothing. Then, about half-way through, Robert had a brainwave. Why, he asked, did the experts have to draw all the maps and ask all the questions? Why could the farmers not do this themselves?

From then on we increasingly involved the farmers in the exercise, not just as passive objects of investigation but also as genuine partners in the process of description and analysis. What they knew and how they expressed it, was a revelation for most of us. I remember sitting down with two farmers while they described, using a fascinating process of spatial and temporal mapping, the number of days of rain per month – for the previous ten years! One day Robert and I with our respective teams developed two different types of ranking procedures for the farmers to use. The purpose that day was to determine which trees they would like to plant (their priorities turned out to be very different from those of the forest department extension workers). Robert's technique was called matrix ranking and mine was pairwise ranking. To this day we argue their respective merits. Last year I got a kick, standing in a field in western Kenya, listening to a woman farmer rank the six different maize varieties in her trial plots. How long, I asked, have you been doing pairwise ranking? She gave me a withering look and replied 'We have always done it in Kenya.'

A few weeks after the Wollo exercise, Jenny McCracken went to a coastal district of Gujarat in India and tried out a fully participatory exercise for the Aga Khan Rural Support Programme (India) (AKRSP(I)). When I asked her how it went, she said that on the final day of the work in one village, they held a meeting to discuss the analyses and, rather than the 60 or so villagers they had expected would attend, they were overwhelmed by a turn-out of 700! A key innovation from this work with AKRSP(I) was that the farmers not only played the main role in constructing the visual analyses, but they also took charge of presenting these analyses to the rest of the village. This meant that the village-level review had an altogether different dynamic than before, as the villagers were less deferential to their peers than they would have been to the 'outside experts', and were more apt to question and correct the findings.

In the same year Jules Pretty and I went to the Alpuri Valley in northern Pakistan to carry out a participatory exercise on behalf of the Swiss Development Corporation (SDC). SDC felt that the valley might be an appropriate setting for a fruit and vegetable development project. It is a somewhat inaccessible place, off the Swat Valley. With a small team of Pakistan agricultural and development experts we spent the first night in a Forest department guesthouse on the ridge high above the Alpuri valley. As was customary on these trips we listened to the BBC World Service which rewarded us with a reading of Kipling's poem about the six serving men – who, what, why, where, how and when. This was an ideal prompt for a discussion of inter- viewing techniques (we felt rather like partisans in occupied France who had just received a special coded broadcast from London's Bush House).

The next morning we went down into the valley, marvelling at the fine chalet-like dwellings perched on the mountainsides. No wonder, we thought, that the Swiss felt it had promise! Our first interviews soon provided an explanation. Most of the men of the valley spent nine months of the year working in the coal-mines of Quetta. They were relatively well paid – hence the fine houses, and hence also a lack of interest in becoming fruit and vegetable gardeners. It was a good lesson in the role of semi-structured interviewing. However, the exercise did provide another example of the value of participatory approaches, in this case leading to an agroecosystem mapping of the valley. Like so many participatory appraisal techniques, it was simple. We went to one village and asked them to describe how their village and its farmland differed from another village we could see across the valley; then we went to the other village and reversed the process. By the end of the week the valley was zoned, effectively by the farmers themselves.

These were some of the beginnings of what came to be known by a bewildering plethora of names, 'participatory rapid rural appraisal' by us at IIED, and later 'participatory rural appraisal', following parallel innovations by colleagues at the National Environment Secretariat, Kenya, and Clark University, USA. (Other names such as 'participatory analysis and learning methods' (PALM), 'méthode accélére de recherche participative' (MARP), reflected the different approaches that mushroomed at the time, driven by local needs and customs). Robert and I felt that it was crucial for this not to become a bureaucratized methodology, and set ourselves against manuals and textbooks. Instead, we established an informal newsletter, based at IIED, initially called *RRA Notes*. Later, the newsletter was renamed *PLA Notes* (PLA for 'participatory learning and action') in recognition of the widening array of participatory research and development approaches. The idea was to provide a forum for practitioners to describe their experiences and innovations and so disseminate good practice. We envisaged that new ideas reported from an African village one week would be tried out in an Asian village the next – and that has happened.

Today *PLA Notes* has an audience of several thousand individuals and institutions scattered throughout the world. Since its launch in 1988, 42 issues of the *Notes* have been published, documenting methodological challenges and innovations across a wide range of sectors and thematic areas, from community water management to participatory monitoring and evaluation, and from sexual and reproductive health to participatory urban appraisal.

Looking back, it is fair to say, the process has been a revolution. PLA embodies a set of methodologies, an attitude and a way of working which has finally challenged the traditional top-down process that has characterized so much development work. Participants from NGOs, government agencies and the research centres have rapidly found themselves, usually unexpectedly, listening as much as talking, experiencing close to first hand the conditions of life in poor households and changing their perceptions about the kinds of interventions and the research needs that are required. But, of course, it has not been without its problems. At times it has had the trappings of a fad. Banks and other aid agencies have inserted it as a requirement in project designs without ensuring just how genuine was the participatory element. In the beginning, some critics saw it primarily as an academic exercise. But the practical value soon became apparent, and hundreds, if not thousands, of development projects and programmes are demonstrably better for adopting the approach.

At IIED, however, PLA was only one of our preoccupations. We continued to be exercised by what is meant by sustainable agriculture. At the invitation of Johan Holmberg, then at the Swedish Agency for International Development (SIDA), we began a series of small bulletins that he christened *Gatekeepers*. The idea was to provide busy policy-makers and development experts with some windows into the theoretical and practical world of sustainable agriculture, emphasizing new findings in a clear and concise manner. The first, which Jenny and I wrote, described the findings of one of my then students, Michael Loevinsohn, that pesticide use on rice in the Philippines was apparently causing heavy mortality and morbidity among farm workers. That was *Gatekeeper 1*, issued in 1987, and the series has continued ever since, going out to several thousand policymakers, planners and academics in over 120 countries. *Gatekeeper 100*, entitled 'Agri-Food Systems, Livelihoods and the Environment in a Globalizing World', by members of the current Sustainable Agriculture team, was published in mid-2001.

We also continued to publish books and monographs. One important books was *After the Green Revolution*,[1] which I co-authored with another IIED researcher Ed Barbier. He is a resource economist, now at York University; the discipline of combining agriculture, ecology and economics was a challenging experience. The other noteworthy book was *Unwelcome Harvest: Agriculture and Pollution*,[2] authored by Jules and myself. It was a very large book (my wife irreverently referred to it as a very expensive doorstop), but to this day it is the only authoritative compendium of the polluting effects of agriculture.

## INTEGRATED AND COMPLEMENTARY APPROACHES

As I indicated at the beginning of this chapter, one of the problems of sustainable agriculture, as so often defined today, is that it means all things to all people. It has become an all-embracing term. Almost anything that is perceived as 'good' from the writer's perspective can fall under the umbrella of sustainable agriculture – organic farming, the small family farm, indigenous technical knowledge, biodiversity, integrated pest management, self-sufficiency, recycling, and so on. The problem with this is that it ignores the inevitable trade-offs in agricultural development – between productivity, equitability, stability and sustainability. Ignoring them is not only self-delusory, it is also dangerous since it lulls both expert and farmer alike into believing that the problem is solved and everyone is content.

The classic example of an approach to the trade-off issue is integrated pest management (IPM), which preoccupied me in the 1960s. Pesticides are frequently highly effective means of killing pests, and hence can be very productive, resulting in high and stable crop yields. But their use is often not sustainable – pests can evolve resistance and pesticides can wipe out the natural enemies of pests, so producing pest resurgences. Pesticides can also be inequitable in their effects – expensive to use and also hazardous, with the poor suffering most.

The alternatives may be better in some respects – biological control, or the use of cultural techniques such as intercropping – may be more sustainable, but they may be less effective. The trick in IPM is to combine these different techniques, making minimal use of safe pesticides, only when and where wanted, along with appropriate biological and cultural controls. There are now countless examples of IPM working in the developing world, the best known being the control of the brown planthopper in Indonesia. But it has taken the best part of 30 years for that to happen, in part because the trade-off question is still insufficiently addressed. For example, biological scientists find effective ways to control pests but often ignore the cost to farmers – especially the labour costs – and, as a consequence, the approach is simply not adopted on a wide enough scale.

An allied concept is integrated nutrient management (INM). In some respects this is an approach that is nearly a hundred years old. Farmers, soil scientists and agronomists have long known that organic matter – broken-down plant material and animal manure – is essential for healthy agriculture. When applied to and incorporated in the soil it creates a soil structure that allows for root development and the uptake of nutrients – both macro- and micro-nutrients. But organic matter is often relatively poor in the nutrients themselves. In some situations the nutrients can be created by nitrogen-fixing bacteria or blue-green algae. But the kind of high yields that developing-country farmers now need are, with a few exceptions, possible only with the application of synthetic fertilizers containing nitrogen, phosphorus and potassium and, where appropriate, micronutrients.

INM is an approach that recognizes this essential complementarity. Its greatest potential today lies in Africa. There are some who argue that what Africa needs to feed itself is organic farming. But this ignores the reality of current practices. In some respects, Africa is already following a form of organic farming. Pesticides are rarely used, and synthetic fertilizer inputs are only about 4 kilograms per hectare (compared with 42 kilograms per hectare in Asia). As a consequence, cereal yields average only 1 ton per hectare (yields comparable with those in Europe under the Roman Empire 2000 years ago) while in Asia the average is nearly three times more. Such low yields mean, in turn, that there is little organic matter to put back into the soil.

A case in point is production in Central Uganda of bananas, a key staple for many hundreds of years that is in severe decline, partly because of pests and diseases, but primarily because of the nutrient exhaustion of the soil. Bananas take out large quantities of potassium, and unless it is replaced yields inevitably fall. Over much of Africa the soil is being effectively mined in this way. (In parts of western Kenya the nitrogen is being removed at some 125kg/ha – equivalent to what European farmers regularly put on their land each year.)

Part of the problem is the cost of synthetic fertilizers. In countries such as Malawi the cost to poor farmers is many times greater than what European, or even Asian, farmers are paying. On average, fertilizer cost in Asia is equivalent to the price of 2–3 kilograms of grain, but 6–11 kilograms in Africa. It is not surprising that African farmers use so little fertilizer. Subsidies are part of the answer, at least until efficient small-scale private marketing systems are developed, but European and US governments, who subsidize their farmers to the tune of over $70 billion a year, have, through their influence on the World Bank and the IMF, insisted that fertilizer use should not be subsidized in the developing countries.

However, synthetic fertilizers, it must be stressed, are only part of the answer. The essence of INM is to use organic and inorganic techniques in partnership. Legumes, in particular, have been proven to contribute to high sustainable cereal yields. But again, the costs in labour and time have to be factored in. Far too often, experimental results are difficult for farmers to replicate. There is much talk today of the need for scaling-up of such approaches, but this can happen only if the demand and the feasibility are evident and can be easily built upon.

These were the kinds of issues we debated during the two years of my stay at IIED. They continued after I left. Jules Pretty took over the team for a couple of years, producing an excellent book, *Regenerating Agriculture*[3] that persuasively argues the case for the role of indigenous resources in agriculture. This was followed by another book, *The Living Land*,[4] with a focus on agricultural systems in industrialized countries. Jules then became Professor of Environment and Society at the University of Essex where he has recently produced an important review of more than 200 sustainable agriculture programmes worldwide. These programmes and projects include organic farming, strictly defined, but also IPM and INM approaches. As he demonstrates, together these have been adopted at a phenomenal rate over the last decade. The combined area within such programmes is now 29 million hectares, up from only about half a million hectares in 1990. The current total is about 3 per cent of the agricultural area of developing countries.

As I was leaving IIED, Ian Scoones, another of the Imperial College team, joined the programme and continued his work on the ecological and socio-economic approaches to range management by pastoral communities in Africa. In this he teamed up with Camilla Toulmin and the Drylands Programme at IIED. He is now at the Institute of Development Studies (IDS) in Sussex, and has several important books to his name, including *Range Ecology at Disequilibrium*,[5] and *Living with Uncertainty*[6]. Jenny McCracken stayed at IIED until 1991 before going to work in Washington DC, partly with the World Bank. She is now a freelance consultant in Switzerland, working with a number of different international development institutions.

After Jules Pretty left IIED at the end of 1996, John Thompson took over the leadership of the group, which was renamed the Sustainable Agriculture and Rural Livelihoods (SARL) Programme, and established a multi-disciplinary team of six researchers and four information and communications specialists. It has continued to prosper, focusing on the political ecology of agri-food systems in both developing and industrialized countries. Today, SARL maintains an integrated programme of collaborative research, information exchange, and advocacy and advisory support with partners on six continents.

As for myself, I left IIED in 1989 to take up the post of Representative for the Ford Foundation in New Delhi. There I managed to find some time to continue the IIED work, especially during the year when Robert Chambers was in Hyderabad. On holiday at Kulu in the Himalayan foothills we produced an IDS discussion paper on the topic of sustainable livelihoods – arguing against the sectoral approach to alleviating poverty and instead taking a holistic perspective that saw people's livelihoods as the basis is for integrated development. For a short conceptual paper it has had considerable impact. Many aid agencies (including the Rockefeller Foundation!) now take sustainable livelihoods as their basic paradigm.

From India I moved to Sussex in 1992 to become Vice-Chancellor of the University of Sussex. Very little of my time was taken up with issues of sustainable agriculture – except for one important period when I headed a small committee to produce a new vision for the Consultative Group on International Agricultural Research (CGIAR). The vision – which eventually became a book, *The Doubly Green Revolution*[7] – owed much to the IIED work. It called for a new agricultural revolution for the developing world, which was as productive as the old Green Revolution, but sustainable, equitable and environmentally friendly.

In 1998 I took over as President of the Rockefeller Foundation in New York. A major theme of the Foundation is Food Security, especially for Africa, and a great deal of the $30 million plus that we spend annually on this topic goes in grants to universities, research institutions and NGOs, primarily in the developing countries, who are working on techniques of IPM, INM and other related approaches to productive, sustainable and equitable agriculture.

To the traditional concerns of sustainable agriculture is now added the challenge of biotechnology and, in particular, genetically modified (GM) crops. I want to finish by discussing briefly some of these issues. At the Foundation we have spent the last ten years funding the training of Asian scientists in rice biotechnology. It has been a highly successful programme and there must now be nearly 1000 biotechnologists working on rice and other crops in universities and research institutes in countries such as China, the Philippines, Vietnam, India and Thailand. Now we are turning our attention to Africa, and at the same time trying to move forward the intense public dialogue that revolves around GM crops.

We acknowledge that biotechnology approaches raise many legitimate questions. There are many potential hazards; some real, others imaginary. These need addressing by clear trials subject to public scrutiny, in both developed and developing countries. But there are also many potential benefits, especially relevant to creating more sustainable and equitable agricultural systems. For example, there is already evidence from China and Mexico of dramatic reductions in pesticide use following the introduction of 'Bt' cotton (incorporating the *Bacillus thuringiensis* gene). In the US, Roundup Ready soybean, in addition to significantly reducing farmers' costs ($0.75 billion per year in the US), is resulting in less herbicide pollution of rivers, and, more important, the widespread adoption of various no-till rotations that are helping soil conservation.

In the developing countries there is considerable potential for pest- and disease-resistant GM crops, especially as part of IPM programmes. Control of the weed *Striga* that causes enormous damage in parts of Africa, could be aided in this way. Higher soil nutrition helps, and there is promise in cultural control methods, for example, intercropping with the legume *Desmodium*, but it may not be enough. Another alternative may be herbicide treatment of the seed, but this will require herbicide-resistant cereals. Another is to transfer, using a biotechnology approach, *Striga* resistance to maize from sorghum or from wild maize relatives. It is a complex problem and there will be no simple magic bullet but biotechnology could play an important role in an integrated programme.

Many of these benefits are some way off, but other techniques of biotechnology – particularly tissue culture and marker-aided selection – are already producing real benefits in farmers' hands. Pioneering work in Kenya and Uganda involving local universities and government research institutes has produced bananas, using tissue culture, that are free of viruses and other pests and diseases. Farmers are setting up their own nurseries in villages and selling on the banana suckers to their neighbours.

Most exciting, however, has been the development of the new rices at the West Africa Rice Development Association (WARDA), based in Côte d'Ivoire. Rice consumption is growing dramatically in West Africa, partly fuelled by population growth, partly by increasing consumer demand. But local production is falling even further behind demand. The region is importing about half of its requirements, some 3.5 million tons at a cost approaching 1 billion dollars.

But now WARDA has achieved the daunting task of crossing the African rice species (*Oryza glaberrima*) with the Asian species (*Oryza sativa*). The crossing is difficult, because of the high incidence of resulting sterility. But the application of embryo-rescue tissue culture has overcome the problem, and the use of another advanced technique of biotechnology, anther culture, has enabled WARDA scientists to fix some 3000 new rice lines resulting from the crossing, backcrossing and subsequent selection.

The rices have many of the characteristics of their African ancestors. They grow well in drought-prone, upland conditions and their early vigorous growth crowds out the weeds that ordinarily require vast amounts of labour for their removal. They are resistant to local pests and disease, tolerant of poor nutrient conditions and mineral toxicity. But as they mature they take on some of the characteristics of their Asian ancestors, producing full panicles of non-shattering grain, and they are ready for harvesting in about 100 days.

Under low inputs they yield up to 3 tons per hectare, and with high inputs up to 5 tons (current average yields in the region are barely above 1 ton). WARDA has also brilliantly combined the high science of biotechnology with a central role for farmer participation. Given the great diversity of African ecologies, the traditional top-down extension approach is inappropriate. In several countries, farmers are conducting their own farm trials of over 300 of the new lines. Dissemination of the new seed is also relying on the traditional village systems of barter and sales among farmers. As a consequence the spread of the varieties is very rapid.

In Guinea, some 160 farmers evaluated the first new lines in 1997, just a year after they were produced at WARDA. With World Bank assistance, 20,000 hectares were planted in Guinea in 2000, and this year it will approach 90,000 hectares. Guinea's increased rice tonnage will save some $13 million in import costs.

In many respects this is the Doubly Green Revolution in action. It marries the best of modern science with genuine farmer participation in a way that is highly productive, sustainable, equitable and environmentally friendly. The sustainable agriculture programme at IIED can claim no direct credit, but many of the concepts, ideas and techniques that we developed have become part of the agricultural mainstream and helped to inspire and shape efforts such as this. We can be reasonably proud of ourselves – not a bad job!

# NOTES

1  Conway, Gordon and Edward Barbier (1990) *After the Green Revolution*, Earthscan, London.
2  Conway, Gordon and Jules Pretty (1991) *Unwelcome Harvest: Agriculture and Pollution*, Earthscan, London.
3  Pretty, Jules (1995) *Regenerating Agriculture: Policies and Practice for Sustainability and Self-Reliance*, Earthscan, London.
4  Pretty Jules (1998) *The Living Land*, Earthscan, London.
5  Behnke Jnr, Roy H, Scoones Ian and Carol Kerven (eds) (1993) *Range Ecology at Disequilibrium: New Models of Natural Variability and Pastoral Adaptation in African Savannas*, Earthscan, London.
6  Scoones, Ian (ed.) (1993) *Living with Uncertainty*, IT Publications, London.
7  Conway, Gordon (1995) *The Doubly Green Revolution*, Comstock/Cornell Paperbacks, Cornell University Press.

# 10

# Setting an urban agenda: Human settlements and IIED-América Latina

## *David Satterthwaite*

The last decade has brought increasing recognition by governments and international agencies of the need to develop urban policies, both to address urban poverty and in recognition of the importance of well-managed urban centres for economic growth. Many have also recognized that these require more capable, competent and accountable local (urban) governments. There is also the shift in the understanding of what constitutes urban poverty from a narrow focus where poverty is equated only with inadequate income or consumption levels to a broader recognition of the multiple forms of deprivation suffered by much of the urban population (see Box 10.1). Perhaps the most critical implication of this shift is the much increased focus on the role of local institutions in reducing urban poverty since many of the aspects of deprivation noted in the box depend on more competent, effective local institutions that are also accountable to local populations and local democratic political systems.

Three factors have helped to produce this change. The first is the recognition of the long-term trend towards increasingly urbanized populations and economic structures in almost all nations. Most of the world's urban population and most of its large cities are now in low- and middle-income nations. Asia now has close to half the world's urban population. Africa may still have more rural than urban dwellers but its urban population is now larger than that of North America, and it grows far faster than its rural population. Latin America has more than three-quarters of its population in urban centres.

# Box 10.1 The different aspects of urban poverty

**1. Inadequate income**, and thus inadequate consumption of necessities including food and, often, safe and sufficient water; often problems of indebtedness with debt repayments significantly reducing income available for necessities

**2. Inadequate, unstable or risky asset base**, non-material and material, including educational attainment and housing, for individuals, households or communities

**3. Inadequate shelter**, typically poor-quality, overcrowded and insecure

**4. Inadequate provision of 'public' infrastructure** such as piped water, sanitation, drainage, roads and footpaths, which increases health burdens and often work burdens

**5. Inadequate provision for basic services** such as day care, schools and vocational training, health care, emergency services, public transport, communications, law enforcement

**6. Limited or no safety net** to ensure basic consumption can be maintained when income falls; also to ensure access to shelter and health care when these can no longer be paid for

**7. Inadequate protection of poorer groups' rights through the operation of the law**, including laws and regulations regarding civil and political rights, occupational health and safety, pollution control, environmental health, protection from violence and other crimes, protection from discrimination and exploitation

**8. Poorer groups' voicelessness and powerlessness** within political systems and bureaucratic structures, leading to little or no possibility of: receiving entitlements; organizing, making demands and getting a fair response; and receiving support for developing their own initiatives. No means of ensuring accountability from aid agencies, NGOs, public agencies and private utilities, nor of being able to participate in the definition and implementation of their 'urban poverty' programmes

The second factor is the growth in urban poverty. Many governments and some international agencies now acknowledge that they
have long under-estimated the scale of urban poverty, largely because
of inappropriate criteria used to define and measure it, and that action
in urban areas is required if the internationally agreed poverty-
reduction targets are to be achieved by 2015.

The third factor is the recognition that new urban policies and
investment patterns are needed if sustainable development goals are
to be met, not least because a high proportion of the world's production, consumption and waste generation (including greenhouse-gas
emissions) is concentrated in urban areas. Large sections of the urban
population in low- and middle-income countries are also particularly
vulnerable to the likely direct and indirect effects of global warming.
The changes towards more democratic governments at national and
local levels, and to more decentralized political and administrative
structures, over the last 10 to 20 years have also helped to highlight
the key role of urban governments in achieving both environment and
development goals.

But this recognition of a need for more attention to urban issues
has not come easily. International concern for environmental issues
has always tended to focus on natural resources rather than on the
environmental-health issues that are so pressing in most urban (and
rural) areas because large sections of the population lack safe and
sufficient water supplies and adequate provision for sanitation,
drainage, health and emergency services, and live on land sites at high
risk from floods or landslides. There have been many inappropriate
transfers of the urban environmental priorities of high-income nations
to low-income nations so, for instance, the loss of agricultural land or
wetlands to urban expansion receives more attention than the
environmental-health problems that are the main cause of ill health,
injury and premature death of much of the population. There have
been many inaccurate assumptions about the contribution of urban
poor groups in environmental degradation when it is overwhelmingly
the middle- and high-income groups in urban areas that are responsible for the resource use and waste generation that underlie
environmental degradation.

When the failure of development policies to bring benefits to
most lower-income groups was recognized in the late 1960s and early
1970s, the world was much less urbanized. Then, as now, there has
been a tendency by international 'experts' to see urban populations as
privileged, in part because major cities usually concentrate invest-

ments in housing, water supply, sanitation, schools and health care systems. What these 'experts' so often fail to notice is that most poorer groups in these cities do not have access to these services and that most of the urban populations outside the major cities are as ill served as most of the rural population.

When IIED was asked by the secretariat of World Commission on Environment and Development (The Brundtland Commission) to draft a chapter on urban issues for its report *Our Common Future*[1] in 1985, this was strongly opposed by some members of the Commission – as if the Commission's emphasis on 'the needs of the present' did not include the 600 million urban dwellers who survived on very inadequate incomes and who lived in homes and neighbourhoods lacking provision for the most basic urban infrastructure and services (safe sufficient water, provision for sanitation and drainage, schools and health care). Many international agencies developed urban policies and strategies only in the last few years and none did so without opposition both from within the agency and outside. As late as 2001, the World Bank could produce a *World Development Report* on poverty that still refused to recognize the scale of deprivation in urban areas and the fact that urban poverty has characteristics and causes that are not the same as those of rural poverty.[2]

Although the World Bank has many staff with long experience in urban projects, it could still produce estimates for the scale of poverty worldwide based on a single income-based poverty line (US$1 per day), as if the income that a household needs to avoid deprivation is the same in rural areas as in the major cities. There are still some academics and many politicians and bureaucrats who insist that the priority is rural development and that any support for urban development will simply exacerbate urban problems – as it encourages more migrants to move into cities. There are those who still cling to notions about urban migrants moving to cities being attracted by 'the bright lights', despite 30 years of evidence, showing rural-to-urban migration flows to be logical and usually carefully planned responses to changing economic circumstances.

This chapter charts the development of IIED's work in urban areas from its origins in 1974, through the formation of its Human Settlements Programme in 1976 to the setting up of a Latin American office in 1979 and its development into an independent Argentine non-profit organization in 1988. It also describes how it sought to change the way that policy-makers view urban centres and their inhabitants. The Human Settlements Programme not only formed an important strand of IIED's work but also helped to develop new forms of collaboration with partner institutions in Africa, Asia and Latin America. The story of IIED's work in urban areas is also, in large part, the story of the work of Jorge E Hardoy, the Argentine urban specialist who founded and developed IIED's Human Settlements Programme and who subsequently founded IIED-América Latina. Although he died in 1993, the work on human settlements issues both in London and within IIED-América Latina in Buenos Aires still follows the lines and structures he helped to establish.

## IIED'S HUMAN SETTLEMENTS PROGRAMME

The need to address both urban and rural problems in Africa, Asia and Latin America was recognized from the Institute's earliest years, as can be seen in the book *Only One Earth: The Care and Maintenance of a Small Planet*, written by IIED's President, Barbara Ward and the Nobel laureate, René Dubos in 1971–72[3]. This book was prepared for the first of the large UN conferences held to draw attention to key global problems – the 1972 UN Conference on the Human Environment in Stockholm – at the request of the Conference's Secretary-General, Maurice Strong. This proved to be one of the best selling books on the environment during the 1970s. Unlike most other books on the environment at that time, it combined environmental concerns with concerns for human development and social justice. It also contained what was later to be taken up by the Brundtland Commission as the defining goal of sustainable development, as its introduction states that the 'charge of the U.N. to the [Stockholm] Conference was clearly to define what should be done to maintain the earth as a place suitable for human life not only now, but also for future generations' (p25).

After the success of *Only One Earth*, in 1974, Barbara Ward was asked by the Canadian government to write a popular book on human settlements issues, as the Canadian government was to host Habitat, the UN Conference on Human Settlements in Vancouver in 1976. This book, entitled *The Home of Man*,[4] covered such issues as the rapid growth of cities in Africa, Asia and Latin America, the growing proportion of city populations living in tenements and illegal and informal settlements and the large proportion of rural and urban populations lacking safe and sufficient supplies of water and provision for sanitation. It also demanded a greater priority from governments and international agencies to improving provision for water and sanitation and this was a point that Barbara Ward stressed in the many speeches that she made and articles that she wrote for newspapers during the preparations for the conference. This point received enthusiastic support from the Canadian government and from the UN Secretariat which organized the Conference. The need for a greater priority for water and sanitation was then formally endorsed by the 132 governments who were represented at the Habitat Conference and this subsequently led to the 1980s being declared by the UN General Assembly as the International Drinking Water Supply and Sanitation Decade, after a special UN Conference on water in 1977.

One of Barbara Ward's main advisers for the preparation of *The Home of Man* was the Argentine urban specialist Jorge E Hardoy. Writing from the Institute that he had founded in Argentina, the Centro de Estudios Urbanos y Regionales (CEUR), from 1974, he sent material to Barbara Ward to help her prepare the book, and also comments on her drafts. Here was someone who, nearly 30 years ago, was highlighting the urban issues that were to come to the centre of international concerns during the 1990s – the importance of developing more accountable, effective, democratic urban governments and more 'bottom-up' urban approaches that supported the actions and priorities of the urban poor and their organizations. These issues became so central to the discussion of urban development that perhaps their importance now seems self-evident. But few people were stressing the issue of 'good governance' at this time. Also, very few were stressing that it was good policy and practice by local governments in low- and middle-income countries that was the priority, rather than concentrating on the role of international agencies.[5]

IIED's contact with Jorge Hardoy was much strengthened when he accepted the Institute's invitation to work with it in Vancouver, during the UN Conference on Human Settlements in 1976. He took part in The Vancouver Symposium, a small group of urban specialists invited by IIED to meet just before the UN Conference and to define the priorities that the Conference should tackle, and also to draw the attention of the world's press to the Conference. Its declaration to the Conference included a very strong statement about the need for a much greater priority to be given to water and sanitation. Barbara Ward presented these points in a memorable address to the entire Conference; it was a measure of how highly regarded she was, since very few 'non-governmental' people have ever been invited to give a presentation to the plenary of these large governmental conferences.

The Symposium itself received considerable press coverage and prominence at the Conference – helped by the fact that the Symposium included some of the most famous 'global' thinkers of that era, for instance not only Barbara Ward but also Margaret Mead, Maurice Strong and Buckminster Fuller. The Symposium also received the full support of the official conference's host government (Canada) and the UN Secretariat, and the recommendations for a higher priority to be given to water and sanitation were already in the draft recommendations prior to the Conference.

In 1976, Argentina was in the midst of one of its most tragic political episodes, as the military government detained and murdered thousands of its citizens without charges and without trial. Jorge Hardoy had already had problems with the Argentine government. In 1976, when he went to renew his passport, he was seized and detained without trial and without charges. Only after a flood of protests to the Argentine government from academics from around the world through phone-calls, telegrams and telexes was he released. When in Vancouver, Jorge Hardoy received advice through a contact from the Ford Foundation that his life would be in danger if he returned to Argentina after the Conference. He accepted an invitation from the Institute of Development Studies in Sussex to join them as a senior fellow and from IIED to develop a new programme on human settlements. His wife and children also had to leave Argentina, and joined him in England; many other members of his institute, CEUR, also had to leave Argentina.

The initial goal of IIED's new Human Settlements Programme was to evaluate the extent to which governments and international agencies changed their policies and practices in line with the relatively radical recommendations they had formally endorsed at the Habitat Conference in Vancouver. Initial funding for the Programme came from the Canadian government; Barbara Ward received an enthusiastic response from the then Prime Minister of Canada, Pierre Trudeau, to her request for support. Jorge Hardoy agreed to direct the Programme, but on condition that it was formed by teams from different regions in the South. It was initially made up of teams based in the Sudan, Kenya, Argentina and India who visited countries in their region and prepared reports on conditions and trends in housing, basic services and other human settlements issues.[6] Thirty-one national assessments were prepared.

Meanwhile, staff based in London began to monitor the (usually very low) priority given by aid agencies and development banks to water supply, sanitation, slum and squatter upgrading, primary health care, education, and other projects that sought to bring direct benefits to low-income groups in urban and rural areas. Much of this work was done in collaboration with Yves Cabannes who, at that time, was with the French NGO GRET. Yves Cabannes remained a key partner and adviser to the Programme when he moved to work with community groups in Northeast Brazil and later came to head the UN Urban Management Programme for Latin America and the Caribbean – helping to develop IIED's work on housing finance and collaborating in the organization of work and seminars on Local Agenda 21s and on poverty reduction in the region.

From 1977 to the mid-1980s, collaborative research programmes were implemented on a range of topics. This included work on the role of small and intermediate-size urban centres in rural, regional and national development. The need for more attention to smaller urban centres is now recognized as an important issue, since most of the urban population in Africa, Asia and Latin America does not live in large cities, and the proportion of population lacking adequate housing with basic infrastructure and services is usually higher in smaller urban centres than in the large cities. But in the early 1980s, it was difficult to convince funding agencies of the relevance of this work. The work also stressed the importance of understanding rural–urban linkages, as the economy of so many smaller urban centres relies heavily on demand from rural producers and consumers and economic linkages with rural production. This too was a subject for which it was difficult to get funding as few international institutions wanted to fund urban research and institutions that funded rural work did not want to fund anything that had urban components.

IIED's work on small and intermediate urban centres was to lay the ground for its work on rural–urban interlinkages developed under the direction of Cecilia Tacoli during the 1990s. In the early 1980s, work also began on the multiple links between housing conditions and health in informal or illegal settlements and this led to a warm and fruitful working relationship with the World Health Organization (WHO) as IIED staff sat on WHO working groups and contributed to WHO technical reports. Perhaps surprisingly, this also increased IIED's knowledge of Moscow and St Petersburg. WHO received funding from the (then) Soviet Union in the form of roubles – and since these had no value outside the Soviet Union, WHO organized the meeting of various technical committees in Moscow and St Petersburg (at that time, Leningrad).[7]

During 1989, the head of the Lagos team, Tade Akin Aina, came to spend a year at IIED, developing work on housing and health and on the links between sustainable development and cities – and he also helped to develop the early issues of the Human Settlements Programme's journal *Environment and Urbanization*.[8] The Programme has also long drawn on the advice of staff at the London School of Hygiene and Tropical Medicine, especially Sandy Cairncross who developed the book *The Poor Die Young: Housing and Health in Third World Cities*[9] with Programme staff, became a member of the advisory board of *Environment and Urbanization* and later joined IIED's Board, and Carolyn Stephens who helped prepare a special issue of *Environment and Urbanization* on city inequality.[10]

IIED's Human Settlements Programme was unusual in comparison to most research programmes based in Europe and North America. First, much of the funding it raised went to the research partners in the South, with only a small staff based at IIED in London. Second, the intention from the outset was to increase the capacity and influence of the partners – the Institute for Development Studies in Mysore, CEUR (Centro de Estudios Urbanos y Regionales) in Buenos Aires, the University of Khartoum and the University of Lagos – and each was supported in developing its own publication programme, in the languages of its region. The long-term goal was also that each of the four partner institutions develop their own collaborative research programme with other institutions in its region.

A third unusual aspect was the Programme's stress on collaborative research, not comparative research. The intention of having teams in Latin America, Asia, Africa and the Arab World was not so much to compare national and regional experiences as to consider a set of common issues and concerns, recognizing that how they were addressed by governments was rooted in very different political, economic, social and ecological circumstances. IIED staff and representatives from the four teams met regularly to review progress and plan future research. Barbara Ward took a keen interest in the programme and hosted one of the meetings that brought together the directors of the collaborating teams. David Runnalls, who directed IIED from its formation in 1973 until 1983 when he moved to the US to direct its North American Office, also took part in many of the Programme's meetings and helped to nurture and support its development.

Although in the early years the Programme concentrated on research, from the early 1980s it began also to work in action-projects or in linking research with action. All four of the partner teams sought to provide technical and legal advice to those living in illegal settlements and to support initiatives to address housing and health problems, as part of the research work documenting the health problems in illegal settlements. This combination of research and action had become common practice in Latin America during the 1970s but was less common in Asia and Africa and among development researchers based in Europe and North America.

## IIED-América Latina

The Human Settlements Programme became even more decentralized in 1979, when Jorge Hardoy and his family returned to Argentina and founded what began as the Latin American office of IIED in Buenos Aires and was later to become IIED-América Latina. Argentina was still under the rule of the military dictatorship. The level of repression had reduced, although Jorge Hardoy was still not permitted to teach, and no official institution in Argentina would have been able to offer him work. (This was to change dramatically when Argentina returned to democratic rule in 1983 and Jorge was asked whether he would consider becoming Under-secretary for Housing – which he refused.) Later, political circumstances permitted the development of IIED's Latin American office into an independent Argentine-registered foundation, IIED-América Latina.

Jorge Hardoy's return to Latin America led to a great expansion in the research undertaken within Latin America (often with CEUR) and to a Latin-America-wide programme of seminars, workshops and publications (usually organized with the Latin American Social Science Research Council and often with the Inter-American Planning Society). This programme of seminars and workshops – often ten or more each year, organized in different places in different nations – had particular importance in promoting new ideas among hundreds of young researchers and NGO staff. There had been little possibility for such discussions within universities and government research institutes under the non-elected (often military) governments common in the region during the 1970s and early 1980s. Jorge Hardoy was one among many of Latin America's outstanding scholars in environment and development issues who had been forced out of universities and government research institutions for political reasons. Many of those who had been forced out had also set up independent research groups or NGOs in different Latin American nations. The programme of seminars and workshops was organized in partnership with a great range of such groups, many of whom remain today among the best-known centres of urban research, for example, DESCO in Peru, SUR in Chile and CIUDAD in Ecuador.

This annual seminar programme had several important character-istics. First, each seminar was jointly organized with one or more NGOs or other institutions. Second, each seminar sought to ensure that young researchers had the chance to participate and to present papers. Third, the papers presented at each seminar were published, giving many young researchers their first opportunity to publish, and providing the basis for a new literature on urban issues within the region. Fourth, certain themes were identified that were of particular importance to urban areas and these became the themes for seminar series – so each year, one or more seminars considered themes as 'small and intermediate urban centres', 'rethinking the Latin American city', 'housing and health' and 'natural disasters'.

To promote new thinking and new ideas requires constant support and stimulus, although many external funders did not understand this ('why do you want to hold another seminar on natural disasters when you had one on this topic last year?') Jorge Hardoy's particular inter-est and expertise in urban history also led to a series of seminars and publications on different aspects of Latin America's urban history, often on topics that helped to shed new light on contemporary urban problems. It also led to research on how to protect the rich historical patrimony of many of the region's cities without displacing the low-income groups which were so often concentrated there in tenements and cheap boarding houses[11] and this work helped to generate a new interest in such themes throughout the region.

It often proved difficult to obtain funding for this annual seminar programme and the publications associated with it, since these were not regarded as 'research'. The support of the international NGO Division of the Canadian International Development Agency (CIDA) was particularly important. Indeed, Ron Leger who directed the programme at that time always commented that he was not sure about the relevance of research but saw the great validity of the seminar and publication programme as it promoted new ideas throughout the region. This programme brought a whole new genera-tion of Latin American researchers and activists into debates about housing and urban policies and many went on to form or staff some of the region's most influential research groups and NGOs. Many also went into national and municipal government or back to the universities, in countries which returned to democracy – including some who subsequently were elected as mayors of major cities or who became directors of planning.

In 1982, IIED's Latin American office (which was to become IIED-América Latina in 1988) founded the journal *Medio Ambiente y Urbanizacion* with the Latin American Social Science Research Council (CLACSO). This was originally conceived as a bulletin more than a journal, to keep the growing network of people and institutions involved in urban research, and in the seminars and workshops, in touch with each other. It was also another way of reaching a wider audience in Latin America with the findings of IIED's research and of providing a larger circulation for the papers presented in the seminar programme. This developed into one of the region's most widely read and circulated journals; over 50 issues have been published since it was founded.

During the 1980s and early 1990s, the Human Settlements Programme remained jointly managed by IIED in London, IIED-América Latina in Buenos Aires and collaborating teams in Asia and Africa, with a small staff in IIED's London office (never more than two people) responsible for coordinating the work in Africa and Asia and working with IIED-América Latina on fundraising and publications. IIED-América Latina also widened its focus as a new programme was set up to provide direct support to the improvement of housing conditions and basic services in informal settlements (set up by Ana Hardoy)[12] and with the establishment of the FICONG programme, a Latin-America-wide programme of training workshops and seminars for NGOs and municipal authorities.

## EXTENDING THE INFLUENCE OF RESEARCH: THE ROLE OF NETWORKING

One concern of researchers working on environment and development issues is how to ensure that their findings influence professionals and, where possible, politicians, in governments and international agencies. The research undertaken by the teams in Africa, Asia, Latin America and the Arab nations on subjects such as the extent of the health problems associated with poor-quality housing and the role of small and intermediate urban centres needed to reach a wider audience than through conventional academic publications. Publishing research findings in even the best-known academic journals is no solution since most have very little circulation outside Europe and

North America, because of their high subscription costs. Many journals cost several hundred pounds a year and have no provision for cheaper subscriptions for individuals or institutions in low- and middle-income countries.

There is also much less interchange between academics and professionals in the South through journals, seminars and conferences, and little contact between researchers and NGOs and municipal authorities. The Human Settlements Programme sought new means to reach a wider audience, following the precedent set within Latin America through the programme of seminars and workshops and through publications that had a large circulation in the South. Of particular importance in this were two book series: one in English published with Earthscan (with nine books published between 1989 and the present [13]), the other, published by IIED-América Latina in Spanish.[14]

Staff from the Programme also recognized that preparing key documents for international agencies also helped to ensure a wider circulation for the Programme's research findings – as in the drafting of the urban chapter for *Our Common Future* (the report of the World Commission on Environment and Development/The Brundtland Commission) published in 1987, and in the preparation of other widely distributed publications for WHO, UN-Habitat and the OECD.[15] The preparation of each of these documents drew on the work and advice of a large network of individuals and institutions. Programme staff also contributed to the work of the Inter-Governmental Panel on Climate Change.

This network also helped to develop the Programme's English-language journal, *Environment and Urbanization* which was founded in 1989. It drew on the precedents set by the success of IIED-América Latina's journal, *Medio Ambiente y Urbanizacion*, and sought to demonstrate new ways by which professional journals could operate. First, it took measures to ensure that most authors were from Africa, Asia and Latin America rather than having the list of authors dominated by academics from Europe and North America. Second, it encouraged practitioners as well as researchers to write. Third, it ensured a wide circulation in Africa, Asia and Latin America by allowing any NGO or teaching or training institution in low- and middle-income nations to obtain it free. It also became one of the most widely circulated and cited journals in Europe and North America and provided the key text in many postgraduate and professional training programmes. It could not have fulfilled its initial goals, without the help of this network of researchers and NGO staff, yet none of these individuals received funding for this help. It would also not have been possible without the support of the Swedish International Development Cooperation Agency (Sida) which helped to fund the launch of the journal and has always helped to cover the cost of printing and distribution to institutions in low- and middle-income nations which cannot afford to subscribe.[16]

## FUNDING RESEARCH TEAMS IN THE SOUTH

For any Northern-based research institution, collaborative research with Southern partners changes the nature of the tasks they undertake. The work within the Human Settlements Programme has been less the undertaking of primary research and more the development of new research lines with Southern partners, raising finance, coordinating research projects, spreading new ideas, methodologies and concepts from one country or region to the next, and disseminating the research findings within the North and the South.

The emphasis on supporting Southern teams stemmed from the recognition that external agencies often misunderstand local contexts and distort local priorities. The importance of human settlements projects involving local NGOs and drawing on local knowledge and expertise came to be more widely recognized from the mid-1980s. In some cases, international non-governmental funding agencies have withdrawn from implementing projects themselves and now prefer to support local projects and local implementers. But research is still viewed somewhat differently. Most funding for 'development research' from funding institutions in Europe and North America goes to researchers from Europe and North America. Most national funding bodies used to require that funds were spent entirely (or primarily) on researchers in their own countries, and some still do so. Among the few Northern research-funding institutions that have given a priority to funding researchers in the South, there has been a growing pressure from their funders and from researchers in their own countries to fund more researchers in their own countries.

Two advantages to decentralizing the direction and management of research to local groups need to be stressed. The first is that local research groups have an understanding of local context which is central to research in human settlements. It is rare for external researchers to develop a deep understanding of local context. Second, and perhaps of most importance, most local research groups are committed to their locality and to building up local knowledge and feeding and developing local networks. The work that they do is more accessible to other researchers and other local groups. Research outputs often have an importance greater than their direct results. They are disseminated through many informal routes and are brought together with research in other related areas. In addition, and particularly important for work on issues relating to urban poverty or to urban development within predominantly low-income areas, the research results can also be easily linked with local NGO activity in both action research and operational programmes.

IIED's work with Southern teams led to two other work areas. The first was in response to the request from international agencies for overview studies, each focusing on a different aspect of the urban environment, which draw together the work of Southern partners. These include the books published by Earthscan such as *Environmental Problems in Third World Cities* in 1992 (with a new edition published in 2001 under the title *Environmental Problems in an Urbanizing World*) which was originally prepared as an overview for DFID before the 1992 UN Conference on Environment and Development (the Earth Summit) and *The Environment for Children* (prepared at the request of UNICEF) in 1996. The second is to respond to requests from particular international agencies for help as they develop their urban programmes. Human Settlements Programme staff have worked with Sida, DFID, Danida and WaterAid as they developed urban policies, and with many other international agencies in seminars and workshops seeking to develop their work in urban areas.

## THE SHIFT IN RESEARCH PARTNERS

The Programme had long stressed that cities are the result of an enormous range of investments of capital, expertise and time by individuals, households, communities, voluntary organizations and NGOs, as well as those investments made by governments and the private sector. Many of the most effective initiatives to improve housing conditions among low-income groups have come from local NGOs or community organizations. Yet in most cities, the individual, household and community efforts that help to build and manage cities have long been ignored by governments and international agencies, and these are often constrained by unnecessary government regulations. This had been a constant theme in the Programme's work – and in the writings of Jorge Hardoy – and it was a central theme of *Squatter Citizen*, the book he and I co-wrote.

During the late 1980s, two changes helped to reinforce the Programme's focus on community development. The first was the establishment of the community-development team in IIED-América Latina by Ana Hardoy. Initially, this worked in Barrio San Jorge, an informal settlement in one of the peripheral municipalities in Buenos Aires, and later in many other low-income settlements. Unlike previous work areas, this was not research but direct, hands-on support to community-based development and to working with community-based organizations to negotiate with external agencies (including municipal agencies) for support, services and land. The work of this team constantly fed ideas back to the researchers, including a better understanding of possibilities and constraints. It acted as a 'reality check' on the relevance of research in other areas – and helped to reveal the limitations of conventional policy research.

The second change was the shift in research partners in Latin America, Asia and Africa from academic institutions to activist NGOs who worked directly with urban poor groups and with urban governments but who also had research interests. This change was, in part, because the academic institutions with which the Programme had worked during the 1980s were less able to work directly with low-income groups. It was also, in part, due to the difficulties that IIED faced in raising funds for them; the academic institutions were far more dependent on IIED for funds for research. None of IIED's early partners managed to become centres of research for their wider region, which had been the original intention.

Working with more action-oriented NGOs and with the community-development programme in IIED-América Latina has brought many insights about how it was possible for external agencies to support participatory, community-driven development. Apart from the work of IIED-América Latina, among the key NGOs that have helped to reshape the approach of the Programme are: the Indian NGO SPARC (and its work with cooperatives of women pavement dwellers, *Mahila Milan* and the National Slum Dwellers Federation), the People's Dialogue on Land and Shelter in South Africa (and its partner the South African Homeless People's Federation), the Asian Coalition for Housing Rights (with its secretariat in Bangkok) and Orangi Pilot Project (in Pakistan). A considerable part of the Human Settlements Programme's research over the last eight years has been with these groups or has drawn on their work. Staff from these NGOs have also been partners in the organization of seminars and workshops for staff from international agencies and also advisers for the preparation of different issues of the journal *Environment and Urbanization*. One other critical characteristic of these NGOs is that they have never depended on IIED for funding. This enables a much more equal relationship between partners.

Working on urban environmental problems, the partnerships with IDEA in Manizales (Colombia), Ecociudad (Peru) and the Centre for Science and Environment (India) have been particularly important. So too has the Programme's long association with the urban environmental research programme of the Stockholm Environment Institute and its partners in Indonesia, Brazil and Ghana. The director of this programme, Gordon McGranahan, came to join IIED in 2000. From this developed IIED's work documenting innovative Local Agenda 21s and other environmental action plans developed by local authorities and local NGOs. These include case studies in Manizales (Colombia), Ilo and Chimbote (Peru), Durban (South Africa), Jinja (Uganda), Penang (Malaysia), Surabaya (Indonesia), and Rufisque (Senegal), all prepared with local partners.

This collaboration with Southern NGOs helped the Programme focus on the means to support low-income groups and their community organizations. One consistent theme has been the need for international funding agencies to support grassroots initiatives directly and to consider new institutional means to do so – including setting up Funds for Community Initiatives located within cities in the South. Such funds would allow the setting of new standards in terms of speed of response to requests for funding, and in terms of accountability and transparency to urban poor groups themselves. The clearest starting point of work in this area was a paper co-authored by staff at IIED and IIED-América Latina in 1989 which considered how bilateral and multilateral donor agencies might be more effective in targeting funds to support low-income households and their community organizations. Its main proposal was that funding be allocated to foundations or non-profit institutions based in cities in the South that would then encourage and support community-based initiatives with decisions taken locally about what should receive funding.

The paper was circulated to a small number of people in some of the major agencies. Although the paper received little reaction initially, some of its ideas were subsequently incorporated into the initiatives of certain international agencies, including UNDP's LIFE

Programme and DFID's C3 City Challenge Fund. The European Commission requested IIED's help in developing city-based grant and loan funds for community initiatives in sub-Saharan Africa in 1995 but despite the enthusiasm of its staff (and a lot of preparatory work over 18 months), the idea was halted. It was never made clear why, except that some European Community representatives within sub-Saharan African countries had objected to funding channels over which they had little influence. Ironically, the very strength of these local funds – that priorities are determined by local demand from urban poor groups – was the very reason why the concept proved unacceptable to senior staff within the European Commission.

The work with groups such as SPARC, the Asian Coalition for Housing Rights, Orangi Pilot Project and People's Dialogue for Land and Shelter highlighted the importance of community-based savings and credit schemes that helped low-income households to organize, save and develop their own priorities in regard to housing and basic services. IIED's work in this area was developed by Diana Mitlin, an economist who had joined the Programme in 1989. She also took leave of absence from IIED during 1999–2000 to spend 18 months working with the South African Homeless People's Federation. IIED's work in this area has included a study of credit programmes for housing and infrastructure development,[17] the preparation of a special issue of *Environment and Urbanization* on this theme, case studies by the Orangi Pilot Project (Pakistan) and the Urban Poor Associates (the Philippines), a series of seminars, and a newsletter *HiFi News* which circulates among a large network of NGOs and other institutions interested in community-based finance systems. IIED has also commissioned and published many studies of innovative housing and infrastructure finance schemes, both within its working papers series and in *Environment and Urbanization*.

## OTHER PRESENT AND FUTURE AREAS OF WORK

Three other work areas have taken on increasing importance during the second half of the 1990s: children and the city; rural–urban linkages; and what the achievement of sustainable development goals implies for cities.

Work on children and the city began in the mid-1980s, driven initially by work in IIED-América Latina that sought to highlight how inadequately the needs and priorities of children and young people were being addressed in cities in the region. The work began with a series of seminars and publications. IIED and IIED-América Latina also began their association with UNICEF and its Innocenti Research Centre in Florence. IIED worked with UNICEF's urban advisers to develop its work in urban areas. Jorge Hardoy helped the Innocenti Research Centre to develop work on the urban child, and, during meetings of the advisory board there, he met Roger Hart of the Children's Environments Research Group (CERG) in New York. I had also helped UNICEF to develop its position paper for the 1992 UN Conference on Environment and Development (the Earth Summit). When I was asked by UNICEF to prepare a report on the links between children and the environment after the Conference, I called on Roger Hart for help, along with Carolyn Stephens and David Ross from the London School of Hygiene and Tropical Medicine, Caren Levy from the Development Planning Unit (University College London), who had long served as a source of advice and joint work, and Jac Smit of the Urban Agriculture Network.[18]

Roger Hart subsequently spent some months working in IIED's London office, with one of his colleagues (also a child-development specialist) Sheridan Bartlett. During this time, the two of them worked with IIED on preparing a second book for UNICEF, also published by Earthscan, called *Cities for Children*. This focused on the role that city and municipal authorities could and should have in meeting the needs and priorities of children and youth. Sheridan Bartlett also came to work part-time for IIED, both in developing the work on children and, when Diana Mitlin went to work in South Africa, taking over as Managing Editor of the journal *Environment and Urbanization*.

The work on rural–urban linkages was a conscious attempt to link the work of IIED's Sustainable Agriculture and Rural Livelihoods Programme and the Human Settlements Programme. It was based on the obvious but often forgotten point that rural–urban interactions affect both rural and urban development and are often critical influences on rural resource use and management. Yet most governments and international agencies still have institutional structures that treat 'rural' and 'urban' development separately. Cecilia Tacoli joined IIED in 1996 to develop this work which has centred on research with partner institutions in Tanzania, Mali and Nigeria. The work has helped to highlight the importance of both 'rural' and 'urban' components for the livelihoods of many poor (and non-poor) households. It has also highlighted the need for 'rural' components to most urban development programmes and for 'urban' components to most rural development programmes, based on evidence from case studies. Various international agencies including DFID, DANIDA and the World Bank have drawn on IIED's work on rural–urban linkages in their publications or training seminars.

The work on identifying what changes are needed in policy and practice for urban centres to contribute more to sustainable development goals began when Programme staff were asked to brief the Secretariat of the Brundtland Commission in 1985. The work has included:

- drafting of the urban chapter in *Our Common Future* (the Brundtland Commission's 1987 report);
- setting out the basis by which an urban policy can meet sustainable development goals in 1992 (within the book *Environmental Problems in Third World Cities*) and developing this over time (with four special issues of the journal *Environment and Urbanization* and an Earthscan reader devoted to the theme of sustainable cities);
- helping to organize *Global Forum*, the Conference in Manchester in 1994 that brought delegations from 50 cities around the world to develop how urban policy and practice could contribute more to sustainable development goals;
- developing a framework to ensure more complementarity between the 'brown agenda' focusing on environmental health, and the 'green agenda' focusing on ecological sustainability;[19]
- supporting the documentation of innovative Local Agenda 21s in Africa, Asia and Latin America;
- contributing to the reports of the Inter-governmental Panel on Climate Change;
- drafting policy guidelines on the urban environment for the OECD Development Assistance Committee;
- working with the UN Institute for Advanced Studies on the spatial dimensions of different urban environmental burdens.

Before ending this chapter with some reflections on the future, here are a few comments about the people who created and sustained the Human Settlements Programme. I joined IIED in 1974 with the intention of working there for six months, before going to Canada to take a Masters course on arts and theatre management. My task was to help organize the literature that had been collected for Barbara Ward to write the book *The Home of Man*. When Barbara Ward's research assistant left, I was asked to stay on. It was impossible to refuse; the work was a joy, as was working with Barbara and with David Runnalls, who were building the Institute at that time. The temporary job turned into a permanent job and I have been working at IIED ever since, apart from time off to undertake postgraduate studies. Perhaps my greatest good fortune was to be asked to work with Jorge Hardoy as he began building the Human Settlements Programme in 1977 – and I worked with Jorge until his death in 1993 and was the Director of the Human Settlements Programme until Gordon McGranahan took over in 2002.

In the end, the history of IIED's Human Settlements Programme is one of the collective efforts of many people and institutions. Many individual contributions have not received sufficient acknowledgement in this chapter, and four need special mention. The first is Diana Mitlin, an economist who joined IIED from the UK government's Civil Service in 1989 who, more than anyone else, developed the Programme's links with activist NGOs in Africa and Asia. She also developed our work on housing finance systems and managed the journal *Environment and Urbanization* for its first decade. The second is Jane Bicknell who joined the Programme in 1983 and who subsequently came to work part-time as the co-editor of *Environment and Urbanization*. The quality of the journal and its regularity owes much to her work. She has copy-edited every issue from its foundation in 1989 – and has also helped to edit many other IIED publications. The third is Julio Davila who worked with the Programme from 1984 to 1990, including undertaking research on small and intermediate urban centres and managing the Institute's research on urban change in Latin America from 1850 to the present. In 1990, Julio joined the staff of the Development Planning Unit (University College London), but he has been on the editorial board of *Environment and Urbanization* from its foundation and continues to work with IIED in joint research initiatives. The fourth is Gordon McGranahan who may have only joined the Programme in 2000 (and who became the Programme's director in 2002) but with whom the Programme had worked for much of the 1990s, when he was at the Stockholm Environment Institute.

There are also the many former and current staff members of IIED-América Latina who have contributed much to the work of the Human Settlements Programme including Ana Hardoy (Executive Director of IIED-América Latina and also a Board member of IIED), Hilda Herzer, Silvia Blitzer, Silvina Arrossi, Alfredo Stein and Ricardo

Schusterman. There are also people such as Somsook Boonyabancha (Asian Coalition for Housing Rights), Sheela Patel (SPARC, India), Anil Agarwal and Sunita Narain (Centre for Science and Environment, India), Arif Hasan (working with Orangi Pilot Project in Pakistan) and Jorge Anzorena (SELAVIP), on whose advice and support the Programme has long drawn.

There are also certain key individuals in funding agencies without whose support, enthusiasm and advice the Programme could not have existed, especially Ron Leger (CIDA), Goran Tannerfeldt (Sida), Joep Bijlmer (Dutch Development Cooperation), Michael Mutter (DFID) and Francoise Lieberherr (SDC). In addition, there is a network of people scattered throughout Africa, Asia and Latin America and within some research centres in Europe and North America, who have provided advice and guidance and been partners in organizing seminars and publications – most of whom have never received funding from IIED. These people have also been central to the development of the journal *Environment and Urbanization* as they contributed papers, provided suggestions on potential authors and themes, and reviewed papers submitted to the journal.

Perhaps the Programme's greatest challenge for the future is to help to ensure changes in institutional structures within governments and international agencies so that they become far more effective in addressing the problems that the research has highlighted, and more accountable to low-income groups. In 2002, there are many positive developments that were not there or hardly present when the Programme began. First, there are organized federations of the urban poor in increasing numbers of countries, and these are demonstrating cheaper, more effective, more participatory ways to address poverty and homelessness.[20] Second, far more local NGOs have learnt to work with urban poor groups and their organizations in ways that are more participatory and accountable. Many such NGOs and the community organizations they work with have also developed new models for working with (and changing the approaches of) local governments. Third, in most nations, local governments have become more democratic and many have become more effective. Fourth, more international agencies have developed urban programmes and have recognized the need to support accountable and effective local institutions (including community organizations and the federations formed by urban poor groups, as well as local NGOs and local govern-ments). There is also the hope that the Cities Alliance formed by the World Bank and the UN Centre for Human Settlements (renamed in

2001 UN Habitat), with support from many of the OECD nations' bilateral agencies will bring more coherence and a greater scale of impact to international assistance to urban development.

However, there are also many failings and weaknesses. Urban poverty continues to grow in most nations, and most governments and international agencies show little capacity to address it, or little interest in doing so. The promises made in the 1970s by governments and international agencies greatly to improve provision for water and sanitation to both rural and urban areas have not been met in most nations; one wonders whether the promises made during the 1990s to halve poverty by 2015 will be met. Despite the innovation shown by some NGOs and local authorities in developing Local Agenda 21s, these are the exceptions, not the norm. Meanwhile, the innovations in urban policy and practice shown by international agencies remain far short of the needed scale. In 2002, we have the precedents to show how urban poverty can be reduced (most of them developed by urban poor groups themselves) and how urban governments can integrate environmental concerns into their development plans (including meeting global as well as local environmental responsibilities). But we have little evidence of national governments and international agencies changing their institutional structures and funding mechanisms to act on these precedents.

## NOTES AND REFERENCES

1   World Commission on Environment and Development (1987) *Our Common Future*, Oxford University Press.
2   World Bank (2000) World Development Report 2000/2001; *Attacking Poverty*, Oxford University Press, Oxford and New York.
3   Ward, Barbara and René Dubos (1972), *Only One Earth: The Care and Maintenance of a Small Planet*, Andre Deutsch, London.
4   Ward, Barbara (1976) *The Home of Man*, W.W. Norton, New York.
5   I had begun work at IIED in 1974 as Barbara Ward's research assistant, for the preparation of the book *The Home of Man*. I remember well the letters and memos written to Barbara Ward by Jorge Hardoy. Also the fact that these were raising issues that other advisers were not. At the time, I had no inkling that I would come to work with Jorge Hardoy from 1978 until his death in 1993.
6   The findings from this work were summarized in: Hardoy, Jorge E and David Satterthwaite (1989) *Squatter Citizen: Life in the Urban Third World*, Earthscan, London. The book is still in print.

7 Despite the logistical nightmare of getting specialists from all the world to meet in Moscow or Leningrad/St Petersburg and the need for WHO staff to import all equipment (including photocopiers since the Soviet hosts would not provide these), the meetings were remarkably productive. They also produced some strange events – I remember searching for somewhere to eat supper in St Petersburg with a Filipino water engineer and a Brazilian public works specialist and finding no café where they could understand us, until in one, there was an Ethiopian student who was washing up who helped us to order a meal.

8 Although Tade Akin Aina is now with the Ford Foundation, he has remained on the journal's editorial board ever since.

9 Hardoy, Jorge E, Sandy Cairncross and David Satterthwaite (eds) (1990), *The Poor Die Young: Housing and Health in Third World Cities*, Earthscan Publications, London.

10 *Environment and Urbanization 8* (2), October 1996

11 When Argentina returned to democratic rule, Jorge Hardoy accepted the inv.itation of the Argentine government to head its National Commission on Historical Monuments. Although he refused to accept a salary for this work, he built up a team at this Commission which rescued many of Argentina's most important historical buildings and locations; he also pioneered the integration of social concerns into this work.

12 See Hardoy, Ana, Jorge E Hardoy and Ricardo Schusterman (1991) 'Building community organization: the history of a squatter settlement and its own organizations in Buenos Aires', *Environment and Urbanization* 3(2), October, pp104–120.

13 The Earthscan books included: *Squatter Citizen: Life in the Urban Third World* (1989); *The Poor Die Young: Housing and Health in Third World Cities* (1990); *Environmental Problems in Third World Cities* (1992); *Funding Community Initiatives*, (1994); *The Environment for Children* (1996); *The Earthscan Reader on Sustainable Cities* (1998); *Cities for Children* (1998); and *Environmental Problems in an Urbanizing World* (2001).

14 More than 20 books have been published in Spanish, most of them by Grupo Editor Latinoamericano (GEL) including: Feijoo, Maria del Carmen and Hilda Herzer (eds) (1991) *Las Mujeres y la Vida de las Ciudades*; Pírez, Pedro with Claudia Minoliti and Marcos Novaro (1991) *Municipio, Necesidades Sociales y Política Local*; Hardoy, Jorge E (1991) *Cartografia Urbana Colonial de America Latina y el Caribe*; Nora Clichevsky et al (1990) *Construccion y Administracion de la Ciudad Latinoamericana*; Hardoy, Jorge E and Richard Morse (eds) (1988) *Repensando la Ciudad de America Latina*; Hardoy, Jorge E and David Satterthwaite (1987) *La Ciudad Legal y la Ciudad Ilegal*; and Caputo, Maria Graciela, Jorge E Hardoy and Hilda M Herzer (eds) (1985) *Desastres Naturales y Sociedad en America Latina*.

15  This included the drafting of the book *Our Planet, Our Health* working with the World Health Organization's International Commission on Environment and Health in 1992, preparing *An Urbanizing World: Global Report on Human Settlements 1996* (Oxford University Press, 1996) for the UN Centre for Human Settlements and helping to prepare *Shaping the Urban Environment in the 21st Century: From Understanding to Action* for the Development Assistance Committee of the Organization for Economic Cooperation and Development in 2000. During 2000–2001, programme staff also contributed to the US Academy of Science's report on urban demography in the Third World and to a CD-ROM on urban environmental issues prepared by the World Bank.

16  Among the other agencies that subsequently helped to support the distribution of this journal and IIED's seminar and publication programme are the Dutch Ministry for Development Cooperation, the Swiss Agency for Cooperation and Development, the UK Government's Department for International Development and DANCED (Danish Cooperation for Environment and Development). The support of the latter two has allowed Environment and Urbanization to have its full text available on the Web and to have a widely circulated summary of each issue sent to staff from governments and international agencies.

17  The findings were published in Arrossi, Silvina et al (1994) *Funding Community Initiatives*, Earthscan, London.

18  Roger Hart was one of the co-authors of *The Environment for Children* which IIED prepared for UNICEF and which was jointly published by UNICEF and Earthscan in 1996.

19  These are described and discussed in two new Earthscan books to which Programme staff contributed: Hardoy, JE, D Mitlin and D Satterthwaite (2001) *Environmental Problems in an Urbanizing World: Supporting Local Solutions to City Problems in Africa, Asia and Latin America*, Earthscan, London; and McGranahan, G, P Jacobi, J Songsore, C Surjadi and M Kjellén (2001) *The Citizens at Risk: From Urban Sanitation to Sustainable Cities*, Earthscan, London.

20  See the October 2001 issue of *Environment and Urbanization* (13(2)) for more details.

## *11*

# Drylands: A history of networks

## *Camilla Toulmin*

Heavily pregnant with my second child, I heaved myself up one of the endless stairwells towards the attics of Endsleigh Street, and staggered into a smoke-filled room. I could see Richard Sandbrook through the haze, a massive plane tree casting heavy shadow through the window. 'Don't smoke in front of Camilla – it's bad for the baby', barked Sue, Richard's PA – she should really have been IIED's Director. I cadged a cigarette from Richard and hoped Sue couldn't see.

It was early 1987 and I was on a visit from the Overseas Development Institute where I had been working on the pastoral and irrigation management networks. I had met Ed Barbier, who was working on environmental economics at IIED, while preparing a paper for The Other Economic Summit. I had also met Geoff Barnard who was then working on agricultural residue use, and had come across my work on cattle, crops and dung in Mali. But despite this contact, I had very little idea of what IIED was, and did. Nor did I have any sense of where it got its money from, nor why it had so many staircases, and how you got from one part of the basement to the other. Only gradually have some of these queries become clearer, though several questions remain remarkably enigmatic even after 14 years.

Richard had successfully raised some funds from the United Nations Environment Programme to set up the Dryland Networks Programme, was looking for someone to run it and had heard my name from Ed Barbier. There was already a cast of nomadic characters associated with African drylands who passed through the IIED building – Charles Lane when he wasn't in Tanzania, and Ian Scoones when he came back from Zimbabwe. Robin Sharp was also a partner on the early programme – an experienced journalist, he was key in establishing *Haramata* and the Issue Papers. We had one difficult moment with the UNEP funds, when we were told that actually we could have the money promised, but only if we took it in roubles – 'come on Camilla, surely you can set up some of your activities in the Soviet Union? Hold a meeting in Samarkard, get your printing done in Vladivostock', challenged Richard – but fortunately we persuaded UNEP to give us dollars instead, and offload their unwanted roubles onto someone else.

## THE PROGRAMME RATIONALE

The Drylands Programme was set up soon after the 1984/85 droughts which had ravaged East and West Africa, bringing famine and disaster to many, and displacing huge numbers. Many donors set up new programmes to promote more sustainable patterns of dryland development, and NGO activity mushroomed in the North as well as in-country. Band Aid and SOS Sahel were set up and the big NGOs like Oxfam and Care launched major development projects in the Sahel and Horn of Africa. There was a widespread perception among many commentators that dryland areas of the world were becoming more and more hostile, and that people would need to be moved elsewhere, if necessary by force, for their own good. The Ethiopian Derg's strategy, which got underway in 1985, was to transport people from the northern highlands to the southwest of the country. Elsewhere, like in West Africa, people moved under their own steam, seeking out land in wetter regions and looking for new ways of making a living. There was also pessimism among many donors regarding technical answers to Africa's drought-prone areas, given their perception that irrigation schemes had failed in many areas. Equally, the potential of Green Revolution technology for raising yields in marginal rainfed farming areas was seriously questioned, while little research had been done on many of the dryland staple crops, such as millet, fonio and cassava.

Despite such pessimism, there was also increasing awareness that promising alternatives were starting to emerge to challenge conventional approaches to dryland agriculture. These involved a variety of activities involving low external inputs, such as simple soil and water conservation structures, agro-forestry work, support to pastoral associations, community-based systems for managing woodlands and pasture, and so on. These alternatives seemed to provide evidence that yields and productivity might be improved significantly without jeopardizing the longer-term sustainability of the agro-ecosystem, as well as being compatible with social and institutional structures. Often small in scale, frequently the product of the NGO sector, such activities pioneered new methods of managing land and making decisions. Projects where things worked best involved close participation by local people identifying priorities, planning what should be done, and allocating responsibilities for implementation.[1]

The Drylands Programme sought to identify common concerns and make better known to the pessimists some of the promising options which might be followed. Thus, the major initial emphasis for the programme was its information and networking activities – the *Haramata* newletter and the Issue Papers – prepared in both English and French language editions. The newsletter was intended to provide short articles giving an overview of key issues, new research and publications, resources, training and meetings. *Haramata* is the name given to the Harmattan wind in the Ewe language of Ghana. This cool wind from the north starts to blow across much of West Africa in December and January, bringing welcomed relief at the end of the harvest. We hoped that *Haramata* could provide such a breath of fresh air. The Issue Papers provide a more in-depth treatment of particular questions, offering a quick way to get material published and circulated, and for which we sought African authors where possible. We have now published 40 editions of *Haramata* and more than 100 Issue Papers, which together constitute a veritable archive on drylands development.

Bit by bit, the programme started picking up speed, with both Charles Lane and Ian Scoones returning from the field and taking on major roles. Charles had been working in Tanzania for Oxfam and then with Barabaig herders who had lost much of their land to a Canadian-inspired mechanized wheat-farming scheme. Ian had just finished his field work in Zimbabwe, looking at herding patterns and grazing dynamics. Together, we identified a niche in African drylands, spanning francophone West Africa, East African pastoralism and Zimbabwe. I went off to Norway to explain our plans and strategy, and was greeted with great warmth by Mie Bjonness, responsible then for the NORAD Sahelian programme, who immediately pledged support. We also worked with Danida staff to flesh out their drylands strategy, the beginning of a relationship which continues to be central to our programme today. I began to understand how the programme might develop, by taking on work, finding good people to help carry it out, and building alliances with African partners.

I also began to understand more about how IIED worked institutionally, and about its failings. We all felt the need for a more systematic and transparent approach to people-management – hence the emergence of the union, the job evaluation system to grade different posts, and appraisal process for discussing performance and expectations. I began to get to know the other groups who inhabited both the basement and the attic – the Campaign for Lead Free Petrol, the Institute for European Environmental Policy, and Earthscan. I started to recognize the characters who passed through the reception area, such as Gerry Leach trailing a cloud of smoke and an inch of ash balanced on the tip of his cigarette, stooping to clear the lintel of the door, and Lloyd Timberlake in cycling gear, juggling bells under his arm.

When I came to set up Drylands, I brought with me a draught of enormous respect for the many millions of small farmers who succeed in making a living in difficult circumstances in the Sahel. I had lived for a couple of years in a small village in Mali, Dalonguebougou, having been hired by Jeremy Swift as a researcher for the International Livestock Centre for Africa (ILCA). Jeremy had become an ardent advocate of pastoral nomads in Africa, having often seen them displaced by projects to set up wildlife parks, irrigation projects, and mechanized farming schemes. His task at ILCA was to demonstrate the rationality of pastoral production systems, through a series of field research projects. Dalonguebougou was chosen to investigate the deeply enmeshed relations between livestock and crops in the millet farming zone, and the value of 'black gold' in the form of cattle dung.

I am sure that Dalonguebougou is not special, but it represents for me a spirited expression of how productive and successful local farmers can be – helped by being distant from government, able to continue many aspects of traditional ways of life without too much dependence on outsiders; proud in the maintenance of tradition, but eager to look at and adopt new ways of doing things. I knew from Dalonguebougou that farmers come in all shapes and sizes; some were much brighter and more aware than others, some had a clear vision and strategy for what they wanted to do and were eager to try new methods. Many observed and experimented, adapting to new circumstances and opportunities. Others were happier following others. But all tried to balance the varied parts of their lives, keen to ensure good relations with kin and neighbours, needing to negotiate with family members seeking a bit more personal space, and working out strategies to make their families more secure in future. So it continues to provide for me a touchstone against which to judge proposals for interventions.

A recent visit showed how much things have changed over the last 20 years, as seen by a survey of what Babou Dembele has in his shop now, compared with then. Babou, now in his early fifties, is the head of an 80-strong household, reputed for its bulging granaries and large cattle herd. With so many younger brothers in the field, Babou concentrates on running a shop, the benefits from which go to the whole family. In 1980, you could buy nine items from his table-top shop – green tea, sugar, soap, Liberté cigarettes, salt, petrol, sweets, kola and dates. Nearly 20 years later, when you walk into his store, he has more than 100 things for sale, including nail varnish, rope (nylon and baobab bark), batteries, chocolate biscuits, scissors, tomato concentrate and moped spare parts.[2] The village is booming, with migrants from elsewhere seeking to settle and farm, while village households themselves have an ever more extensive set of economic and social ties to Bamako and beyond. Such changes bring their own challenges, but they also demonstrate great dynamism and an outward-looking approach by the Sahel's 'traditional' peasants.

## PROGRAMME ACTIVITIES: PASTORAL RIGHTS, SOIL CONSERVATION, PARTICIPATION

Digging in an old cardboard box recently, I came across the drylands programme strategy for 1992, drawn up for discussion of funding opportunities with the Norwegian government. The emphasis then, as now, was on equitable, sustainable management of natural resources on which the livelihoods of so many depend and to combine a variety of approaches and disciplines. The small size of the programme – in 1992 we were only two-and-a-half researchers and one administrator – meant that we had to establish close collaborative links with partners in Africa with whom to carry out a common set of activities. Our role then, as now, was seen as being to catalyse, coordinate and facilitate policy research and analysis, to challenge and re-think policy towards dryland development, and to feed findings from the field into broader national and global debates.

## Pastoral rights and development

Charles Lane campaigned for the rights of East African pastoral groups to be recognized, working with indigenous peoples' organizations, challenging government behaviour in the courts, and allying with key figures in the debate. In the case of Tanzania, foremost among these figures was Professor Issa Shivji, who had chaired the Presidential Commission on Land in 1991. His clear-sighted recommendations were largely ignored by the government, particularly his argument in favour of vesting land title in the village assemblies, thereby divesting the state of its control over land matters. Issa has remained a powerful voice in favour of supporting local people's rights and spreading knowledge and understanding of legal provisions, through the Hakiardhi organization.[3]

Charles also spent much time encouraging East African pastoral groups to come together in association to press for change and greater recognition of their rights. Thus support was given to Inyuat e-Maa for the first conference of Maa people, held in Arusha in 1993. The association's charismatic leader, Saruni Oitesoi ole Ngulay, came to IIED as a Drylands Visiting Fellow and spent some weeks in London to gain time to think and reflect on strategy. Charles' work also brought him into contact with groups supporting land rights in Uganda and Kenya, such as the Centre for Basic Research in Kampala, led then by Mahmood Mamdani, and the African Centre for Technology Studies in Nairobi, which Calestous Juma had turned into a major centre for policy research.

The plight of the Maasai in the Ngorongoro Conservation Area (NCA) was also a focus of his attention, and represents one among many such conflicts between wildlife bodies and local resident Maasai pastoralists. The former see the Maasai as a problem and barrier to achieving effective long-term management of this extraordinarily beautiful World Heritage site. Pro-Maasai groups contend that the resident pastoral population are in fact the best custodians of the Ngorongoro crater and plains, and protectors of key species such as rhino. As such they are essential to maintenance of grazing lands and control of poaching. The Maasai should thus be assured long-term rights within the NCA, a proper share of revenue from visiting tourists, and more effective representation on management and decision-making bodies. Charles brought together the various stakeholder groups to try and find common ground at a meeting in London in 1997. But there remain serious differences in view between those promoting wildlife conservation and those who argue that previous commitments to Maasai residents have been repeatedly betrayed.

Drylands' work on West African pastoral issues was taken on by Richard Moorehead in 1993. I had known him since 1980, when he had met me in my first days in Mali. We drove out together for a first visit to various villages, and sat up much of the night chatting at the height of the hot season beneath a classic African sky, black as pitch save the thousands of holes burnt through by stars. Richard had spent several years in the heart of the inner Niger delta of central Mali, a magic complex swampland renewed by the annual flood of the River Niger. These lands are of enormous value to rice farmers, herders seeking lush grazing, fishermen tracking the shoals of catfish, and latterly the international conservation movement because of its wonderful bird life. Richard worked for IUCN trying to see how best to stitch together the diverse interests of each group into an agreed management plan. The strategies and shifting bargaining powers of different groups are well illustrated in his PhD thesis which Robert Chambers and I examined one summer afternoon in 1991.[4] Richard, so talented and such good company, left us in 1996 to join the Department for International Development (DfID) as a social development adviser in Bangladesh where, in 1998, in a moment's black gloom he killed himself. The letters we received from Sahelian colleagues were testament to his love of West Africa and commitment to the pastoral cause.

Ced Hesse, formerly with Oxfam's Arid Lands Information Network (ALIN) in Dakar, took on the pastoral agenda for the Drylands Programme in 1997. I had first met Ced in 1981, when he was newly arrived to join Jeremy Swift's research group at ILCA, Mali. Ced was settled in Hombori to study a group of Bella agro-pastoralists. Under Ced's management, the pastoral programme has developed a wide-ranging set of activities in both West and East Africa. The principal objectives have been to help pastoral organizations understand the institutional framework within which they operate, identify policy openings to lobby for their interests, and better represent their membership.

Work on pastoral issues seems to generate a network of colleagues who may move to new jobs but maintain their interest in pastoralism. Soon after the Drylands Programme was set up, we were asked by the National Livestock Programme in Chad to help them with a study of pastoral organizations in the Sahel. We were given the name of Djeidi Sylla then working for ACORD in Gao, the hottest, most isolated corner of northeast Mali, as the River Niger bends itself round from the north to the southeast on its plunge towards the Gulf of Guinea, still more than 1500km away. We needed to draw in Djeidi's experience and wisdom gained from many years of dealing with support to pastoral organizations. So Djeidi set off from the banks of the River Niger to come to IIED for a fortnight in late November 1988, amid the cold and dark of London in late autumn. His report was a model of clear-sighted analysis which persuaded us to see how we could encourage him to work with the programme whenever possible. He made a major contribution to the Woburn Conference on management of grazing dynamics in savanna Africa,[5] and has repeatedly helped to support our work in Mali. He has also had a spell as an IIED Board member.

## Soils as the basis for dryland sustainability

Soil and water conservation is evidently of great importance for gaining better yields and ensuring some kind of harvest in years of low rainfall. This had become obvious from the work of Chris Reij of the Free University of Amsterdam who had shown that most farmer practices provide an excellent basis for trapping rainwater and topsoil. Development of the film and book, *Looking after our Land – Lessons from Successful Soil and Water Conservation Practice in East and West Africa* was an early activity for Drylands, in collaboration with ALIN. This project was realized thanks to funding from Comic Relief and Oxfam. Will Critchley did much of the footwork around the six countries covered and made sure we got the footage and cutting to make the film and prepare the book. It shows very clearly why soil and water conservation matters, and demonstrates the huge importance of ensuring that adapted technologies suit people's wants, priorities and means. Star of the film was Mathieu Ouédraogo, then the project coordinator of Oxfam's flagship *Projet Agroforestier* (PAF) in Ouahigouya, northwest Burkina Faso.

PAF achieved great prominence because it combined many of the characteristics of the new generation of 'success' stories. It helped to forge new attitudes to field-level development, by demonstrating the potential of working with local people, providing training in technical skills and building on local knowledge. It helped to turn opinion among donors, government and NGOs in favour of simple, community-led measures. Years of research by soil scientists and agronomists had led to little beyond 'tied ridging' techniques which no one wanted, and a dismissive attitude towards the unscientific approach of NGOs. Yet, it was just such a practical 'can do' attitude which was bringing results and leading to massive take-up of simple soil conservation techniques.

PAF's iconic status has led some to question how successful it has in fact been, whether poorer farmers have been able to benefit from its activities, and how far its approach can be replicated.[6] Travelling around the Mossi Plateau of central Burkina Faso provides strong evidence for the replicability of an approach like that of PAF and other projects which have focused on improving local soil conservation methods. Enormous areas of farmland have been treated with rock bunds and terraces, making a great contribution to increased yields, improved tree cover and rising water tables throughout the region.[7] Farmers from neighbouring Mali and Niger have also benefited from the lessons gained by PAF and others, having been brought to see with their own eyes what was being achieved, so they could take back ideas to try at home. PAF may have received too much credit for the astonishing spread of such simple soil conservation methods, since many other projects were following similar pathways. But being able to demonstrate a 'success story' by focusing on a single case can be the most effective means of conveying a message of hope to government and donors about how to support Sahelian farmers. PAF served as an emblem for a people-centred approach, which could be used to counter the pessimists who saw the Sahel as a basket-case which would never be able to feed itself.

## Strengthening participatory approaches

As well as being our film star, Mathieu Ouédraogo from PAF was also a key figure in developing and spreading participatory tools and approaches to local development in the francophone Sahel, as part of the MARP[8] programme led by Bara Guèye. At the beginning of the 1990s, it became increasingly apparent that the many actors involved in support to Sahelian communities needed a more systematic set of skills and methods for participatory development. Governments since 1984 had been using the rhetoric of participation but achieving little in practice. IIED's Jules Pretty had done a one-off training session in Senegal in 1989 for 15 people, organized by the International Development Research Centre (IDRC) in Senegal. Bara had been among those first trainees, being based then at the Ecole Nationale d'Economie Appliquée, Dakar.

From our first meeting in Dakar, Bara and I planned work on how to promote better links between NGOs and research organizations. Robin Sharp and I had got some funds from UNSO to see how best to promote greater collaboration between these groups, in the belief that their complementary skills might generate a common interest in working together. This had all stemmed from an earlier study which we had commissioned through the Small Grants Fund (thanks to Band Aid's support). Pape Sène, a Senegalese forester, had carried out a study looking at all the mistakes which NGOs make when engaging in tree-planting programmes. He provided convincing evidence that NGOs do not always get things right and that it would make more sense for them to work with researchers who could provide some of their missing expertise. So Bara prepared a study of the links between NGOs and researchers engaged in horticultural work. This study was complemented by others, and then formed the basis for two sub-regional meetings in Uganda, and Senegal, to promote greater engagement by researchers and NGOs in each others' activities.

But Bara and I also started discussing how to set up a network of people interested in developing skills in participatory methods to strengthen community-based programmes of natural resource management in the Sahel; this was known as the *gestion des terroirs* approach. The first meeting was held in Ouahigouya with help from Mathieu Ouédraogo, in recognition of the significance of PAF's experience with participatory methods. The workshop brought together a dozen people from Senegal, Mali, Burkina Faso and Niger, generated great energy and enthusiasm and helped to create the core group of MARPeurs of today. A series of grants from BMZ, NORAD and UNSO allowed us to get things moving over the first year.

I then made an ill-fated approach to the World Bank, to see if they would like to buy into our MARP programme, given their strong emphasis on *gestion des terroirs*. There had been much enthusiasm from Sahel regional staff, but recognition that we would need to deal directly with the people in Washington DC. Early encouragement for our initiative was followed by rising levels of mutual incomprehension and the overwhelming difficulty faced by World Bank staff in conceiving of making a contribution to someone else's programme, that they did not control. After six months of fruitless dialogue, the quarter-million-dollar support which had been dangled in front of us had vanished, and we realized we would be better off running our own programme without them.

Bara not only developed a very effective network of those devoted to MARP, but has also established a dynamic group of young colleagues in IIED Sahel, Dakar, Senegal: Fatou N'Diaye, Mansour Tall, Awa Ba and Marième Fall. Together they have been instrumental in reflecting critically on what is meant by participatory natural resource management, creating a partnership of structures in the Thiès Region of Senegal. Equally, they have provided methodological support to ARED/CERFLA[9] in Senegal, which has generated path-breaking work with newly literate Pulaar communities to help them gain skills in community development, conflict management and civic rights. These materials, known by their Pulaar acronym, LOHU, have put into the hands of local people a set of participatory tools and methods for their own use, rather than having to rely on outsiders to initiate such community consultation processes. The work being led by ARED's Sonja Diallo now forms an integral part of our work on supporting decentralization in the Sahel, as we seek opportunities for groups in Mali, Burkina Faso and Niger to learn from what can be achieved by such methods.

## THE INTERNATIONAL CONVENTION TO COMBAT DESERTIFICATION: A SUCCESS?

IIED's response to the process around the 1992 Rio Earth Summit, driven by Johan Holmberg and Koy Thomson, provided an opportunity to reflect on the importance of local management systems for achieving more sustainable livelihoods in the Sahel.[10] It strongly argued the case for placing faith in local structures and ensuring a broader framework of law and institutions to facilitate such local control as the only way forward. The Rio process also generated an enormous body of new work for the programme associated with the decision by governments at Rio to negotiate an International Convention to Combat Desertification (CCD). Earlier initiatives such as the United Nations Conference on Desertification (UNCOD in Nairobi 1977), and UNEP's assessment of desertification in 1984 and 1991 had provoked considerable dissatisfaction from both governments and researchers who lacked confidence in the methods, definitions and purpose of such activities.

Developed countries involved in the preparation for Rio had been strongly pressed by African countries to agree to negotiating an International Convention to Combat Desertification. The latter felt that their particular interests and priorities had been neglected by the

Rio process, since they did not fit neatly into issues of either climate change or biological diversity. If Rio was to gain international acclaim and support from Africa as well as the rest of the world, some gesture was needed to demonstrate commitment to the needs of poor, drought-prone, highly indebted countries in the Sahel and parts of Eastern and Southern Africa. But it was a commitment poorly thought through, which has landed us with an unworkable and poorly focused convention, unable to achieve its high ambitions. Desertification, or dryland degradation, is not and has never been an environmental issue of global dimensions; it is much more broadly tied into wide-ranging development, global trade opportunities, debt and aid relations.

Ian Haines at ODA threw us in at the deep end by commissioning a paper[11] to provide a first cut on what the CCD might seek to do, which then formed the basis for a meeting of EU member state experts, the UK holding the EU Presidency in the six months following Rio. The meeting in London was memorable for several reasons, not least the whispered consultations among French delegates and request for help on tips to distinguish the coffee from the tea – both mid-brown warmish fluids. At the meeting we needed to see how far there might be a common EU position on the CCD. What should it seek to do? How might it work? What kind of commitments and policy measures? There was a remarkable degree of consensus around the table. On the basis of my paper, I was proposed by ODA to be a member of the International Panel of Experts on Desertification (IPED), set up to provide technical assistance to the International Negotiating Committee on Desertification (INCD) proceedings.

The series of IPED meetings and INCD negotiation sessions provided a roller-coaster ride of emotions, with moments of exhilaration, that we might get agreement from governments North and South to sign up to far-sighted commitments to decentralized management of natural resources, the importance of pastoral systems, and the central role of participatory approaches. This sense of advance received a rude shock, when we realized that the IPED was more of a public show than a forum for achieving serious influence on the proceedings. We were two social scientists out of 14 experts. All the funds available for studies were allocated to review 'scientific issues' – such as climate change, and biodiversity – despite the recognition by all that degradation issues are intimately linked to social, economic and institutional dimensions.

My fellow social scientist, Brigitte Thébaud, counselled me early on: 'don't believe this is going to do any good Camilla – it's all for show!'. I found this viewpoint hard to accept, but it was ultimately borne out. The technical bias continues, with emphasis in the Committee on Science and Technology (CST) and other bodies on 'proper' scientists, agronomists, rangeland scientists, climatologists, and so on. Nevertheless, the meetings could be enjoyable, due to an engaging collection of members, such as Moulaye Diallo from Mali, Stein Bie from Norway (currently head of the International Service for National Agriculture Research (ISNAR)), and Youba Sokona from Environmental Development Action in the Third World (ENDA-TM) Senegal who now works in collaboration with IIED's climate programme. We met, we discussed, we argued, often vehemently. But I don't think much of it made any difference. As Ambassador Bob Ryan admitted, he had got the draft text prepared already by cutting and pasting the relevant chunks from Agenda 21.

Going along to the INCD gave me an insight into international policy-making processes. There was a certain fascination about observing people and groups at work, along the corridors as well as in the plenary chamber, and in the restaurants of Geneva. You could get obsessed with questions such as: why are the Australians pushing a line on indigenous rights? What can the delegate from Japan be discussing so intensely with her colleague from Haiti? Have all the square brackets come off article 21? Does anyone know what the Global Mechanism might actually do, and who will get the job? But after a few days of this, I would be desperate to return to something which more nearly represented normal life. The ten sessions of the INCD have now been followed by five conferences of the parties (COPs), and the expected structures associated with all international conventions have been set up – COP, Secretariat, CST, Bureau meetings ...

At an early session of the INCD in New York, an *ancienne combattante* for the Sahel, Anne de Lattre – who had set up and run the OECD's Club du Sahel for 15 years – asked with her elegant good manners whether the whole process was not becoming just a trifle complicated. Surely we could simply agree a code of good practice on which to base future activities in the drylands – might this not be a better way forward? But for many, the CCD had become a totem. The CCD had to have exactly the same structure and status as the other Rio conventions on climate change and biological diversity. Anything less than this would be a slight on poor drought-prone countries, pushing for recognition of their particular problems within a crowded international agenda. But the end has been a green cul-de-sac. Institutional politics and global empire-building have triumphed over getting effective action in the field.

Donors have maintained a lukewarm adherence to the CCD, anxious not to appear the agents of its demise, but at the same time funding a range of parallel activities through bilateral and other channels. They have repulsed attempts to set up a special CCD fund, having seen the poor results from earlier enterprises, such as the DESCON, the Desertification Fund established after the UN Conference on Desertification. However, it looks as though the Global Environment Facility (GEF) will now open a window for drylands in its future strategy. Meanwhile, the agenda for dryland nations has moved on to debt relief, poverty reduction strategies, decentralization, and land reform – all areas of great relevance to the principles underlying the CCD, yet the process of drawing up National Action Plans by ministries of the environment has often involved very little buy-in from neighbouring ministries.[12]

There was a flurry of hope and activity in CCD circles when it looked possible that the Clean Development Mechanism might provide lots of new money for carbon sequestration in drylands, if only you could get the peasants to plant lots of trees. There is also a growing consortium of NGOs and researchers who think there is good money and a living to be made from linking into the Kyoto accords. If farmers can grow cotton, cocoa and coffee for world markets, why not trees? Maybe you could also sell-out carbon storage credits through improved soil management? At one level, it seems weird and improbable, yet, perhaps no more unlikely than farmers in Europe being paid to conserve the landscape and provide animal welfare benefits, rather than producing food. Its success and sustainability at local level will depend on how it is done, what share of benefits farmers will receive, and whether government will see this as an opportunity to renew a policing role over their peasantry, on the grounds of needing to ensure compliance with this international accord.

Ten years on from Rio, we need a reassessment of the CCD and whether it makes sense to continue along this track. Can anyone provide evidence that the CCD has made a difference to the livelihoods and opportunities of poor drylands peoples? I feel that the CCD has not been the right mechanism for drylands, partly because 'desertification' or drylands degradation is not a global environmental problem of the same sort as climate change, or ozone depletion. The causes, manifestations and solutions are far broader and more diverse. Equally, there is no clear common global interest equivalent to that driving the other environmental conventions. There would have been,

conventional development projects. Instead, the history of soil and water conservation in Africa has been one of imposing external solutions without regard for local practice. There is a remarkably diverse range of locally developed and adapted technologies for the conservation of water and soil, well suited to their particular sites and socio-economic conditions. *Sustaining the Soil*[20] documents the many farmers' practices we could find, illustrating their ingenuity, and exploring their origins and adaptations carried out by farmers over generations, in response to changing circumstances.

## West African land and the FBI

In early 1996, we were contacted by the Overseas Development Administration (ODA) to help with a new programme of work which involved collaborating with the French government in West Africa. A meeting had recently taken place between John Major, then UK Prime Minister, and Jacques Chirac, then the newly elected President of France. They had discussed the prospects for a Franco-British Initiative (FBI) to include collaboration on a wide range of issues, from defence and aircraft design to education and health. Policy development in West Africa was also included, and three fields chosen: cocoa policy among producer nations, strengthening collaboration between farmer organizations and agricultural research institutes, and opening up national and regional debate on land-tenure issues and options for intervention.

West Africa offers the opportunity to witness the marks of history and colonial heritage in patterns of government, legislation and attitudes. The FBI has helped to bring together researchers from anglophone and francophone countries in West Africa, with support from IIED, the *Groupe de Recherche et d'Echanges Technologiques* (GRET) and the *Institut de Recherche pour le Développement* (IRD) – our principal French partners – supported by an advisory committee established by the French Ministry of Foreign Affairs. The FBI started with a big meeting in the *triste* atmosphere of the island of Gorée,[21] Senegal where the slave boats would dock to pick up unwilling passengers for the sugar plantations of the West Indies. The Gorée meeting provided a chance to get English- and French-speaking West Africans talking about common issues.

At the same time, our French colleagues generated a set of fascinating perspectives on how land issues might be addressed, based on much experience recently acquired such as through the *Plan Foncier*

*Rural* in Côte d'Ivoire.[22] Foremost among our French collaborators have been Philippe Lavigne Delville from GRET, and Jean-Pierre Chauveau of IRD, both bringing a powerful mix of practical experience from field level, with capacity to conceptualize and analyse the different kinds of institutional arrangements we have been studying with our West African partners. It has not been an entirely easy process, trying to broker the multiple barriers of language, intellectual tradition and approach. But it has been highly productive, with a series of studies now being generated from our joint programme on 'derived rights of access to land'.[23]

This research project has been investigating the wide range of secondary rights which people try to negotiate in order to gain access to land, including tenancy, loans, land pledges and share-cropping. Each location provides a diversity of practical detail which makes it difficult to draw up water-tight categories. Regardless of the detail, however, our recommendation seems clear – that local practice needs to be set within a broader government framework which can confer validation and legality on arrangements which are acknowledged locally as legitimate.[24] A new programme on shifting claims to land in West Africa with our francophone colleagues is now underway and will provide an in-depth framework for investigating whose land rights are changing, and how government policy might support poorer groups to assert their claims more effectively.[25]

## Networking land issues

Our work on land tenure in West Africa provided the basis for support to DfID's Conference on Land Rights and Sustainable Development in sub-Saharan Africa, held at Sunningdale in February 1999. We were a group of 70–80 people, including many professionals from East, South and West Africa – researchers and government officials with responsibility for land tenure issues. The combined experience of the group provided a heady mix of much in-depth knowledge and wisdom[26] from which grew the Landnet Africa programme. Launched in Addis Ababa in January 2000, this has established networks at national and regional levels among a broad mix of people engaged in land issues, providing a means to share lessons and ideas about making land rights more secure. We currently support Michael Ochieng from RECONCILE, Kenya and Hubert Ouédraogo of GRAF, Burkina Faso as coordinators of their respective regional networks. Both have been highly effective advocates on land issues within their regions, and are helping to generate wider debate on different options to approaching land-rights management. The challenge now is to see how Landnet can actively engage in the various land reform policies underway in many African countries. Judy Longbottom and Julian Quan have been key figures in facilitating Landnet's growth.

## CURRENT AND FUTURE THEMES: DECENTRALIZATION AND GLOBALIZATION

Two main themes dominate the current Drylands Programme agenda – the decentralization process in West Africa, and sustainable livelihoods. Decentralization of government responsibilities and activity from central to local levels has been strongly advocated by both donor agencies and many national administrations. The hope is that decentralization will bring more effective local governance, better-tailored service provision, and the greater generation of resources for investment in local economic development.

Experience so far, however, provides little evidence of such benefits. Decentralization provides a setting with enormous potential benefits – but will they ever emerge? Who will gain? Will it provide cover for a local elite to seize power in the name of local democracy? How will questions of land allocation and administration be addressed, and what kind of compromise will be achieved with customary chiefs? Decentralization raises fundamental questions about power and governance within West African countries (as it does in many European states as well). Local government needs some measure of financial independence as well as firm commitment towards local accountability and willingness to listen to diverse voices, not all of which sing the communal hymn. But central governments remain unwilling to translate the rhetoric of decentralization and local responsibility into practical measures to ensure an effective transfer of powers and resources.

Drylands' new programme – Making Decentralization Work – aims to address the major challenges and opportunities that such a process of decentralization can open up, to strengthen community-based approaches to natural resource management, and to identify with partners how best local-level practice can inform more effectively the national policy-making process. This means helping local institutions to become more inclusive and accountable, and trying to ensure that local voices and perspectives, and those of less powerful groups, are heard in national-level policy debates. Working in four

Sahelian countries – Mali, Niger, Burkina Faso and Senegal – we hope to enable the exchange and dissemination of ideas and experience with new approaches.

In 2000, we finalized work with the Institut d'Economie Rurale (IER) in Mali and the Institute of Development Studies (IDS), Sussex, examining what make up the elements of a sustainable rural livelihood in Mali, Ethiopia and Bangladesh. It was an unrivalled opportunity to work with in-country partners and IDS research staff in understanding the different opportunities open to rich and poor, men and women, young and old, urban and rural. What strategies do people pursue? How does agriculture fit with migration and off-farm activity? What social, institutional and political constraints influence the choices people face? Working with Karen Brook of IDS and N'Golo Coulibaly of IER allowed us to go back to Dalonguebougou in Mali to see how people's lives had changed over nearly 20 years. It helped us to remember that such lives do not fit into neat boxes labelled 'farmer', 'trader', 'migrant' or 'herder'. Instead, they combine an ever-changing range of activities in a myriad of fashions which allow people to pursue new things, try out emerging niches, experiment with new crops, explore the benefits of trading with a donkey cart, even fortune-telling. Rural households are highly inventive and able to seize new opportunities as they arise, in contrast to some perceptions of poverty in Africa which tend to categorize 'poor people' as victims, lacking in spirit and ever vulnerable to shifts and changes in economic circumstance.

## Drylands and globalization

After 14 years of work, it is clear that the problems facing Africa's drylands must be seen as part of a much broader system, in which multiple inter-relations demonstrate the dense integration of much global activity. Sahelians find their way around the world, identifying opportunities where they can make a better living. The incomes of dryland peoples and nations also turn to an increasing extent on the operation of world markets in cotton and groundnuts, the price of gold, and demand for rare metals, as well as immigration policy in Europe and the USA. The new policy paradigms from Downing Street and the White House are tried out on sceptical developing-country governments, through the conditionalities attached to debt-relief agreements. Thus, it is not just users of the London underground who are exposed to the tensions inherent in public–private partnerships, but also families in Ghana seeking more assured water supplies.

Legislation in developed countries has its own impact, often far away, and not just directly related to trade. The EU chocolate directive of 1999 is a good example, with mixed impacts for West Africa. The directive established revised standards for levels of non-cocoa fat which would be allowed in products sold within the EU that can call themselves 'chocolate', the consequence of lobbying by the British confectionery industry. A lower proportion of cocoa fat is now acceptable, which has brought further downward pressure on world market prices for cocoa, damaging incomes and livelihoods in Côte d'Ivoire (with 40 per cent of world cocoa production) as well as Ghana. Yet, the shea-nut-oil producers of Mali welcomed the chocolate directive, having lobbied for its adoption, since it provides new market opportunities for output of this non-cocoa fat from a largely female dry-season activity in the savannah.

There are new health-related controls on imported foods brought into Europe aimed at protecting domestic consumers from high levels of pesticide residue and other potential toxins. Groundnut imports from drylands are particularly at risk, given the incidence of aflatoxin, thought to contribute to liver cancer, generated by a mould which grows too readily on the crop after harvest when inadequate drying has taken place. West African producers will need to find ways of raising the quality of their harvested crop if European markets are not to become closed to them. Equally, fruit and vegetable crops – from green beans to mangoes – will need to demonstrate conformity to tighter health requirements.

For centuries, the peoples of West Africa have adapted to changing circumstances and opportunities by moving. The creation of nation states and frontiers has partially checked such easy passage, though flows of people and goods within the region remain very important. The drought years of the 1970s and 1980s prompted many Sahelians to seek out new lands in higher rainfall areas. Thus, Côte d'Ivoire now provides homes and land to more than 3 million people from Burkina Faso and Mali. While cocoa and coffee prices were high, such massive rates of migration were positively encouraged, since this labour formed the backbone of the export economy. But now, as many commodity prices hit their lowest levels for decades, there are tensions between migrant settlers and local people.

New legislation passed in late 1998 circumscribes the rights to land which non-citizens can claim, so that only Ivorians themselves can be property holders in land. Conflict and expulsion of migrant farmers have taken place in some areas, leading to a significant return movement by Sahelian families to their homeland. Yet the incomes from migration and settlement in Côte d'Ivoire remain critical to the livelihoods of a huge number of farming families in the Sahel. At the same time, the production and harvest of cash crops in Côte d'Ivoire are highly dependent on the energies of their settler farmers. Such regional issues require mechanisms to defuse tensions and find solutions which build on the complementary interests of all parties.

Overall, it is not clear what 'globalization' will bring for drylands. On the climate front, predictions from modelling activity present a range of scenarios, some bringing more rain, others less. As in other regions of the world, it is difficult to specify the impact of global climate processes at local level. The Inter-governmental Panel on Climate Change argues that whatever happens to rainfall, dryland regions will become more vulnerable to climatic risk, and exposed to higher variability in the amounts and distribution of rainfall. Hence, countries will need to strengthen systems for monitoring rainfall, to detect as early as possible any adverse impacts and trends, while evolving responses to adapt to new circumstances in future.

As far as biotechnology is concerned, great play has been made by proponents of genetic modification that it could provide new varieties able to withstand drought, grow in highly saline conditions, or even absorb nitrogen from the atmosphere thereby obviating the need for inputs of fertilizer. But the process remains vague by which such 'miracles' might be achieved, the skills and funding found, and corporate power and broader public interest aligned. The highly diverse range of crop varieties found within drylands, and the need to maintain capacity for self-provision of seed stock within such farming systems, argue for an agnostic approach to prospects for a new green revolution for marginal agriculture, at least in the short term. More immediate benefits could be reaped through improving the incentives and access to marketing opportunities faced by many farmers, and increasing their access to new thinking and practice about soil conservation and fertility management which make best use of local knowledge and resources. Putting GMOs on one side, simpler forms of biotechnology, such as marker-assisted selection and cloning techniques, are more likely to produce crop varieties with the range of characteristics needed to help them survive in harsh conditions, rather than focusing on a single gene.

## Where next for IIED Drylands?

Our future depends on effective collaboration with a range of actors, with partners in Africa at the heart of the strategy. Our role remains to strengthen and support their activities, and act as broker, facilitator, catalyst and meeting ground for sharing new ideas. We continue to publish in both English and French, with the aim of making better links between people working in what remain different language areas. Promoting exchange between East and West African groups working on similar challenges is a significant component of the programme's work. A continuing role for IIED demands that we go on changing, so that our 'partnership' approach with Southern organizations really does live up to the values we claim. To this end, we have developed a code of conduct for collaborative research which outlines our goals for how we want to work with Southern partners. It recognizes the potential tensions involved in such relations and argues for greater responsiveness to partner priorities, more transparency and clearly accountable procedures. We must make more time at the beginning of projects to ensure that we share a joint vision of the work to be done, openness about the division of tasks and budgets, and negotiation of how results will be published and credited.

Our record here has been good, with a very large output of books, articles and reports clearly authored by both Southern partners and IIED staff. Such principles of collaboration and shared responsibility are key to IIED's capacity to sell itself in future yet, given our lack of core funding, we are also forced to be opportunistic, seizing new opportunities and openings as they arise, and hoping to mould them to fit our broader strategy. We must also evolve a different pattern of activity in which we work harder at trying to change the policies and practice of our own governments, where they damage the interests of poorer nations. Equally, we should be looking at the impacts of global trade, aid and finance initiatives on the particular interests of poorer African nations, so that our arguments for change have force and legitimacy. The New Partnership for African Development (NePAD) needs to keep the interests of more marginal countries in mind.

Over the last 14 years, it has been heartening to see in much of dryland Africa the serious policy advances made in favour of local institutions for managing resources, and the value accorded to farmer knowledge and perspectives. Now that the arguments in favour of decentralization have been won, come the challenges of putting such principles into practice. I trust that the next 14 years will demonstrate how the rhetoric in favour of more sustainable livelihoods for the poor can translate into tangible improvements to the opportunities faced by dryland peoples.

## NOTES AND REFERENCES

1   Chambers, Robert (1998) *Farmer First: Farmer Innovation And Agricultural Research*. ITDG, London; Conroy, Czech and Litvinoff, M (1991) *The Greening of Aid*, Oxfam, Oxford; Harrison, Paul (1987) *The Greening of Africa*, Paladin, London; Rochette, RN (1989) *Le Sahel en lutte contre la Désertification: Leçons d'Expériences*, CILSS/Verlag, Weikersheim; Shaikh, A et al (1988) *Opportunities for Sustained Development*, E/Di for USAID, Washington.

2   Brock, Karen and Ngolo Coulibaly (1999) *Sustainable Rural Livelihoods in Mali*. IDS Research Report 35, IDS, Sussex.

3   Shivji, Issa G (1998) *Not yet Democracy: Reforming Land Tenure in Tanzania*, IIED/Hakiardhi/University of Dar es Salaam.

4   Available as: Moorehead, Richard (1997) *Structural Chaos: Community and State Management of Common Property in Mali*, Drylands Programme Pastoral Land Tenure Monograph 3.

5   Scoones, Ian (ed.) (1993) *Living with Uncertainty*, IT Publications, London.

6   Atampugre, N (1993) *Behind the Lines of Stone*, Oxfam, Oxford.

7   Reij, Chris and Waters-Bayer, A (eds) (2001) *Promoting Farmer Innovation in Africa*, Earthscan, London.

8   Méthode Active de Recherche et de Planification Participative.

9   Associates in Research and Education for Development and Centre d'Education, de Recherche, de Formation en Langues Africaines.

10  Bishop, Josh, Ian Scoones and Camilla Toulmin 'The future of Africa's drylands: Is local resource management the answer?' in Holmberg, Johan (ed.) (1992) *Policies for a Small Planet*, Earthscan, London.

11  Toulmin, Camilla (1992) *From 'Combatting Desertification' to Improving Natural Resource Management – A Significant Advance?*, IIED, London.

12  Freudiger, P and O Touré (1998) *Implementation of the CCD in Seven Sahelian Countries*, OECD, Paris.

13  The West African Long Term Prospective Study, OECD (1998).

14  Toulmin, Camilla (1992) *Cattle, Women and Wells. Managing Household Survival in the Sahel*. Clarendon Press, Oxford.

15  Defoer, T and A Budelman (eds) (2001) *Managing Soil Fertility in the Tropics: A Resource Guide for Participatory Learning and Action Research*. Royal Tropical Insitute, The Netherlands.

16  Scoones, Ian (ed.) (2001) *Dynamics and Diversity: Soil Fertility and Farming Livelihoods in Africa*, Earthscan, London.

17 Hilhorst, Thea and Fred Muchena (2000) *Nutrients on the Move: Soil Fertility Dynamics in African Farming Systems*, IIED, London.
18 Scoones, Ian and Camilla Toulmin (1999) *Policies for Soil Fertility Management in Africa*, IIED and IDS, London and Brighton.
19 Hilhorst, Thea and Camilla Toulmin (eds) (2000) *Integrated Soil Fertility Management*. Policy and Best Practice Document 7, DGIS, The Netherlands.
20 Reij, Chris, Ian Scoones and Camilla Toulmin (1996) *Sustaining the Soil: Indigenous Soil and Water Conservation in Africa*, Earthscan, London.
21 Toulmin, Camilla, P Lavigne-Delville and S Traoré (eds) (2002) *Dynamics of Resource Tenure in West Africa*. James Currey, Oxford.
22 Lavigne Delville, P (ed.) (1998) *Quelles politiques foncières pour l'Afrique rurale? Réconcilier pratiques, légitimité et légalité*. Karthala, Paris.
23 For a synthesis of the findings, see: Lavigne Delville, P et al (2002) *Negotiating Access to Land in West Africa: A Synthesis of Findings from Research on Derived Rights to Land*, IIED, London.
24 Lavigne Delville, P et al (2001) *Securing Secondary Rights to Land in West Africa*, Drylands Issue Paper 107, *Haramata* 39, pp12–15.
25 *CLAIMS to Land in West Africa, an EU-Funded Research Project in Benin, Burkina Faso, Côte d'Ivoire and Mali* – see www.iied.org/drylands.
26 Toulmin, Camilla and Julian Quan (eds) (2000) *Evolving Land Rights, Policy and Tenure in Africa*, IIED, NRI, DFID, London.

# 12

# Economics of environment and development

## David Pearce and Ed Barbier

## THE ORIGINS OF BLUEPRINT FOR A GREEN ECONOMY BY DAVID PEARCE

IIED can legitimately claim to have been one of the birthplaces of the economic approach to sustainable development. In 1988 the then UK Conservative Government sought a structured response to the Brundtland Report of 1987.[1] The Brundtland Report was not the first international report to focus on the notion of the sustainability of economic and social activity, but it remains the most celebrated statement of the issues. The new focus was on forms of economic development that would permanently raise the living standards of the world's population, and especially the living standards of the poorest people. The notion of permanent development was intended to avoid forms of economic change that would benefit generations now but impose unacceptable risks for generations in the future. Environmental quality was at the centre of this notion because so many current-day activities are characterized by exactly this inter-generational impact. The benefits of fossil fuel use are secured at the expense of damaging health and ecological effects now and well into the future, and perhaps especially so because of the contribution to climate change. Land-use change now secures benefits in the form of extra agricultural land, but deprives future generations of the life-support functions provided by biological diversity. These 'trade-offs'

are by now well known. Brundtland's challenge to national governments was to explain how they were going to tackle these formidable
problems.

Already in 1988 Prime Minister Margaret Thatcher had made an
historic speech to the Royal Society in which she raised the global
warming issue to a national priority for the UK. Less well remem-
bered is that she also espoused the notion of sustainable development
– 'the health of the economy and the health of the environment are
totally dependent upon each other.... Protecting this balance of
nature is therefore one of the greatest challenges of the late Twentieth
Century'. But if the government of the day was, albeit cautiously,
committed to sustainable development, what was it that they were
committed to and what did it entail for economic and social policy?
The request to provide a framework within which government could
answer these questions came in 1988 to IIED from the then
Department of the Environment (DoE).

Shortly before this, IIED and University College London's
Economics Department had set up the London Environmental
Economics Centre (LEEC), taking advantage of UCL's major research
efforts in environmental economics, and IIED's own economics unit.
I was joined by Ed Barbier (IIED) and Anil Markandya (UCL) to
form the team that was to deliver a report to the DoE. (Ed Barbier is
now Professor of Economics at Wyoming University, and Anil
Markandya is Professor of Economics at Bath University. We had
valuable assistance from Joanne Burgess, now Dr Joanne Barbier, and
Sue Pearce.)

The resulting report, produced in August 1989 and known
somewhat embarrassingly as 'the Pearce Report',[2] as if there was only
one author, was long and detailed. We had set out a framework for the
analysis of sustainability and we also set out the implications (as we
then understood them) for policy. A review of the first draft by the
authors suggested that it did not tell a complete story. More was
needed. We added chapters on 'valuing the environment', 'discounting'
and 'prices and incentives'. These afterthoughts were to have political
consequences none of us foresaw. Because the report was intended as
an input to government thinking it became the subject of a press report
and a small meeting at the DoE. Quite why the press were invited to
hear about a report that was still fairly technical, despite considerable
efforts to make it readable, remains an open question.

The Pearce Report did not contain much that was unfamiliar to
environmental economists, but perhaps it brought those familiar

findings into the public arena for the first time. There is some suspicion that the Report was being used to 'test the water' for potential policy changes. After all, the Prime Minister had already placed the issue of climate change on the agenda, and there must have been many inside government who had thought about the implications of doing that. Since carbon is pervasive to the working of all economies, 'decarbonizing' the economy was not going to be easy. It was extremely unlikely that it would happen with the traditional regulatory policies. The Report addressed those issues and perhaps it served the purpose of seeing how the public, and, probably more importantly, the media would greet the policy change.

The press meeting was, in retrospect, odd, although we did not think so at the time. The Report had quite openly said that we needed to revise the way we accounted for economic progress. We recommended a 'green' measure of gross national product (GNP). There were not many questions on that issue. The Report also called for more economic appraisal of policies using cost-benefit approaches in which environmental impacts were 'monetized', using techniques we described and illustrated. There were more questions about that. But most of the questions were about the 'prices and incentives' chapter. While that chapter set out a short menu of policy instruments, the one that attracted most attention was the notion of an environmental tax. What kinds of things would be subject to taxes, we were asked. We listed energy, emissions, pesticides, fertilizers, and so on. The DoE press officer was showing signs of unease as the questions continued, and the meeting was called to a close.

In the meantime, Chris Patten succeeded Nicholas Ridley as Secretary of State for the Environment. Within a day of this, I was asked in to discuss an advisory position. So it was that I became Special Adviser to Patten. In turn, Patten gave a fairly enthusiastic endorsement of the Pearce Report. The result was an explosion of press interest in the Report. The *Today* newspaper spoke of a 'Green Tax Shock'. The *Daily Mail*'s headline was 'Tax the Polluters'. Charles Clover of the *Daily Telegraph* ran a long article headed 'This man is working out the bill for saving the planet. And he wants you to pay for it'. The *Sunday Express* declared 'Tax the polluters and save the world'. Economics and financial correspondents spoke of the 'greening of economics'. Some local newspapers went over the top: 'Boffin plans to save the world' said the *Bedford Herald*! (I lived in Bedford at the time.) Looking back, Patten did promise a sea-change in how environment was to be treated and he had taken a calculated risk in backing the Report. The press attention was therefore largely understandable. But it was also August, the 'silly season' when newspapers are usually starved of news. So, how far it was stage-managed and how far accidental I don't think we will ever know.

The Pearce Report was quickly published as *Blueprint for a Green Economy*[3], through IIED's publishing arm, Earthscan. This served only to magnify the press attention as the original report had proved difficult to obtain (I think we printed only about 20 copies). My role for the next few years was to expand on the messages, but mainly to communicate the ones already in *Blueprint*. It is interesting to note how the system works: I became an 'opinion former' in the eyes of the media and, for that matter, industry and commerce too. I took on various advisory roles for corporations and public relations companies, all of which helped get the 'green economics' story across to a wider public. Convincing politicians was harder since they perceived the real problems in advocating a new economic approach to the environment: the public does not like the word 'tax' and much of what was being argued for would require that households and corporations should pay the full social cost of production, ie a cost that included the value of the environmental resources also being used up. The message also went international and was picked up by environmental economists on the continent. Bodies like the OECD in Paris had long advocated solutions of the kind envisaged in *Blueprint*, so there was a sound base for extending the audience for the notion of using market signals to improve the environment.

## Some sustainability economics

The irony of *Blueprint* is that it did set out the beginnings of a coherent approach to sustainability. What the media focused on, fairly understandably, were the policy implications. The underlying theory was quickly passed over. Yet that has proved to be extremely productive and has been explored in much more detail in the subsequent *Blueprint* publications.[4] The essence of the argument is that future generations will indeed be worse off than current generations if they have less capacity to generate 'well-being' than we have. That capacity depends on the assets available to them. Traditionally, economists would have defined this capacity in terms of human-made capital, labour and land – the famous three 'factors of production'. A more modern classification would be human-made capital, natural capital (environmental assets), human capital (skills and knowledge, as well as labour), and social capital.

Social capital refers to the sets of relationships between individuals and institutions, relationships which cement contracts and understanding, thus reducing the need to have costly arrangements for guaranteeing contracts. So, one basic rule for sustainability, which in turn is defined as increases in well-being that last through time, is the 'constant capital' rule. This says that sustainability is more likely (it is not guaranteed) if the sum total of all forms of capital increases through time. This generation's obligation to the next one is to pass on that increased stock of capital assets. Some obvious modifications to the rule (which should be 'constant or rising capital' but is usually abbreviated to 'constant capital') involve making sure that it is *per capita* stocks that increase over time, and allowing for technological change. If population is growing, increases in per capita stocks are likely to be harder to achieve – hence the importance that the theory places on the negative consequences of population change. If technology raises the well-being that can be secured from any single unit of capital, it follows that capital stocks could decline and well-being could simultaneously rise. Population and technology therefore tend to work in opposite directions.

As *Blueprint* made clear, one could have a variation on the constant-capital rule. This would involve paying special attention to natural capital. The idea is that 'too much' environmental degradation has already taken place, so that further reductions should not be countenanced. If so, the constant-capital rule becomes a two-part rule: first ensure overall per capita asset stocks rise through time, and then ensure that the stock of environmental assets does not decline. In its general form the rule is known as 'weak sustainability'. In its two-part form it is known as 'strong sustainability'. A huge literature has grown up debating the merits of the two approaches, much of it unfortunately not very enlightening. But the basic distinction is that weak sustainability allows environmental capital to decline as long as overall capital increases (and, of course, vice versa: weak sustainability could also involve substituting natural capital for other forms of capital). Strong sustainability requires overall capital to rise (though this is often forgotten in the literature) and, in addition, environments must not degrade.

The economic approach to sustainability is at least coherent. Far too little of the literature on sustainable development has any theoretical underpinnings. The result is a mass of confusing and confused statements whereby almost anything passes for acceptable policy on sustainability. Not only is the theoretical foundation of the economic approach fairly rigorous, but it lends itself to measurement. Procedures for measurement were set out in Blueprint 3 and had been hinted at in the original *Blueprint*. The essence of the procedure is as follows.

Consider any corporation. It has assets upon which the production of the corporation depends. Those assets depreciate over time. Hence any sensible manager puts resources to one side to provide a depreciation fund. When, say, a machine wears out, the fund is available to replace the machine and production can be sustained. Call the resources put to one side 'savings'. Then the 'sustainability' rule for the corporation is that savings must exceed depreciation. The analogous idea for the nation (or region or, indeed, the world) is that nations must save more than the depreciation on their capital assets, but this time the assets in question are *all* of the forms of capital described above. In this way, a nation correctly accounts for its demands it makes on the asset base of sustainable development.

Savings can be measured directly by looking at the national accounts. Depreciation on human-made capital is also recorded in the national accounts. Human capital tends not to decline because knowledge and skills are added to every year – so in this case there is an *appreciating* asset. Natural capital tends to depreciate (but not necessarily so) and, provided it can be valued in monetary terms, that depreciation can also be recorded.[5] Environmental economists have made great strides in placing money values on environmental assets, so it is possible to get some estimates. Social capital has yet to be studied carefully in terms of measurement, and this remains a challenge for the future.

The consequent rule for sustainability can now be stated. If S is savings, $d_M$ and $d_N$ and are depreciation on (human-)made and natural capital accordingly, and $a_H$ is appreciation on human capital, then we require that:

$$(S + a_H) > (d_M + d_N)$$

This can be rewritten in terms of a rule that 'genuine savings' – SG – (savings plus appreciation minus depreciation) should be greater than zero for sustainability to be (probably) guaranteed:

$$S_G = S + a_H - d_M - d_N) > 0$$

Since all the elements are now measurable, we have a measure of sustainability. Since this idea was produced back in 1993, considerable advances have been made in measuring genuine savings for many different countries, and the procedure has been adopted by the World Bank.[6] Measures of genuine savings are published annually in the World Bank's *World Development Indicators* and are available on the World Bank's web page.

As one would expect from such a rule, countries that fail to save significant portions of their GNP fail the genuine savings test. In other words, their genuine savings are below zero – they are 'consuming capital'. Many developing countries thus fail the test. But, contrary to some commentaries, it is not the case that the genuine-savings rule divides the world into sustainable rich countries and unsustainable poor ones. Countries like the USA, which have notoriously low savings rates, also risk being unsustainable on the genuine-savings rule. Indeed, once population growth is introduced into the rule, as it has been in very recent work, the USA looks distinctly marginal in terms of sustainability. The UK also fails a genuine-savings rule for the 1980s, the period when oil revenues were being used to expand consumption rather than investing in the asset base of the economy.[7] So, the genuine-savings approach turns out to provide considerable insights into policy. Countries that fail to reinvest the proceeds of natural resource exploitation can quickly risk being unsustainable, even if they are rich in the short term. Countries that fail to save also risk unsustainability, giving some rigorous meaning to that other much over-used and confused notion of 'over-consumption'. Countries that fail to invest in technology, training and education also risk being unsustainable. While many people might think we already know these lessons – and one can take leave to doubt even this – there is virtue in having them revealed through a logical process.

## Future challenges for the economics of sustainability

What are the remaining challenges to the economics of sustainable development? There are several, and four key challenges are outlined here. The first, and probably the most important, is to explore further the linkages between technological change and sustainability. Past approaches to technology have suggested that technological change just 'happens'. If so, there is a temptation to conclude that it cannot be the subject of policy initiatives. Yet, technological change is of the utmost importance for sustainability since it provides the means of improving human well-being without depleting natural resources at unacceptable rates. In other words, it offers the mechanism for resource conservation.

There is a great deal of interest currently in this notion of raising the 'productivity' of resources, and *Blueprint for a Green Economy* actually highlighted the issue over a decade ago. The options are essentially three: continue to achieve economic growth and face a deteriorating environment; grow and decouple the environment from the growth process; or not grow. The last alternative is in fact not an option because what determines long-run growth is not short-run government policy but technological change and investment in human capital. The idea that any government would deliberately set out to reduce growth by reducing investment in education, training and R&D is not credible. Hence, the options are grow and suffer a reduced quality of life, or grow and decouple. Only the latter is acceptable.

To achieve this, there has to be a renewed focus on incentive measures for environmentally beneficial technology. The dismal state of initiatives to switch all of us out of carbon-dependent technology explains much of what is going on. Even environmental and energy economists have focused too much on taxes rather than payments to bring on new technology such as renewable energy. There are enormous external benefits to be obtained by jump-starting environmentally sound technology so that movements down very steep learning curves can be secured. Resource productivity means better and cleaner technology, and better and cleaner technology means a technology policy. No doubt some technological change will just 'happen' but modern theory suggests that most of it is the result of conscious decisions.

The second key challenge concerns population change. Some have argued that population change is itself a stimulus to economic growth. It creates demand and increases the labour supply. Potentially more important, it pushes societies to their ecological limits, and this induces technological change. Ester Boserup[8] is the name most closely associated with this view, but it has surfaced more recently in the work of Mary Tiffen and others.[9] The problem with this view is that one can find as many, if not more, examples of population change causing decreased well-being as cases where it has generated increased well-being. Nor is it clear that the gains in well-being that occur in the relevant cases would not have occurred without population change. The opposite is hard to demonstrate.

The sustainable development literature is very clear that the dominant effect of population growth is to dissipate the capital assets on which sustainable development depends. Only if capital assets are 'public goods' can population growth be compatible with rising levels of services from the available capital stock.[10] The negative effect of population change on indicators of sustainability is, for example, firmly demonstrated in the work of Kirk Hamilton at the World Bank,[11] work that had as its stimulus an original paper by Pearce and Atkinson[12] which in turn arose from the original *Blueprint* work.

Yet there is an unnerving reluctance on the part of policy-makers to emphasize the destructive features of population change. As an example, the issue is barely mentioned in the UK Department for International Development's strategy papers for poverty alleviation and sustainable development.[13] One clear implication of the economic models of sustainable development is that sustainability is most threatened by even modest changes in population. As is well known, there is little or nothing to be done to prevent world population rising by 50 per cent in the next 50 years, but everything should be done to prevent it rising further than that. Political correctness involving silence on the issue spells disaster for sustainability.

The third challenge is to improve our approaches to valuing the environment. While controversial, the monetary approach remains the most promising. Critics of the approach appear to invest little time and effort in understanding what economists are doing when they derive such values. They are essentially measures of human preference for environmental quality. Somehow, this fact gets lost amid claims that money is 'evil', a confusion of the commodity with a measuring rod. As the techniques are improved, we can get better and better indicators of sustainability, centring on the genuine-savings concept. The insights from this measure contrast starkly with the almost endless array of environmental indicators which masquerade as sustainability indicators. They are nothing of the kind, useful though they might be for other purposes.

The final challenge concerns social capital. While much of the discussion about sustainability has emphasized the importance of environmental quality, there are disturbing signs that what we might call social sustainability is under threat through the destruction of social capital. Social cohesion appears to be threatened from many sources – crime, family break-up, drugs, for example. The question is how far the creation of social capital is a policy-relevant issue. Governments have been notoriously bad at creating socially cohesive values, not because they are incompetent but perhaps because it is not something that governments can do. It can be argued then that some of the focus on sustainability should shift to social issues, and to the particularly perplexing issue of how social capital might be measured.

Apart from the social capital issue, these challenges were all raised in the original *Blueprint*. While one could look at the half-empty glass and say that, more than a decade later, we still have a lot of work to do, I prefer to look at the half-full glass and say that in only a decade we have come a very long way in our thinking about sustainability. IIED's brief but productive alliance with UCL on this issue changed the language of environmental politics. There is more to be done.

## ECONOMICS OF ENVIRONMENT AND DEVELOPMENT: IIED'S CONTRIBUTION *BY EDWARD BARBIER*

Twenty years ago, the application of economics to the environmental problems of developing countries was virtually unheard of. In 1984, I was made painfully aware of this fact as a result of two incidents, both of which occurred while I was working that academic year as a temporary lecturer at the Geneva campus of a US college, Webster University of St Louis, Missouri. During this time I was also completing my PhD thesis, which among other things was exploring the role of environmental economics in economic development.[14]

The first incident occurred when I was asked to give an economics lecture at another US university with a campus in Geneva. After the lecture, the director of that campus's economics programme asked me about the topic of my thesis. Upon hearing my interest in the economics of environment and development problems, the director remarked that in his opinion – which he considered to be the conventional view of the economics profession – not only was the topic too obscure for a PhD thesis but it was also largely irrelevant to economics.

The second incident occurred when I tried to sign on to a register of consultants for a well-known international non-governmental organization (NGO) based in Geneva, which was working on conservation and development issues worldwide. When asked by the person in charge of the register to list my main area of expertise, I explained that I was an economist interested in the analysis of environmental problems of developing countries. The person replied that her organization did not need any consultant with that area of expertise. When I suggested sending in my curriculum vitae in the hope that the situation might change in the near future, she said not to bother as they did not include on their register any consultant without a PhD degree (not surprisingly, I found out some time later that this was untrue).

My main aim in recollecting these two incidents in this introduction is not to try and prove how wrong these two individuals were. Rather, I see these two events as important reminders of how much and how fast attitudes have changed in less than 20 years. Today, the economics profession appears to have accepted that the application of economics to environment and development problems is a legitimate and important area of study. Perhaps the most tangible proof of this was the launching in September 1995 at the Royal Swedish Academy of Sciences of an academic journal, *Environment and Development Economics*, published by Cambridge University Press. Equally, virtually every major bilateral and international donor agency in the world either has one or more full-time staff members engaged in the economic analysis of environmental problems in developing countries, or routinely contracts researchers and consultants to undertake such analysis. Many international NGOs and some NGOs within developing countries have also been sponsoring and conducting research into the economics of environment and development.

However, what is less well known in the international community is the important contribution that the International Institute for Environment and Development (IIED) has made to the rapid surge of research emanating from this new field. Having worked at IIED over the period 1986–1993, I was extremely fortunate to be involved in this contribution.

Hired by Richard Sandbrook and Czech Conroy in early 1996, I initially worked with Czech on setting up an international conference on sustainable development and on the *World Resources Report*, which IIED produced jointly with the World Resources Institute and the UN Environmental Programme. At this time, Richard Sandbrook and IIED were assisting the Commission on Sustainable Development headed by the former Norwegian prime minister Gro Harlem Brundtland to conduct its global enquiry. Published in 1987, the now-famous Brundtland Report *Our Common Future* was responsible for bringing the concept of sustainable development to the world's attention. As a result of the report, economic policy-makers and donor agencies globally began taking environment and development issues seriously, and were asking important policy questions concerning the practical implementation of sustainable development. Sensing this change, Richard Sandbrook encouraged me to set up a one-man Environmental Economics Programme at IIED to initiate policy-relevant economics research into environment and development issues. One of my initial aims was to try to understand both the economic and non-economic components of what the environment and development community was calling 'sustainable development'.[15]

During this period Gordon Conway, who was setting up IIED's Sustainable Agricultural Programme, also asked me to work with him on integrating economic and ecological analysis in the study of the sustainability and development of agricultural systems, particularly in the marginal agricultural areas of the developing world. Through this work, we were able to demonstrate not only the importance of agricultural sustainability for alleviating rural poverty but also a role for economics in assessing the trade-offs between the sustainability and productivity of various agricultural systems.[16]

Meanwhile, an important process was occurring in Washington DC. Since the 1960s, the World Bank has generally been viewed as the premier global agency concerned with economic development, and along with the International Monetary Fund, the Bank has generally led donor policy thinking on development. In the late 1980s an economist at the World Bank, Jerry Warford, among others became increasingly successful in convincing the Bank hierarchy that the economic analysis of environmental problems in developing countries should feature in Bank policy thinking. The so-called 'greening of the Bank' led to the establishment of the Environment Department and several environmental divisions within the regional departments of the World Bank, as well as the launching of several Bank country studies incorporating economic analysis of environmental and resource problems in developing countries.

Other donor agencies were also 'greening': perhaps most notably and publicly, the US Agency for International Development (USAID) in Washington, but also the major UK, Scandinavian, Canadian and West European bilateral donor agencies were developing key environment and development programmes with substantial impacts. Again fortunately for me, the head of IIED's Washington office, David Runnalls, had been both following and encouraging the 'greening' of the North American donor agencies and, as a result, David got me involved early on in some of the environment and development economics studies launched by the World Bank and USAID.

Much of the initial policy research commissioned by Jerry Warford at the World Bank was also being conducted by David Pearce

at University College London, who was based just around the corner
from IIED at UCL's Economics Department. Another UCL econo-
mist, Anil Markandya, was also collaborating in much of the research.
It became obvious that we would all benefit from pooling our
'London-based' research efforts. With the enthusiastic support of
Richard Sandbrook and Johan Holmberg of the Swedish International
Development Authority (SIDA), SIDA was persuaded to provide the
initial seed money for the new venture. Thus in 1988 the IIED-UCL
London Environmental Economics Centre was created, with David
Pearce as Director, Anil Markandya and myself as Associate Directors,
and Joanne Burgess as the first researcher.

Over the next few years, the four of us at LEEC, plus others who
joined us on some studies such as Tim Swanson, set about producing
numerous books, journal articles and research reports concerned with
the economic analysis of environmental problems in developing
countries. Most of this research was concerned with applied policy
analysis, featuring sectoral, country and even global studies of key
environment and development problems. One of the most influential
– and controversial – studies we conducted was on the economics of
the trade in African elephant ivory.[17] Such studies quickly established
LEEC's reputation for pioneering the application of economics to
significant environment and development problems. Other studies
that I personally participated in during this period at LEEC included:
the economics of soil erosion in Indonesia,[18] the economics of rehabilitating gum arabic systems in Sudan,[19] technological substitutions for
greenhouse gas emissions,[20] and various country studies of the
economics of tropical deforestation.[21]

However, no matter how much we tried to accomplish at LEEC
there was always a demand for more; these were the days when the
sudden surge in demand for economists working in our area far
outstripped the available supply. Ironically, however, the most widely
influential publication from this period was *Blueprint for a Green
Economy*, a report commissioned by the UK Department of
Environment on how the UK might implement sustainable development.[22] Written essentially as a sideline to what we thought was our
main area of research at LEEC, the phenomenal success of *Blueprint*
was perhaps partly attributable to the rapidly expanding interest
worldwide in all aspects of economic analysis of environmental policy
and sustainable development, and not just for developing countries. A
companion book that we wrote based on our 'bread and butter' LEEC
research of the time was *Sustainable Development: Economics and
Environment in the Third World*.[23]

In 1990 David Pearce left LEEC in order to devote his time fully as UCL's Director of the Centre for Social and Economic Research into the Global Environment. I agreed to become Director of LEEC, and Richard Sandbrook, Anil Markandya and I decided to return the Centre's focus exclusively to environment and development economics research. In this 'second phase' in LEEC's development, we tried to concentrate on more long-term applied economic studies of various key environmental problems in developing countries, both on our own at LEEC and in collaboration with other economics researchers worldwide. During this period, two additional researchers joined LEEC full time – Bruce Aylward and Josh Bishop, both of whom proved instrumental in the development of LEEC in its crucial second phase. Michael Collins also joined us in my last year as Director. Examples of the topics we studied at LEEC during this era include: the economics of the tropical timber trade,[24] the ecological economics of biodiversity loss,[25] the pharmaceutical value of bioprospecting,[26] the economics of land degradation,[27] tropical deforestation in Mexico,[28] and the environmental effects of structural adjustment.[29]

It was at the end of LEEC's 'second phase' that IIED's long and distinguished record in contributing to the economics of environment and development was finally reaping dividends in the wider international community. Nowhere was this more important than at the 1992 UN Conference on Environment and Development (UNCED), held in Rio de Janeiro, Brazil. For example, in its Agenda 21 preconference declaration, the UNCED Secretariat made the following statement:

> *In the last two decades, there has been some progress through conventional economic policy applied in parallel with environmental policy. It is now clear that this is not enough, and that environment and development must be taken into account at each step of decision making and action in an integrated manner.[30]*

The economic analysis of environment and development problems had finally received the full support of the international policy community, and this could be seen in tangible terms by the community's continued support for the type of research we were conducting at LEEC, as well as the valuable work that continues to be pursued to this day by LEEC's successor, the Environmental Economics Programme at IIED, under the leadership of current Director, Josh Bishop.

## NOTES AND REFERENCES

1  World Commission on Environment and Development (1987) *Our Common Future* (The Brundtland Report), Oxford University Press, Oxford.
2  Pearce, DW, A Markandya and E Barbier (1989) *Sustainable Development, Resource Accounting and Project Appraisal: State of the Art Review*, Report to UK Department of the Environment, London Environmental Economics Centre, IIED, London.
3  Pearce, DW, A Markandya and E Barbier (1989) *Blueprint for a Green Economy*, Earthscan, London.
4  Pearce, DW, E Barbier, A Markandya et al (1991) *Blueprint 2: Greening the World Economy*; Pearce, DW, RK Turner, T O'Riordan et al (1993) *Blueprint 3: Measuring Sustainable Development*; Pearce, DW (1995) *Blueprint 4: Capturing Global Environmental Value*; Maddison, D, DW Pearce, O Johansson et al (1996) *Blueprint 5: The True Costs of Road Transport*; Pearce, DW and E Barbier (2000) *Blueprint for a Sustainable Economy*, all published by Earthscan, London.
5  As it happens, monetization is not essential for some of the approaches to measurement, but the issues are technical and are not elaborated here.
6  Hamilton, K and M Clemens (1999) Genuine savings rates in developing countries, *World Bank Economic Review*, 13(2), pp333–356.
7  See Pearce et al (1993), note 4 above.
8  Boserup, E (1980) *Population and Technological Change*, University of Chicago Press, Chicago.
9  Tiffen, M, M Mortimore and F Gichuki (1994) *More People, Less Erosion: Environmental Recovery in Kenya*, Wiley, New York and London.
10  A public good is one that, if made available to one person, is automatically supplied to other people. Moreover, the consumption of the good by one person does not diminish consumption by others. Some capital assets, such as clean air and much information, are public goods but many are not.
11  Hamilton, K (2001) *Sustaining Economic Welfare: Estimating Changes in Wealth per capita*, Environment Department, World Bank, Washington DC.
12  Pearce, DW and G Atkinson (1993) Capital theory and the measurement of sustainable development, *Ecological Economics* 8, pp103–108.
13  Department for International Development (DfID) (2000) *Achieving Sustainability: Poverty Elimination and the Environment*, DfID, London.
14  The published version of my PhD thesis (Barbier, EB (1989) Cash crops, food crops and agricultural sustainablity: the case of Indonesia,

*World Development* 17(6), pp1378–1387) was updated during my early years at IIED, and owes a great deal to the research experience I gained at the Institute.

15  Particularly influential was a meeting held at IIED in September 1986, in which we attempted to integrate a concept of sustainable development across economic, biological and social perspectives. This 'IIED definition' is summarized in: Barbier, EB (1987) The concept of sustainable economic development, *Environmental Conservation* 14(2), pp101–10.

16  Barbier, EB (1989b) *Economics, Natural Resource Scarcity and Development: Conventional and Alternative Views*, Earthscan, London (223pp); Conway, GR and EB Barbier (1988) After the Green Revolution: sustainable and equitable agricultural development, *Futures* 20, pp651–671; Conway, GR and EB Barbier (1990) *After the Green Revolution: Sustainable Agriculture for Development*, Earthscan, London (205 pp).

17  Barbier, EB, JC Burgess, TM Swanson and DW Pearce (1990) *Elephants, Economics and Ivory*, Earthscan, London.

18  Barbier, EB (1990) The farm-level economics of soil conservation: the uplands of Java, *Land Economics* 66(2), pp199–211.

19  Barbier, EB (1992) Rehabilitating gum arabic systems in Sudan: economic and environmental implications, *Environmental and Resource Economics* 2, pp341–352.

20  Barbier, EB, JC Burgess and DW Pearce (1992) Technological substitution options for controlling greenhouse gas emissions, in J Poterba and R Dornbusch (eds), *Economic Policy Responses to Global Warming*, MIT Press, Massachusetts, pp109–160.

21  Barbier, EB, JC Burgess and A Markandya (1991) The economics of tropical deforestation, *Ambio* 20(2), pp52–54.

22  See note 3 above.

23  Pearce, DW, EB Barbier and A Markandya (1990) *Sustainable Development: Environmental Economics in the Third World*, Edward Elgar, London.

24  Barbier, EB, JC Burgess, JT Bishop and BA Aylward (1994) *The Economics of the Tropical Timber Trade*, Earthscan, London.

25  Barbier, EB, JC Burgess and C Folke (1994) *Paradise Lost? The Ecological Economics of Biodiversity*, Earthscan, London.

26  Aylward, BA, J Echeverría, L Fendt and EB Barbier (1993) *The Economic Value of Species Information and its Role in Biodiversity Conservation: Costa Rica's National Biodiversity Institute*, LEEC Paper 93-06, London Environmental Economics Centre, London; Barbier, EB and BA Aylward (1996) Capturing the pharmaceutical value of biodiversity in a developing country, *Environmental and Resource Economics* 8(2), pp157–191.

27  Barbier, EB and JT Bishop (1995) Economic and social values affecting soil and water conservation in developing countries, *Journal of Soil and Water Conservation*, March–April, pp133–135.

28  Barbier, EB and JC Burgess (1996) Economic analysis of deforestation in Mexico, *Environment and Development Economics* 1(2), pp203–240.

29  Reed, D (ed.) (1992) *Structural Adjustment and the Environment*, Earthscan, London.

30  UNCED Secretariat (1992) *Integration of Environment and Development in Decision Making*, Report to the Preparatory Committee for UNCED, UNCED, New York.

# 13

# Strategies, plans, impacts and people: IIED's role in changing the world of planning and environmental assessment

## *Barry Dalal-Clayton*

The concept of sustainable development began to take shape during the 1980s. Following from the writings of Barbara Ward, the 1980 World Conservation Strategy pushed for the integration of environment and conservation values in development. In 1987, the report of the Brundtland Commission[1] also promoted closer links between environment and development and emphasized issues of social and economic sustainability. Brundtland defined sustainable development as 'development that meets the needs of the present without compromising the ability of future generations to meet their own needs'.

I joined IIED in 1988 when Brundtland mania was sweeping the development community and the Institute was in a period of expansion. Over the next four years our focus was on the 1992 Earth Summit. Agenda 21, one of its main accords, placed sustainable development as the internationally agreed core goal for development. It called on all countries to develop national strategies for sustainable development to translate the words and commitments of the Earth Summit into concrete policies and actions. But no official guidance was forthcoming on how to do this. IIED has been working on this challenge ever since, analysing experience and practices with partners and practitioners in many countries.

To achieve its aims, Agenda 21 also signalled the need for effective, integrated planning supported by appropriate tools such as environmental impact assessment (EIA) and natural resource surveys and evaluations. Yet by this time, planning had somehow earned itself a bad name. As the more participatory and integrated ethos of sustainable development was gaining increasing acceptance, 'planning' was becoming increasingly associated with all that was seen to be wrong with the failures of state-controlled development in the communist-bloc countries. We saw part of our task at IIED as promoting more participatory and holistic approaches to planning through integrating economic, social and environmental concerns.

## STRATEGIES FOR SUSTAINABLE DEVELOPMENT

It was clear to us that the emerging international experience of national conservation strategies, the parallel approaches adopted for developing Tropical Forestry Action Plans and various other strategic planning mechanisms offered a platform on which to build for countries to address the wider challenge of sustainable development. The World Bank had also been pushing the preparation of National Environmental Action Plans (NEAPs). If countries wanted to secure soft loans (under IDA–9), it was required that they complete a NEAP by 1993 at the very latest. This was criticized as a form of conditionality. Guidance to Bank staff was provided in the infamous Operational Directive 4.02. NEAPs, particularly the first generation in Africa, were often developed in a highly top-down manner and usually led by Bank 'experts'.

We began to debate the idea of national strategies for sustainable development, and introduced these ideas into discussions during the preparatory process for the Rio Earth Summit. Later we were responsible for crafting some of the language on the need for strategies for sustainable development which was subsequently taken up and peppered throughout Agenda 21. In the run up to Rio, Johan Holmberg – on secondment to IIED from the Swedish International Development Agency (Sida) – ran the Institute's 1992 programme which concentrated on building awareness of the challenge of sustainable development.

A short explanatory booklet about sustainable development[2] was a key document used extensively by negotiators attending preparatory meetings for Rio. It contained some early ideas on indicators of sustainable development – as opposed to a mix of strictly economic, social or environmental ones. The indicators gave a flavour of what sustainable development would look like – for example, passenger kilometres travelled by public transport were increasing in proportion to those travelled by private motorized transport. These suggested indicators were intended to be easier to monitor than the indicators proposed by the Commission for Sustainable Development and other international organizations, and more conducive to participatory monitoring by citizens' groups.

In the aftermath of Rio, IIED's Environmental Planning Group, funded by the Norwegian Ministry of Foreign Affairs and the UK's Overseas Development Administration, began work on a review of experience in developing and implementing National Conservation Strategies (NCSs), Tropical Forestry Action Plans (TFAPs), National Environmental Action Plans (NEAPs), and a range of other processes in order to learn lessons and provide guidance for developing strategies on sustainable development. At the same time, IUCN embarked on a programme to to learn from its 14 years of experience of NCSs. This was a joint inititiative of IUCN's Secretariat in Switzerland and IUCN's Commission for Environmental Strategies and Planning. In 1992, IIED and IUCN combined forces and, following several regional workshops involving strategy practitioners, developed a handbook for the planning and implementation of national strategies for sustainable development.[3]

Several thousand copies of this handbook were distributed to decision-makers, planners, academics, governments, donors, UN organizations and others, and it became the main source for those charged with developing strategies. The handbook was a great success and we were asked to run a string of workshops and seminars for different donors, and to contribute to conferences on the subject. At IIED, we also produced a series of papers giving more detail on particular aspects of strategies (eg, key dilemmas, participation, the challenge for small island states).

Requests came in from different governments for information, advice and help in developing their strategies. ODA commissioned IIED to help the Government of St Helena with its strategy – on this we collaborated with Kew Gardens which was working on conserving the endemic island species. We also worked with the World Bank to help it reflect on its experience of NEAPs and had some fairly intensive 'discussions' with somewhat defensive Bank staff. But slowly the Bank took on board many of the principles we had pulled together in the handbook, and this contributed to a change in the Bank's policy and behaviour on NEAPS.

Many developing-country practitioners expressed a need for information on how developed countries were developing their strategies.

So, in 1996, IIED produced a study of strategy experience in industrial countries. The problems faced by developing and developed countries in preparing strategies for sustainable development are usually quite different. Most developing countries are occupied with achieving economic development, through industrialization where this is possible, and by expanding production. By comparison, one of the key issues for sustainable development in most developed countries is dealing with the problems caused by high levels of consumption, by existing industries and by technology-based economies (for example, pollution and waste). The study[4] showed some marked differences between the processes followed in the North and South (see Box 13.1) but also suggested that that the developed and developing countries have much to learn from each other.

In 1997, governments met again at the Special Session of the UN in New York to take stock of progress since Rio. It was noted that there had been continued deterioration in the state of the global environment under the combined pressures of unsustainable production and consumption patterns and population growth. This assessment led governments to set a target date of 2002 for introducing national strategies for sustainable development (nssds[5]). In preparing for the UN meeting, the Development Assistance Committee (DAC) of the OECD called for the formulation and implementation of a sustainable development strategy in every country by 2005 (adopting this as one of seven International Development Goals).[6] The document also committed DAC members to support developing countries in the formulation and implementation of *nssds* through a partnership approach.

Despite these international targets, there was a lack of clarity about the nature of an *nssd* (there is still no internationally agreed definition). Nor was there any official guidance on how to prepare one. The DAC therefore launched a project to clarify the purposes and principles underlying effective national and local strategies for sustainable development, describe the various forms they can take in developing countries, and offer guidance on how development cooperation agencies can support them. Because of its acknowledged expertise on strategies, IIED was asked to help design, coordinate and facilitate this work. It was undertaken in collaboration with a donor Task Force co-chaired by DfID and the EC.

Between 1999 and 2001, we coordinated stakeholder dialogues and reviews of a range of different strategic planning processes in eight countries, each led by local teams, and organized three international

## Box 13.1 Basic comparisons between strategy processes in developed and developing countries

| *Developed countries* | *Developing countries* |
| --- | --- |
| *Approach* | *Approach* |
| Internally generated | External impetus (IUCN, World Bank, etc) |
| Internally funded | Donor-funded |
| Indigenous expertise | Expatriate expertise frequently involved |
| Political action | Bureaucratic/technocratic action |
| Brokerage approach | Project approach |
| | |
| *Aims* | *Aims* |
| Changing production/consumption patterns | Increase production/consumption |
| Response to 'brown' issues (eg pollution) | Response to 'green' issues or rural development |
| Environment focus | Development focus |
| | |
| *Means* | *Means* |
| Institutional re-orientation/ integration | Creation of new institutions |
| Production of guidelines and local targets | Development of project 'shopping lists' |
| Cost-saving approaches | Aid-generating approaches |
| Links to Local Agenda 21 initiatives | Few local links |
| Awareness-raising | Awareness-raising |

workshops. An innovation used to support the project was the development of a strategies website.[7] This culminated in the development of policy guidance on *nssds* as a partnership exercise between developing countries and DAC members (the first time this had been done) with IIED drafting the initial text. The guidance was endorsed by aid ministers at the High Level DAC. The project is now in its final stage as we put together a resource book with detailed case studies and methodological guidance.

In the past, many strategic planning initiatives have had limited practical impact because they have focused on the production of a document as an end-product, and not been implemented. It is now accepted that, instead, the focus of an *nssd* should be on improving the integration of social and environmental objectives into key economic development processes. The DAC guidance defines an *nssd* as:

> *A co-ordinated set of participatory and continuously improving processes of analysis, debate, capacity-strengthening, planning and investment, which seeks to integrate the short and long term economic, social and environmental objectives of society – through mutually supportive approaches wherever possible – and manages trade offs where this is not possible.*[8]

Sustainable development strategies require a systematic approach and iterative processes of learning and doing. Different strategic planning processes can be used as starting points for a strategy for sustainable development. The learning from the country dialogues and other experience confirmed that putting a sustainable development strategy into operation would, in practice, most likely consist of improving existing strategic planning processes and their coordination rather than establishing a new process.

## LAND USE AND RURAL PLANNING

Our work at IIED on land use planning was also greatly influenced by my earlier experiences working with the Department of Agriculture in Zambia in the 1970s and 1980s. We undertook soil and land capability surveys, producing beautiful maps. However, we achieved very little by way of effective progress for the rural poor. Our soil maps were never used to any effect. They were far too technical and couldn't be understood except by professionals. They were not wanted by decision-makers. Costly printed maps lay unused in offices, although one office messenger used some to paper the wall of his hut to keep out the draught. The land use plans were prepared mainly in provincial offices and headquarters with no involvement of the beneficiaries.

In Tanzania, there were numerous, expensive, integrated rural development programmes, water master plans, zonal plans and similar initiatives of the 1970s and 1980s, none of which made a lasting difference. One reason why these plans were unsustainable was because they placed very little emphasis on institutional building.

Usually, they were managed by expatriate staff, and all activities tended to grind to a halt when their short-term contracts came to an end. The remaining local staff had limited skills or capacity and were unable to manage and sustain the programmes. Also, the lack of benchmark indicators and adequate data prevented any assessment of impacts of these programmes.

Our work at IIED found these problems to be commonplace in many developing countries, and we used the principles of sustainable development to look for a better way to proceed. In 1991, we began the Planning for Sustainable Development project. This involved detailed case studies of experience of resource assessment and land use planning in Sri Lanka and Tanzania. These were undertaken by local teams based in the Land Use Policy Planning Division, Sri Lanka, and the Institute of Resource Assessment, University of Dar es Salaam, Tanzania. We worked with contacts around the world to prepare a review of resource assessment and the use of land resource information in developing countries.

The reports of this project launched a new IIED publications series – Environmental Planning Issues. The overview study[9] found that large surveys had often been undertaken without establishing who would use the information collected, and how. Much information gathered by costly surveys had been under-utilized and effectively lost. It confirmed that land use planning remained largely sectoral and unintegrated, and usually centralized and top-down. There was little effective participation in land use planning by the supposed beneficiaries. The series also provided examples of emerging practices in participatory planning, and recommended how to change approaches. The overview study, recently updated with new materials,[10] had a significant impact on FAO's planning practices and procedures, has been used extensively by rural planning departments, and has become a key teaching text in universities.

In the mid-1990s, the concept of sustainable livelihoods gained prominence and was adopted by DfID as a key pillar of its thinking. In 1998, DfID commissioned IIED to undertake a study of approaches to rural planning, to learn about potential contributions to sustainable livelihoods. The work involved country case studies in Ghana, South Africa and Zimbabwe (again, undertaken by local partners) and an overview synthesizing global experience.[11] The work led to some key conclusions:

- There is a paramount need for rural planning to operate under a truly domestically driven development vision at national and sub-national levels – not tied to party, ethnic or religious groups.
- The sustainable livelihoods concept offers a powerful focus for development planning, linking natural, human and capital assets of a particular place both with the vulnerability and opportunities of different livelihoods and with potentially transforming institutions (governmental and non-governmental) and processes (eg legal, planning).This contrasts with previous piecemeal support for services, infrastructure and commodity projects. It remains to translate sustainable livelihoods into practical guidelines for effective decision-making and action on the ground. The real value of sustainable livelihoods as a planning concept is that it brings together a small number of key factors. Its value will be lost if it is made over-complicated.
- Two underlying causes of the general failure of top-down planning in poor and emerging countries have been the absence of any local stake or input to the planning process, and the preference of donors to bypass ineffective local administrations by setting up financially and administratively autonomous project organizations, which have further weakened local capacity to plan and deliver development. In reaction to these failures, decentralization and participation are now the watchwords.
- Planning is not a politically neutral, technical activity. It is now increasingly recognized that successful implementation of development plans depends upon common ownership of the problems and the proposed solutions by the people who will be affected. This common ownership may arise from consensus about the goals and the necessary actions, or from a negotiated compromise between groups with different goals and insights.
- If there is to be negotiation of a sustainable future, there must be some forum that commands general respect and legitimacy where all stakeholders can negotiate and contribute to plans. Appropriate platforms for decision-making are needed at each level of planning (local, district and national) and the stakeholders must be equipped to participate.

The need to adopt more participatory planning approaches is increasingly being accepted – particularly with the focus now placed on decentralization. For example, as part of its support to the decentralization process in Tanzania under the Capacity 21 programme, UNDP is promoting participatory planning in two pilot districts. To guide the design of this programme, in 1999, I worked again with Professor Idris Kikula, former Director of the Institute of Resource Assessment (IRA) at the University of Dar es Salaam. This was yet another in a series of fruitful collaborative studies undertaken with the IRA over the past decade (see Box 13.2).

Achieving progress in planning depends on resolving several key questions, which also indicate where we need to concentrate future efforts.

1   Are bureaucrats willing to do things differently, thinking and behaving in more open, participatory ways that provide for dialogue and consensus-building in order to agree what is needed and how to get there. Are they also willing to decentralize? Experience has shown so far that this is not the case. There is therefore, a need to identify motivations to encourage bureaucrats to work differently.
2   Are institutions willing to work in support of each other to achieve cross-sectoral integration and synchronization? Experience shows that, in many countries, cross-sectoral intergration is constrained by government structures even at the lowest levels. Heads of departments are rewarded for performance in their own sectors and not for inter-sectoral activities. There is a need to identify and support, in each situation, the constructive institutional relationships that exist, how to build capacity through action to overcome initial constraints.
3   Is there political will for the necessary changes and new planning frameworks that support rather than inhibit participatory approaches? Such political will needs to be harnessed to achieve realistic objectives and to implement change.
4   What is the appropriate role for government? This needs to be clarified, particularly in relation to private enterprise – the latter represents an important resource (often virtually the only resource in many countries, albeit it at a low level) to drive effective development.

## DEVELOPING ENVIRONMENTAL ASSESSMENT METHODS

Environmental impact assessment (EIA) was first introduced in the USA as a requirement of the 1969 National Environmental Protection

## Box 13.2 Planning and environmental assessment in Tanzania: Reflections on working with IIED

*Idris Kikula*

In 1991, I became the Director of the multidisciplinary Institute of Resource of Assessment (IRA) at the University of Dar es Salaam, and was keen to build links with other organizations. My aim was to help IRA to tap international financial resources for research and also to build our capacity, particularly through exposing IRA colleagues to 'international' approaches to research on sustainable development.

Collaborative research between IIED and IRA began in 1992 when Barry Dalal-Clayton introduced the idea of joint work on land use planning and resource assessment in Tanzania. This study[12] highlighted many issues previously taken for granted, and demonstrated an effective way of conducting interdisciplinary research. This early collaboration was followed by many other joint activities, including:

- capacity building of many IRA staff on environmental impact assessment (EIA);
- capacity building of government staff (from Permanent Secretaries down to staff in regions and districts), and of staff working on a number of donor-funded projects;
- contribution to the preparation of national EIA guidelines;
- Environmental Impact Statements for many development projects within and outside Tanzania (eg Zambia);
- several joint publications, including an evaluation of EIA in Tanzania, and three sets of EIA manuals which have been widely used for training in Tanzania, and also distributed to other African countries.[13]

The IIED–IRA collaboration also widened to include colleagues from the Universities of Bradford and Manchester. This extended ring of collaboration made it possible for IRA staff to collaborate with world-renowned experts in planning and EIA, and has made a tremendous contribution to capacity building in IRA.

Reflecting on the IIED-IRA collaboration over ten years, I would highlight two factors as crucial for success. First, institutional collaboration cannot work effectively unless it is linked to individuals who respect and trust each other, and who are committed to the course of the collaboration. As soon as this factor is withdrawn, for whatever reason, including management changes, the collaboration tends to break down. Second, the collaboration must embrace broader interests. For example, in 1999, I proposed to UNDP that IIED should team up with IRA to conduct a survey on participatory planning in Tanzania, and Barry Dalal-Clayton was able to contribute his international experience.[14]

Act. During the 1970s, it emerged as a procedure for encouraging decision-makers to take account of the effects of development on environmental quality and the productivity of natural resources. More than half of the countries in the world now have a formal EIA system, and increasingly comprehensive and sophisticated procedures have been drawn up by development agencies.

Work on environmental assessment took off at IIED in 1988, with IIED providing various support services to the British Overseas Development Administration (ODA) and then to its successor, the Department for International Development (DfID). We screened hundreds of projects for their potential environmental impact (often also addressing the social issues). Projects ranged from industrial plant and transport infrastructure, hydropower dams and irrigation schemes, to wildlife management and conservation activities. We also assessed projects for other agencies.

In the early 1990s, commissioned by ODA, IIED undertook an impact assessment of the Kilombero Valley Hardwood Project in Tanzania, together with the Institute of Resource Assessment. The Kilombero project was being proposed by the Commonwealth Development Corporation (CDC) and would see the investment of £29 million in a private-sector venture to grow 25,000ha of teak. Rather than conduct a conventional EIA, we based the assessment on sustainability principles, examining social and economic as well as environmental aspects. The process was participatory, involving a range of stakeholders and engaging with local communities through traditional village fora.

The assessment findings were in favour of the project in general terms, but we took issue with a number of elements which were not in the best interests of the local communities. ODA was generally pleased with the report but CDC reacted strongly – more I think out of pique that ODA had insisted on this EIA and that someone had been critical of its plans. In practice, many of our suggestions were subsequently taken up by the project managers and, ironically, CDC did then change its ways of working and adopted EIA procedures consistent with the approach we had followed.

The Kilombero experience signalled the need for a modified approach to EIA based on basic principles of sustainable development – integrating environmental, social and economic concerns – an approach which has been dubbed sustainability analysis.[15] But progress in securing such integration in EA practice remains a major challenge. The problems are not really technical or methodological, they have more to do with lack of institutional and political will.

At the request of the DAC, 1991 saw us launch the International Environmental and Natural Resource Assessment Information Service (Interaise) in collaboration with WRI and IUCN. Over the next five years, three Directories of Country Environmental, Studies were compiled (led by WRI), regional directories were produced for southern Africa and Latin America (by IUCN) and an Interaise information service was established at IIED, providing copies of documents to developing countries. In 1992, we completed a series of environmental synopses assessing environmental conditions and trends in a number of countries.

In late 1992, IIED embarked on a major review in Bangladesh, to provide a balanced assessment of challenges to water management. It was stimulated by misguided international efforts (led by the World Bank) to support the preparation of a Flood Action Plan (FAP) in response to periodic (and devastating) floods. The review[16] reinterpreted some of the vital inter-relationships, highlighted the inadequate attention to environmental issues and participation of floodplain communities in the FAP process, and pointed to the need for strategic planning to provide integrated water resources management. This report added to the weight of criticism of the FAP. In the event, many donors declined (for various reasons) to provide support to implement projects proposed by the FAP. As a result, the FAP died and was replaced by the National Water Management Plan which was influenced by the criticisms made of the FAP by the IIED study and many others.

Collaborative work with the IRA in Tanzania was also central to our attempt to determine objectively the influence of environmental impact assessment. EIA is big business internationally, with countless consultancy companies offering services. But it is questionable whether, as currently practised, it is providing value for money or making any effective difference to steer development down a sustainable path. IIED aims to undertake further studies in other developing countries with different types of EIA frameworks and institutional capacity.

EIA has rarely been attempted at policy level. However, there is increasing recognition of the value of introducing environmental considerations at the earlier stages of the decision-making process. In response, we have recently seen the emergence of Strategic Environmental Assessment (SEA) – environmental assessment at the level of policies, programmes and plans. Several developed countries have also established SEA systems – some mandatory, some informal.

There has also been considerable recent interest in the use and application of SEA in developing countries.

During 1998–99, Barry Sadler and I undertook preliminary study of SEA in developing countries, to investigate experiences, constraints and opportunities for implementing sustainable development strategies. A more thorough stock-taking is now planned, given the momentum which appears to be growing to promote the use of SEA in the South. A key question here is whether SEA, as it is currently understood and applied in the developed world, is an appropriate tool for promoting sustainability in developing countries or those in transition. One element of SEA is scenario planning, which helps us to see options for the future and to agree on what kind of world we want to live in. Scenario planning is an area in which more effort should be invested, particularly to represent the full range of stakeholders.

IIED is perhaps best known in the world of EIA for its Directories of Impact Assessment Guidelines[17] which aim to improve awareness of, and access to, existing guidelines. The directories have gained international recognition as sourcebooks for EIA practitioners. It is hoped to begin work on the third edition in the near future, to include chapters focusing on good practice in environmental assessment.

The ideas of sustainable development can now be found in almost every quarter, and the buzzwords (participation, integration and the rest) are in common use. But an even bigger challenge remains – to put the principles into practice and to implement sustainable development. Here it is not a question of methodologies – there are sufficient tools already available and people who know how to use them. Rather, it means securing the political will, at all levels; bringing governments, the private sector and civil society together to work on creating the future we hope for; and building the skills and capacity to deliver this. Here lies the development agenda for the future.

## NOTES AND REFERENCES

1   WCED (1987) *Our Common Future*. Report of the World Commission on Environment and Development (The Brundtland Report), Oxford University Press, Oxford.

2   Holmberg J, S Bass and L Timberlake (1991) *Defending the Future: A Guide to Sustainable Development*, Earthscan, London.

3   Carew-Reid, J, R Prescott-Allen, S Bass and DB Dalal-Clayton (1994) *Strategies for National Sustainable Development: A Handbook for their Planning and Implementation*, IIED, London, and World Conservation Union (IUCN), Gland, in association with Earthscan, London.

4   Dalal-Clayton, DB (1996) *Getting to Grips with Green Plans: National Level Experience in Industrial Countries*, Earthscan, London. This study analysed strategic planning approaches in 21 case studies of strategic planning in 10 countries and in the European Union.

5   The lower-case letters are used here to indicate that the *nssd* is not a 'brand' but a generic approach to be interpreted locally.

6   OECD-DAC (1997) *Shaping the 21st Century*, Development Assistance Committee, Organisation for Economic Cooperation and Development, Paris.

7   The website (www.nssd.net) contains information about the project, all the key literature on strategies and related subjects, and all project documents and papers produced by the country teams. It is updated every two weeks and has enabled the all interested people to keep track of the project, to see and comment on draft documents as the evolve, and to make their own inputs.

8   OECD-DAC (2001) *Strategies for Sustainable Development: Practical Guidance for Development Cooperation*, DCD/DAC 9, 21 March. Development Cooperation Committee, Organisation for Economic Cooperation and Development, Paris.

9   Dalal-Clayton, DB and D Dent (1993) *Surveys, Plans and People: A Review of Land Resource Information and its Use in Developing Countries*, Environmental Planning Issues 2, IIED, London.

10  Dalal-Clayton, DB and D Dent (2001) *Knowledge of the Land*, Oxford University Press, Oxford.

11  Dalal-Clayton, DB, D Dent and R Dubois (2001) *Rural Planning in the Developing World with a Special Focus on Natural Resources: Lessons Learned and Potential Contributions to Sustainable Livelihoods: An Overview*. Environmental Planning Issues No.20, IIED, London.

12  Kauzeni, AS et al (1993) *Resource Assessment and Land Use Planning in Tanzania.*

13  Mwalyosi, R and R Hughes (1998) *The Performance of EIA in Tanzania: An Assessment*. Research Paper 41, Institute of Resource Assessment, University of Dar es Salaam, Tanzania, and Environmental Planning Issues 14, IIED, London;

14  Mwalysoi, R, R Hughes and D Howlett (1999) *Training Courses on EIA in Tanzania*. Three volumes: *1 Introductory Course; 2 Orientation Course; 3 Review and Quality Control Course*. IIED in association with Institute of Resource Assessment, University of Dar es Salaam, Tanzania

15  Kikula, IS, DB Dalal-Clayton, C Comoro and H Kiwasila (1999) *A Framework for District Planning in Tanzania*. Volume One. Report Prepared for the Ministry of Regional Administration and Local Government and UNDP. Institute of Resource Assessment, University of Dar es Salaam and IIED, London.

16  Dalal-Clayton, DB (1993) *Modified EIA and Indicators of Sustainability: First Steps Towards Sustainability Analysis,* Environmental Planning Issues 1, IIED, London.
17  Hughes, R, S Adnan and DB Dalal-Clayton (1994) *Floodplains or Flood Plans? A Critical Look at Approaches to Water Management In Bangladesh,* IIED, London and Research and Advisory Services, Dhaka.

*14*

# Profit in need? Business and
sustainable development

## *Nick Robins*

## SETTING THE COMPASS

Ours is a bewildering age. General Motors, one of the world's largest makers of automobiles – by far the most environmentally damaging and lethal of mass consumer products – is now signed up to the landmark CERES principles of environmentally responsible behaviour, and pledged to the pursuit of sustainable mobility. Royal Dutch Shell and BP, who provide much of the gasoline that powers the car – and together generate climate-changing emissions from their facilities and products equal to those from a large European nation – have also won plaudits for their commitment to sustainable development and renewable energy. The mining industry that processes so much of the materials for the car and carries such a painful legacy of human and environmental exploitation – from colonial Latin America through apartheid Africa to the present day – has commissioned IIED to broker a process of analysis and dialogue to show how the sector can be placed on a sustainable trajectory.

Is this all spin or do these steps show business really moving towards a more sustainable future? Certainly, when IIED was founded 30 years ago, many of the actions that these and other companies are now taking to reduce their environmental burden, become more accountable and deliver positive social benefits, would have been inconceivable. Even today it is often difficult to comprehend what the array of corporate activities – from charitable gestures through independent social audits to new sustainable services – cumulatively signify. This is not simply a problem of measuring impact, but one of fundamental meaning. For the economic, technological and social foundations on which sustainable development has been built up over the past three decades – and thus the role that the private sector should play in its achievement – have been shaken to their core. The Brundtland report of 1987 and the Earth Summit (of 1992) it inspired, essentially saw the state as the primary agent for achieving sustainable development, just as the wave of privatization, deregulation and fiscal retrenchment in both North and South, was overturning these assumptions. Globalization was not mentioned once in the texts of the Earth Summit agreements; Agenda 21 remains the longest unused shopping list in history.

As a result, many within the sustainable development establishment held decidedly naive views about business as the 1990s began, underestimating both its growing dominance and also its inherent weaknesses. Furthermore, the emergence of the knowledge economy and the consequent rise of service sectors such as finance and retail, meant that the equation of business with industry in discussions of sustainable development was increasingly anachronistic. Significantly, this shift from 'bulk to bytes' also meant that the inextricable link between growing output and environmental degradation could be broken, with spectacular results in some cases. That consumption was becoming steadily more resource-intensive at the same time was an unwelcome reality that most policy-makers and corporations chose to ignore.

Globally, the information revolution both enabled new areas of the South to benefit from trade liberalization and business outsourcing, while further marginalizing countries and continents dependent on commodities and unskilled labour. The rise of civil society, in part a result of a global process of democratization and in part a response to the inadequacies of both the market and the state to meet social and environmental needs, also challenged the managerialism that dominated so much of first-generation sustainable development. All in all, the apparent consensus reached at the Earth Summit masked a crunching of gears. The old statist approach was certainly passing away, and the UN Centre for Transnational Corporations, the archetypal institution of the fading 'New International Economic Order', was closed soon afterwards. A new win–win creed of eco-efficiency was born within the corporate elite, while environmental groups railed against 'greenwash' and the corporate co-option of the summit.

Ten years on, the world is perhaps wiser, though still more than a little confused on how business can be a positive force for environmental regeneration, social justice and quality of life. Despite the frequently cited success stories, scepticism remains the norm. Within business itself, many companies continue to exist in a state of denial – unaware, evasive or openly hostile to the changes that sustainable development requires. This situation should shock no one. Business is hardwired to generate profits for shareholders from satisfying consumer wants: it is simply not programmed to deliver the major public goods – clean water, social justice and accountable governance – that sustainable development implies. As Ray Anderson, the inspirational chief executive of US flooring company Interface, wrote in his eco-biography *Mid-Course Correction* in 1998, 'I am a plunderer of the earth and a legal thief [and] perverse tax laws, by failing to correct the errant market, are my accomplices'.[1]

The past decade has shown that companies do have a broad scope for introducing voluntary pro-sustainability actions – especially when prodded by investors, consumers and citizens. But the scope of their contribution ultimately depends on the prevailing frameworks for institutional behaviour and ethical action: global poverty and environmental unsustainability are system faults – and system solutions are what are needed. The world has learnt the hard way, however, that governments frequently do not have the skills, desire or ability to put these frameworks in place – often, of course, after heavy petting from the more Neanderthal reaches of the corporate sector. Getting progress thus means redefining anew the boundaries of responsibility for the state, the corporation and the citizen.

In society at large, the dissonance between the expanding rhetoric of 'corporate citizenship', accelerating environmental decline and widening global inequality, has become ever more noticeable. The resulting trust deficit has led both to a crisis for the gradualist gospel of sustainable development – based largely it seems on faith in voluntary business programmes – and a profound intellectual backlash against corporate globalization. Increasingly, it is no longer enough for companies simply to improve their performance on social and environmental matters. The issue is now corporate power and the structural place that business plays in the new global economy. The resistance to genetically modified organisms, for example, is as much driven by opposition to private sector dominance over biological resources as it is by precautionary concerns about potential health effects and ecological disruption. More broadly, the extension of the corporations' intellectual property rights through the World Trade Organization's TRIPS agreement is widely recognized as facilitating both the theft of biological knowledge from indigenous communities, and the removal of access to essential medicines for some of the world's poorest countries. From this underlying critique has come the protest movement that shook the bureaucratic niceties of global negotiations on trade, finance and the environment at Seattle, Prague and Genoa, forcing an increasingly public questioning of global capitalism and the role of business in the 21st century.

For a new generation of environmentalists and development practitioners, this wider corporate questioning has opened the space for new forms of social innovation, combining market dynamics with accountability and oversight. Particularly for those corporations where brand value constitutes a high proportion of their overall assets – Nestle, Nike, McDonald's, Shell – exposure of poor practices along the value chain can catalyse action to preserve reputation and consumer loyalty. In the first age of globalization during the 19th and 20th centuries, it was trade unions and their allies that led the way in seeking to regulate business access to employees and thereby humanize the workplace. In our own era, non-governmental organizations are emerging as crucial social gatekeepers, seeking to control corporate access to consumers and thereby produce a responsible marketplace.

Whether it is child labour or sustainable forestry, consumer campaigns, often using labelling and certification, have worked with the grain of the market and stimulated action of a speed and scale that would be unthinkable through traditional state regulation – often with troubling side effects. Out of these initiatives and a new appreciation of the dynamics of the post-industrial economy is emerging an embryonic 'business case' for corporate responsibility – with ethical investors at the vanguard. Anecdotes and analysis suggest that action that aligns corporations with the values and needs of their communities they affect reduces risks, improves efficiencies, stimulates new innovations and builds resilience. The question is now whether these initiatives are prefiguring new regimes for governing global corporations – or just trimming the excesses of the status quo.

If one were to look for signs of hope in the evidence of 1990s, the evidence would yield the growing numbers of corporate codes, management systems and programmes. But just like governments with their Local Agenda 21s, national policies and sustainability strategies, these preparative efforts have yet to result in a substantive shift in social and environmental outcomes. The array of creative market innovations is simply not breaking through the remorseless global trends that are leading, for example, towards further climatic disruption or intensified impoverishment in sub-Saharan Africa. While there can be undoubted enthusiasm about specific initiatives, the long-term prospects for the shift to sustainable patterns of production and consumption looks bleak: an outlook, perhaps, of tactical optimism and strategic despair. Any change in this picture is going to involve a rethink of business as a social, political and economic force. This poses special challenges for IIED as the Institute enters its early middle age with a growing body of experience at the tactical level of corporate change. To respond to the coming disjuncture facing the corporate sector if the world starts to get serious about sustainability, IIED's business agenda will need to become more strategically focused on how to reshape the corporation for a very different world.

## THE WOOING OF BUSINESS

Like many working in this arena over the past three decades, IIED's efforts to understand, advise and ultimately to influence business have often been hesitant and exploratory – necessarily making it up as it goes. From the outset, its founders and early business benefactors viewed IIED as a centre-ground institution: a place to challenge the extremes of conservationist thinking by taking a wider perspective on the imperative for global economic development. This positioning certainly opened up an important arena for independent analysis and debate. But it also left the Institute potentially vulnerable to charges from NGOs that it had 'sold out' to the corporate elite, and from companies that it was no more than a 'fifth column' for radical environmental and social demands – charges that would echo down the years. Yet, despite the sometimes significant financial donations from companies, the Institute's increasingly aid-focused programmes meant that it was not until the preparations for the Earth Summit that IIED began to grapple seriously with the corporate agenda.

The prompt came from a newly established business group that needed help to prepare its submission to Rio. As far-sighted leaders in the corporate world started to recognize that the groundswell behind sustainable development meant more than just additional pollution control devices, so they sought out a vehicle that could help craft a message both to inspire business to act in more sustainable ways in its own enlightened self-interest, and also help to deflect demands for new regulation and taxes. Encouraged by UNCED secretary-general (and IIED founder) Maurice Strong, the Business Council for Sustainable Development was formed to take on the task. Led by the charismatic Swiss billionaire, Stephan Schmidheiny, who had recently divested the family firm of its asbestos holdings, the BCSD aimed to break with the defensive traditions of the International Chamber of Commerce, the traditional lobby vehicle of global corporations. Established as a leadership group, the BCSD consisted of chief executives from 50 major multinationals – many of whom would be attacked at Rio by Greenpeace and others as some of the world's largest polluters. Connections and clout it had in abundance, but what the BCSD didn't have was content.

Looking back, it is sobering to reflect how few organizations there were only a decade ago that had a mature understanding of sustainable development, and IIED was clearly one of this handful. So in late 1990, IIED was commissioned to prepare a background document, setting out an agenda for the BCSD. So successful was this that IIED was even asked to write the Council's report to Rio. A 'palace coup', with the BCSD opposed to the idea of an NGO being so centrally involved, cut this short. But IIED's input into what became *Changing Course*[2] would remain central, if unacknowledged. Richard Sandbrook's strategic input was critical for driving the Council to address the agenda of Third World poverty that business had hitherto been uneasy discussing except in terms of corporate philanthropy. Lloyd Timberlake, with his background on the Brundtland secretariat and the *Only One Earth* series, ended up ghost-writing the final version when the coup plotters in the secretariat proved unable to deliver a coherent text. I prepared the report's case studies and its chapter on innovation, strategically quoting the then Du Pont chairman Edgar Woolard whose words held a potential probably unrealized by the speaker: 'in a sustainable economy world needs rather than existing product portfolios will determine which businesses we enter and which we leave'.

On reflection, this input from IIED could be one of the factors that explains much of the novelty of the *Changing Course* message. The report made clear that reaching sustainable development would require 'far-reaching shifts in corporate attitudes and new ways of doing business', including the assumption of greater corporate responsibilities to match new-won rights in the deregulating and privatizing global economy. The book also found a rare honesty that markets must 'give the right signals', with environmental costs reflected in the prices of goods and services. Beneath these and other signs of fresh thinking, the old verities of multinational business remained: open markets, free trade and economic growth – and it was, of course, around these that the growing movement to challenge corporate globalization focused, as it became clear that elegant exhortation was never going to guarantee responsible practice or get the prices right.

There was nothing hidden about IIED's next venture among the business tribe. Talking with Erling Lorentzen, a BCSD member and head of Brazilian papermaker Aracruz at the Earth Summit, Richard Sandbrook threw down the gauntlet: vision statements like *Changing Course* were important, but it was only through detailed sector assessments that the real opportunities, dilemmas and trade-offs inherent in sustainable development would be appreciated. With his company port blockaded by Greenpeace activists for a variety of alleged environmental and human rights abuses, and his key European markets increasingly affected by demands for increased recycled paper content, Lorentzen soon responded and rallied the world's paper industry behind the 'sustainable paper cycle project'. Essentially an exercise in strategic dialogue and analysis, the project broke new ground as the world's first 'full cycle global multi-stakeholder' study, assessing the social, economic and environmental issues from forest management through production to use and disposal.[3]

The project was always very much a study, with contact and consultation with companies, NGOs and governments focused on trying to enlighten the many areas of considerable disagreement – clear-cutting tropical forests, chlorine bleaching, insufficient recycling and waste – through detached analysis. Although many non-business voices were involved to ensure the independence of the results, the exercise was ultimately driven by the needs of the paper industry, which contributed the bulk of the project's funding. IIED buffered itself from charges of co-option by establishing an arms-length advisory group made up of experts from government, academia and industry, and ensuring that it had full rights to publish regardless of its sponsors' views. At the time, these conditions were as far as business would go – any further involvement (particularly of its more vocal critics in civil society) was anathema. But the narrowness of its governance base meant that there was little buy-in to the study's final results and much suspicion beside. The paper industry's own fragmentation and inability to organize globally – unlike the chemical sector – also meant that proposals for collective business initiatives fell on stony ground.

But these criticisms – easy with hindsight – should not obscure the achievements. A whole series of popular myths were busted – notably that fibre from tropical forests was a significant raw material for paper in the North. Truly innovative research from the University of East Anglia also exploded one of the industry's favourite claims that the paper cycle was carbon-neutral, pointing to methane leaching from landfills as a major greenhouse negative. Steve Bass's far-reaching work also helped to defuse some of the industry's initial unfounded hysteria against forest certification, a movement rising fast on the back of successful consumer campaigns against old-growth logging. By the end of the process, leaders of well-managed forest companies realized the obvious: certification would simply verify that they were well-managed.

Apart from the process lessons that the project would deliver for the governance of the subsequent mining, minerals and sustainable development initiative, the paper project also highlighted a range of sustainability dilemmas – icebergs that stand in the way of real progress across the development spectrum. Thus, how could the asset-stripping of forest resources be tamed in a world of open markets? How to challenge the apparently unstoppable technological trajectory for ever-larger, cleaner and jobless paper plants that were wholly inappropriate for the economic and livelihood needs of developing countries? But perhaps the largest and most immoveable of these icebergs was industry's deep reliance on the continuing growth in paper consumption as a source of rising profits. While many in the industry would grumble and groan, but eventually accept forest certification and zero chlorine bleaching, there was no room for considering 'communist' suggestions that paper itself should be used more efficiently and become more targeted at issues of real need. Out of the window went fashionable ideas of companies thriving by shifting from products to services, and focusing on customers' real needs rather than just selling more stuff.

The paper project generated a new profile for IIED as a serious player in the fast-expanding world of initiatives around business, corporate responsibility and sustainable development. Just as important, it also legitimized a whole series of initiatives within IIED tackling parts of this vast agenda. Work on forests was always furthest ahead, building on the paper project and its pioneering certification work to explore new areas such as how corporate–community partnerships could be made to work for the livelihoods of the poor, and how the tide of deregulation in forest policy could be tailored to support sustainable practices. Another issue of potentially immense leverage was to explore the design of new market frameworks that would encourage users to pay for the variety of non-market environmental services that forests provide (such as watershed protection). Research into the practical application of economic instruments was an equally important theme during the 1990s – taking cost-internalization out of academe and into industrial estates. In India, collaboration with the Confederation of Indian Industry and Tata Steel was the first project to model the impact of pollution charges on producers that involved business as a key stakeholder throughout the process.

For all its innovative analysis on business practice and market frameworks in the South, IIED was late to appreciate the seismic rumblings challenging the fundamentals of corporate globalization, which first became crystallized in David Korten's *When Corporations Rule the World*.[4] Strangely for an international policy institute focused on environment and development, IIED had played no part in the formation of the World Trade Organization (WTO), which provided the global constitution for the growth of corporate rights, not just in the obvious areas of trade, investment and intellectual property, but also indirectly, over environment and development policies. The scope for corporate enrichment was highlighted in the scandalous case brought by the USA against the EU's banana-import regime. Ramshackle and costly the regime certainly was, but it enabled a certain reciprocity between Europe and its former colonies in the Caribbean, highly dependent on the banana trade. Though the USA did not export a single banana to Europe, the chief executive of one of America's leading banana companies had contributed to President Clinton's election expenses, and so the muscle of the US trade negotiator was successfully deployed on behalf of this very private interest.

Against this backdrop, it was almost by accident that IIED started work on the implications of the trade and environment agenda for businesses in both North and South. In the run-up to the five-year review of the Earth Summit, IIED was invited by the secretariat of the UN's Commission for Sustainable Development to explore the scope for new trade opportunities for developing-country exporters of fairly traded and sustainable goods and services – essentially trying to discover whether there were any 'lollipops' for the South in the linkage between trade and sustainability. This was a time of great mistrust and suspicion. With bitter experience of the ability of the industrialized countries to manipulate trade rules to their advantage, the governments of the South were deeply opposed to any attempt to attach environmental or social conditions to their exports, seeing this as a new form of 'green protectionism'. Northern governments countered with essentially disingenuous claims about the potential win–win benefits of trade liberalization for environmental protection and social welfare, failing to recognize how the concentration of market power in the hands of Northern multinationals meant that very little value added returned to the South from its increasing export activities. The WTO had been the first major test for states to be true to their commitment to integrating environmental and social dimensions into economic policy-making, and the assembled governments of the world failed miserably.

This policy stalemate prompted a wave of independent initiatives that sought to introduce some degree of 'civil regulation' to the global marketplace. IIED tried to capture a flavour of these, countering the prevailing denigration of developing-country production standards by profiling pioneering entrepreneurs and communities, and so adding a range of new Southern case studies to the business and sustainability resource. The resulting report, *Unlocking Trade Opportunities*,[5] offered a fresh perspective – pointing to areas of new economic potential for the South, but also highlighting the structural conditions in terms of capacity building and market regulation that would enable these to materialize. Not only was the report one of the few bright spots at the generally dismal Rio+5 summit – no doubt helped along by free gifts of organic cotton T-shirts donated by Patagonia – but it also stimulated a new agenda for promoting sustainable patterns of trade. Careful work with producers on the ground has generated a powerful reform agenda and proposals for a Sustainable Trade Centre to support an equitable 'co-evolution' of standards along international supply chains.

## THE GREAT TRANSFORMATION

The fundamental place of business in a sustainable world is once again under the spotlight. The 1990s have demonstrated the capacity of business for generating innovative solutions, deploying human and technological resources to produce new partnerships and technologies. But this decade of experimentation has clearly not created the conditions for 'take-off' – the irreversible shift of private-sector activities so that they are driven by world needs, respect ecological limits, and are accountable to the communities they affect. IIED now has one of the more creative portfolios of private-sector initiatives – tackling the special challenges facing sectors such as agriculture, mining, forestry and tourism, and expanding the policy and management toolbox to include corporate–community partnerships and new markets for environmental services. Increasingly, the Institute is extending its scope from its primary focus in the developing world to global linkages along international supply chains and the changes required in the North itself.

The nature of the task for the years ahead is of a different kind – to help set the agenda for the transformation of business, as both economic actor and social force. As with the imperial globalization of the late 19th and early 20th centuries, so today's corporate globalization has ushered in a 'great transformation' of economic and social structures. What links these two very different eras of globalization is the unifying faith in the self-regulating market. Writing in London in the depths of World War II, the Austrian émigré Karl Polanyi traced the origins of the war to the crumbling of the pillars – notably, the balance-of-power system, free trade, the liberal state and the gold standard – that had supported the era of imperial globalization.[6] Polanyi's insight was to recognize that the self-adjusting market was a 'stark utopia', which could not exist for any length of time 'without annihilating the human and natural substance of society'.[7] In our own age, the movement for sustainable development is now confronting the same reality: that the global economy is simply not structured to deliver equity or the regeneration of the natural resource base, to ensure the accountability of market actors or the diversity of cultures.

As the capitalist euphoria of the early 1990s fades, as financial crisis extends from the 'emerging economies' of Asia and Latin America to the heartlands of Japan and the USA, and as public debate moves from demands for remedial adjustments to a deeper questioning of global capitalism, so the role for think-tanks such as IIED changes too. Taking a proactive stance does not come easily to many Anglo-Saxon think-tanks which see their independence as being equivalent to a position of neutrality between the contesting forces shaping the sustainable development agenda. Such coyness does not affect other organizations, such as Germany's Wuppertal Institut, which has maintained its integrity, but also driven the policy and business agenda – notably around the need for reductions in material use. For IIED, rethinking the fundamental unit of business – the corporation, and its institutional structures and dynamics – would be a creative place to start.

For, despite the mounting body of experience and analysis on the role of business in sustainable development, the capacity of the modern corporation to exist in its present form in a sustainable world has invariably been overlooked. So far, the sustainability movement has only scratched the surface of corporate change, focusing mostly on modifying particular practices, for example, through health and safety or environmental legislation. But beyond this, there are a further five dimensions along which the corporation may need to change to contribute fully to sustainable development: technology, governance, ownership, scale and purpose. These are briefly discussed below.

The sustainability imperative points to a number of areas where the use of core technologies will need to be radically reduced or phased out if ecological limits and equity are to be respected. Nuclear power, fossil energy generation and genetic modification are the three technologies most in the spotlight. To take an example, considerable pressure is now being placed on oil companies to shift towards renewable sources of energy. But as much as companies such as BP and Shell are doing to invest in new sources of energy, the shift away from fossil fuels is a collective endeavour that individual corporations on their own cannot achieve. For established but ecologically obsolete technologies, the challenge is therefore to organize a managed shift – perhaps learning from the experience with the post-Cold-War defence sector – to ensure that changes are used to inspire a positive boost for employment and dependent communities. Here IIED could collaborate with those sections of the labour movement representing workers in vulnerable sectors that have been developing strategies for a 'just transition'. For emerging technologies, the task is essentially preventive, encouraging governments to re-establish a capacity for foresight and technology assessment, but, unlike the corporatist efforts of the past, to integrate societal perspectives at the heart of the process, for example, through citizen juries.

Environmental and social pressure has brought much innovation to corporate governance in recent years. Companies have set up a range of formal and informal 'stakeholder dialogues'; a few have even appointed individuals with environmental or social expertise to the board of directors. But the exclusive rights of company directors to decide how sustainability should be managed within the firm remain essentially untouched. Again, there is much to learn from efforts to civilize the corporation in the wake of the first era of globalization – the two-tier management boards in German companies, for example – and how these might be adapted to recognize the interests of stakeholders in an ecological and social market economy. Although so far yielding little from a sustainability perspective, the UK's recent review of company law has shown that many of the answers to corporate responsibility lie in the hidden wiring of the corporation. The exclusive focus of companies on profit maximization on behalf of their shareholders is a related area that requires reassessment. Profit is a necessary goal to generate surplus for re-investment and to reward productivity gains. But sustainable development implies an expanded set of corporate objectives. Many companies are already finding that they need to express this extended mandate through individual mission statements: the task for a policy institute is to establish whether these individual codes of good intent need to be formalized through law and regulation.

In the first era of globalization, public ownership became a key lever for governments to regain control over strategic industries and unaccountable multinational corporations. Central to the new globalization has been the rejection of state property and the promotion of privatization as a critical lever for economic development. Public ownership certainly had many faults – most notably soft budget constraints, political interference and poor customer service. But that does not mean that the question of corporate ownership is now irrelevant for the sustainable development agenda. Experience with privatized utilities across the world suggests that while state ownership has its problems, so does private ownership.

In key areas of collective infrastructure – such as energy, transport and water – new corporate models are required that reflect the value of inherent public goods and social interests. In transport, Australia presents an interesting model, where ownership of the infrastructure remains in public hands, and the state leases its management and the operation of trains to private contractors – a model which the UK could learn from in the wake of the disastrous performance of Railtrack. For water and sanitation, inspiration can be found in Wales, where the privatized Welsh Water has been bought from its US owner by Glas Cymru, an independent, not-for-profit company, accountable to 50 members representing its stakeholders and financed by bonds not equity. As protests grow against the excesses of privatization, great scope exists for institutes such as IIED to contribute to this new generation of mutual ownership.

The issue of scale has long been dear to the 'green' movement, lying at the heart of Fritz Schumacher's manifesto against corporate gigantism, *Small is Beautiful*. But a critical view of the political, economic and social consequences of corporate concentration is also essential for an effective and responsive marketplace. One of the deepest frustrations with the impoverished economic theory supporting today's corporate globalization is the assumption of perfect competition at a time when market opening and privatization is leading to ever-greater agglomerations of corporate power. Assertive anti-trust policy was an essential ingredient in the taming of the corporate 'robber barons' during early 20th-century America, and the absence of a global trust-busting agency is one of the biggest holes in today's international institutional architecture. Without this, cocoa farmers will remain at the mercy of multi national traders and processors who retain the bulk of value-added and ensure that the assumed tendency to market equilibrium is distorted. Without effective competition, the negotiating position for developing countries in the face of rival multi national companies, for example, seeking access to oil, gas or minerals, will continue to decline, and with it the ability of their societies to benefit from the use of natural capital. As IIED identified for the paper industry, the current acceptance of increasing economies of scale generates a technological dynamic that ensures little effort is dedicated to developing decentralized production processes that could utilize the developing world's huge labour resources.

Yet for today's consumer capitalism, the sustainability agenda means more than simply restructuring institutional frameworks – it also demands a reassessment of fundamental corporate purpose. Making profit just one of a number of indicators of success is clearly important. But the wider challenge is to recognize the power of business as a social force – not just in terms of creating livelihoods, but shaping lifestyles also. For many on the development end of the sustainability spectrum, questioning the excesses of consumption has often appeared a relatively frivolous exercise compared with the urgent task of eliminating poverty. Globalization has changed all this, with the creation of increasingly common aspirations for material advancement throughout the world, stimulated by the spread of television and advertising. But it is blindingly obvious that these legitimate desires for a better life cannot be met at the current levels of resource use achieved in the post-industrial North: nine more worlds would be required.

Business does not just generate goods and services for sale – it also manufactures the dreams and desires that underpin them. Study after study shows that there is no consistent relationship between national or individual consumption levels and happiness – and yet business strategy remains fixated on encouraging consumers to spend ever more. It is therefore no surprise that corporate branding (remember: a term derived from singeing cattle flesh to mark owner-ship) has been at the forefront of recent consumer campaigns against the occupation of people's minds by commercial fantasies. Yet, for business, like government, questioning the ethical or environmental basis of consumption is simply not on the agenda – not 'up for negoti-ation' in the words of George Bush senior at Rio a decade ago. The 'grand dialogue' that philosopher Amitai Etizioni has called for on the links between affluence, social justice and personal fulfillment has yet to begin.

Here, the capacity of business for social innovation needs to be deployed to a different purpose than perpetuating the cycle of work and spend. Opportunities for green and ethical consumerism certainly exist, but remain limited by awareness and entitlements to a narrow elite. The real zone for business to exert its creativity is in the gener-ation of new lifestyles that rebalance the private, social and public spheres of consumption, curb the excesses of over-consumption among the global middle-class, and transform the material basis of consumption through far greater resource efficiencies. For IIED, this agenda would imply working more in its own backyard to generate a 'popular case' for sustainable development – and the new 'Race to the Top' project to benchmark the performance of Britain's supermarkets as a way of encouraging consumers to choose those supporting sustain-able agriculture and rural livelihoods is a potent example of this. Similar work is also vitally important to generate aspirational 'low-carbon lifestyles' to curb the growth in greenhouse gases from private consumption.

By the time IIED collects its ethically invested pension in 2031, these and other transformations yet to be conceived will need to have taken place if we are to have some hope of doing what is so frustrat-ingly possible, yet tantalizingly far away: create an economic culture that rewards enterprise in the service of people and planet, and which earns a modest profit from the needs of current generations and those yet to come.

# REFERENCES

1   The second edition (Donnelly, A, DB Dalal-Clayton and R Hughes (1998) *A Directory of Impact Assessment Guidelines*, IIED, London) contains over 800 bibliographic references and abstracts for more than 90 countries and 45 agencies. Also included are country status reports summarizing the legislative and administrative context within which the guidelines operate, and introductory chapters addressing areas of particular interest and current debate.

2   Anderson, Ray (1998) *Mid-Course Correction*, The Peregrinzilla Press, Atlanta.

3   Schmidheiny, Stephan / BCSD (1992) *Changing Course*, MIT Press, Cambridge.

4   IIED (Maryanne Grieg-Gran et al) (1996) *Towards a Sustainable Paper Cycle*, IIED, London.

5   Korten, David (1996) *When Corporations Rule the World*, Earthscan, London.

6   Robins, Nick and Sarah Roberts (1997) *Unlocking Trade Opportunities*, IIED, London.

7   Polanyi, Karl (1945) *The Origins of Our Time*, Gollancz.

# PART IV
## ENDPIECE

## 15

# Globalization, civil society and governance: Challenges for the 21st century

## *Anil Agarwal*

*Anil Agarwal, the Director of the Centre for Science and Environment in India, died on 2 January 2002. Anil had planned to contribute to this book – reflecting on the two years he spent at IIED, helping to develop its information and media service Earthscan, before returning to India to set up the Centre for Science and Environment in Delhi in 1981. He and his colleagues at the Centre set so many new standards. Their first* State of India's Environment: A Citizens' Report *in 1982 inspired many other national reports – yet this and the subsequent editions (including the 1999 two-volume edition) still remain among the best of all national assessments. Their fortnightly journal* Down to Earth *remains the essential journal for keeping in touch with environment and development concerns in Asia (and elsewhere). Their documentation of global environmental negotiations (for instance in the two seminal volumes,* Green Politics *in 1999 and* Poles Apart *in 2001) not only keep all those interested in these negotiations informed but also point to their weaknesses and inadequacies.*

*This text is included as a memorial to one of the world's most inspiring and innovative environment and development specialists. Its key themes – of the ways in which conventional development does little to support those suffering from ecological poverty, of the need for development solutions that strengthen and support civil society – are ones that have always been central to IIED's work. Anil helped to ensure that this was so. He also remained an active adviser and supporter of IIED's work, after his return to India. This text is drawn from a lecture he delivered at NORAD's Environmental Day held in Oslo on 15 December 1998, organized by NORAD and the Norwegian Forum for Environment and Development. Special thanks are due to Sunita Narain, his long-term co-author and colleague at the Centre for Science and Environment, for suggesting this text.*

## INTRODUCTION

It is impossible to talk of the 21st century without recognizing the backdrop of the phenomenon of globalization. The term 'globalization' is usually used to denote 'global economic integration', which despite all its problems, contradictions and criticism, now appears to be inevitable, built as it is on the backs of an irreversible 'technological globalization process' and an increasingly integrated global communications systems. This process will increase world trade and, hopefully, global wealth, too. But with global wealth, production and consumption growing, environmental problems created by one country will increasingly cross over national borders and affect the people, economies and ecologies of other countries. It is, therefore, inevitable that there will have to be a harmonization of global ecological laws. Since the mid-1980s, this process of 'global ecological integration' or 'global environmental governance' has, in fact, gained considerable strength and momentum, and numerous international environmental treaties have already been developed and many more are in the process of being developed.

Since economic concerns are often in conflict with ecological concerns. There is sufficient reason to argue that some form of 'global political integration' is also necessary to ensure that the global market works in the best interest of the public and that global regulations ensure that the market works for the global common good. But this is unlikely to happen in the near future. Nations will be extremely hesitant to hand over sovereignty, especially in a world in which military and economic power and, hence, political power is highly concentrated. The United Nations is likely to remain for a long time, as it is today, a Federation of nation-states, largely reflecting the agendas of different nations, and often veering towards the agendas of the more powerful nations. The 'global political integration' of the form represented by the United Nations suffers from the weakness that it is not built on principles of 'global democracy' which give equal political rights to all citizens on Earth.

While this, too, may become inevitable over time, it is clear that in the immediate decades of the 21st century the processes of global ecological and economic integration will proceed far faster than the process of global political integration. In such a political vacuum, it is absolutely vital to develop a key element of 'global democracy', namely a powerful global civil society which can ensure that the trade-offs between ecology and economy and between the interests of the empowered and the disempowered are decided within the full consciousness of a global debate, dialogue and mass awareness.

In the ongoing process of globalization, the processes of economic and ecological integration are already happening. However, without global political integration, we must develop and strengthen a global civil society. I see human society in the 21st century, at least in its early decades, grappling hard to strike a balance between two critical trade-offs: between economic development and marginalization; and between economic development and natural integrity.

Let us try and understand the implications of each of these two challenges.

## ECONOMIC DEVELOPMENT AND MARGINALIZATION

There is now ample evidence to show that the globalization process is going to bypass or neglect at least a billion people for several decades until they pick up the capacity to integrate themselves with national and global markets. The human condition, as far as these marginalized people are concerned, is, to say the least, abysmal. Lack of access to even basic necessities like safe drinking water, adequate food and health care means that almost a third of the people in the developing world have a life expectancy of just 40 years. As noted by Gus Speth (UNDP's former Administrator), 'For them, poverty is a denial of the most basic of all human rights: the Right to Life.'

The 21st-century human society will, therefore, have to address itself to the following critical question: do we forget these marginalized people until they learn to integrate themselves with the rest of the world, or do we do something for them meanwhile? Will the 21st century be marked by a world that remains compartmentalized between extremely rich and extremely poor people, or will it become a humane world in which nobody goes to bed hungry and nobody has to die young because of lack of basic needs?

This question is obviously as important a national concern for several nations on Earth as it should be of global concern. The neglect of the marginalized will clearly lead to mass distress and starvation, social violence and wars, and distress migration within and between nations. The 1980s and 1990s have seen these problems on a massive scale in several parts of the world. If we further recognize the fact that most of these marginalized people, especially the rural poor, live in highly degraded lands – in Africa, Central America, South Asia and China – then the emerging problem of global warming and the resulting climate instability will make life for the world's poor even harder in the decades to come. The answer to this problem is obvious: if the market cannot reach the marginalized, we must at least do something to help them to help themselves.

But first we will have to get rid of a lot of the mental cobwebs of the 20th century. Economic growth has dominated the human mind in the 20th century to an extent that everybody sees everything in the economic context. Economists, for instance, have come to see poverty almost exclusively in economic terms. But by the end of the century, this one-track mindset is starting to be questioned. The UNDP, for instance, with the help of some better thinking economists like Amartya Sen and Mahbub ul Haq has begun to argue that the per capita income cannot be used as the sole index of wealth or poverty. It has developed a Human Development/Deprivation index that factors in a number of other indicators to measure literacy, child health and other important concerns of human life. But even economists like Sen and ul Haq have failed to recognize the problem of 'ecological poverty' that affects most of the world's poor. It is these mental cobwebs that the 21st century will have to clear with great care and commitment.

'Ecological poverty' can be simply described as the lack of a healthy natural resource base that is needed for a human society's survival and development. The 20th century's economic and demographic transformations, including its colonial phase, has left nearly a billion people with a highly degraded resource base and, hence, high levels of 'ecological poverty' which today prohibits them from helping themselves to improve their economic condition. Healthy lands and ecosystems, when used sustainably, as they were for millennia, can provide all the wealth that is needed for healthy and dignified lives. The benchmark lifestyle need not be the one of modern New York or London which has come to dominate the minds of the intellectual leaders who today speak from the mounts of Oxford and Harvard, distant and cut off from large parts of the real world.

The 21st-century challenge lies in empowering and mobilizing the labour of the marginalized billion to get out of their ecological poverty, create natural wealth, and develop a robust local economy based on that natural wealth. It means that natural resource degradation must stop and natural resource regeneration must start. As soon as possible. Experience worldwide shows that natural resource regeneration and management demands community participation. Experience in India during the 1970s and 1980s has repeatedly shown outstanding economic change in rural communities wherever they have organized themselves to regenerate and manage their resource base. There has been nothing more heartening in the entire world in the last two decades of the environmental movement than the transformation that these communities have been able to achieve. On the other hand, bureaucratic resource management systems have invariably failed or have been totally cost-ineffective, which makes them irrelevant in the world of the poor where financial resources are limited.

This means that good governance, built on people's empowerment to deal with the problem of ecological poverty, is going to be critical for addressing the problem of economic development and marginalization in the 21st century. Civil society can help to push this process by doing a number of things. I will draw attention to the following four which I consider to be most important.

Firstly, civil society must spread and share knowledge that inspires people to act. The way the world's knowledge and communications systems are organized, dominated by the Western–urban–upper-class mindset, means that they will inevitably marginalize the best efforts because no attention is being paid to them. These systems will notice a change only when it reaches a large scale and impact. They will totally disregard many, many other smaller struggles to change. It is wrong to think that the poor and marginalized are not trying hard and struggling to change their fate. They are, every day. It is just that we are not prepared to notice. This is a problem that is not merely restricted to the knowledge–communications systems of the developed world. The 20th-century knowledge–communications systems of the developing world have disregarded the struggles of the marginalized with as much impunity, if not more. This 'mental poverty' is, in fact, at the heart of the problem, and must be addressed if ecological poverty is to be challenged.

Second, civil society must argue for appropriate global and national policies that help the marginalized to help themselves. Third, civil society should work with disempowered communities to develop and demonstrate participatory natural resource regeneration. Fourth, civil society must teach (I would rather use the word 'force') all those who are today 'empowered' with modern knowledge to respect the poor, their own survival strategies, technologies and management systems.

There will be more answers available in this disempowered 'knowledge base' of the poor for addressing the problem of marginalization than there will be in the empowered 'knowledge base' of the 20th-century paradigm. Though, of course, this does not mean that the latter cannot make a useful contribution to the economic growth of the marginalized. In sum, I would say that there is absolutely no reason why anybody should go hungry. But if that problem has to be addressed, the 21st century will have to deal with the 'mental poverty' created by 20th-century governance and knowledge systems before it can start reducing 'ecological poverty' which marks the lives of the world's poor and prevents them from creating economic wealth.

## ECONOMIC DEVELOPMENT AND NATURAL INTEGRITY

It is the fervent hope of governments today that globalization will create economic wealth. Let us hope that that is indeed what will happen and that this economic wealth will touch even those who have not yet reached the living standards of Western populations. But few people realize that the Western economic model, built on highly energy- and material-intensive technologies, has proved to be an extremely 'toxic model'. The postwar economic boom immediately landed cities from Tokyo to Los Angeles into devastating air pollution problems even as all aquatic systems began to be poisoned to death. Having learnt from this mistake, Western societies have conducted themselves with much greater discipline with respect to the environment and have also invested substantially in relatively environment-friendly technologies. Even then, the battle is far from won. Huge amounts of toxins still enter the global ecosystem as a result of economic processes, and the disruption of the global carbon and nitrogen cycles still continues to throw a pall over humanity's future.

As Western-style economic growth takes into its sweep more and more masses of humanity, it becomes important to ask: what will this do to the integrity of the world's natural ecosystems? The answer looks frightening. The processes of wealth generation will clearly put increasing pressure on natural ecosystems and generate huge amounts of pollution. During the 1970s and 1980s, Southeast and East Asia grew at a rate unprecedented in human history. Today, this region is also the most polluted on Earth. Literally every city is gasping for air – from Taipei to Delhi. 'Hydrocide' – that is, murder of aquatic systems – is widespread across the region. In India, innumerable small streams have today been reduced to toxic drains.

Very few people understand the speed with which Western-style economic growth brings pollution. In 1986, when Prime Minister Rajiv Gandhi had asked me to address his Council of Ministers on the environmental challenges facing the nation, I had advised the country's leaders that rural environmental problems – because they affect many millions of poor people – are far more important than urban environmental problems. Ten years later I realized my mistake. I had no clue about the speed with which the pollution problems would grow and Delhi, my home, would rapidly turn into a toxic hell. Studies carried out by the World Bank now tell us that when the economy (GDP) of Thailand doubled during the 1980s, its total load of pollutants increased an amazing tenfold. A study conducted by the Centre for Science and Environment for India shows that when the Indian economy doubled in the recent past, its industrial pollution load went up by four times and the vehicular pollution load by eight times.

These are very disturbing figures. What happens to the pollution load when the rest of the developing world – from South Asia to South America – begins to emulate the economic growth of Southeast and East Asia? The whole world may find itself being poisoned to death – just as the hapless Eskimos are today suffering from unbelievably high levels of PCBs, DDT and other persistent organochlorines produced and used by the rest of the world but which the Eskimos have never touched. The spread of chemical wastes that are endocrine disrupters through the global ecosystem, and global sperm-count decline, have emerged as deeply disturbing and as yet poorly understood global problems.

The prospects appear frightening indeed, but it is my firm belief that any problem facing humanity can be resolved. However, we need to ask: if the West has realized that economic growth brings heavy pollution, then why have industrializing countries like India, China, Thailand or Indonesia not also learnt that lesson? The scale of pollution in Asia is clear evidence of the fact that they have not done so. I would highlight four reasons why inadequate attention is paid to pollution in the industrializing nations.

First, the economic and demographic transformations that the rapidly industrializing developing countries are going through are unprecedented in human history. In terms of scale and speed, the Western experience is almost irrelevant and, thus, offers very few prescriptions even though there is a huge global knowledge industry which makes a living – or rather a killing – doing so. The speed with which urbanization, industrialization, agricultural modernization and population growth are taking place in and around cities like Delhi or Bangkok makes the management of a city like London or Paris look like a puny intellectual task. It is not surprising that national leaders across the developing world are failing to address the problem.

Second, the economic transformation is rapidly bringing large numbers of poor people into Western-style consumption patterns and lifestyles. This poses an additional problem. The urban poor and the lower-middle-class constitute a highly price-sensitive segment of the emerging market. This group wants Western lifestyles but it is able to invest only in cheap technologies. The extraordinary growth of two-wheeled vehicles in the Asian urban market, built upon the discarded and heavily polluting but cheap two-stroke engine, is a fine example of this phenomenon. In an electoral democracy, very few politicians will go against the desires of this segment of the electorate, which is extremely powerful because of its numbers and growing economic power. But this means that the economic transformation will remain dependent on polluting and environment-unfriendly technologies for a long time, and few political leaders will be able to do much about it.

Third, the political mindset will also tend to disregard these concerns because of its exclusive focus on economic development, which is only to be expected when a poor nation begins to grow economically. Why would anyone want to disturb a dream, especially when it is just coming true?

Lastly, given global economic integration, a nation's economic managers will also tend to focus on macro-economic concerns – issues like balanced budgets, trade balances and rates of foreign direct investment – rather than micro-economic concerns, which incorporate most environmental and quality-of-life issues. It is easy for an economic manager to say. 'Well, if the micro-economics has to suffer while I am dealing with my macro-economics, then so be it.'

It is clear that all these trends and tendencies will continue to dominate until there is mass consciousness of the threats that this is posing to public health and to long-term survival.

## THE NATURE OF THE FUTURE STATE

The biggest challenge of the 21st century will be the creation of a governance system able to deal with the two trade-offs outlined above. If this is indeed going to happen, then the nature of the state that emerged in the 20th century will have to change considerably, and it is heartening to note that indeed the world's governance systems are undergoing considerable transformation.

By the last decade of the 20th century, highly statist governance systems had either already disappeared or were rapidly changing. The current paradigm is a state built on electoral democracy and competitive markets. But this paradigm is inadequate to deal with the problems of the 21st century. If the two tensions that have been identified above are to be resolved adequately, the world's governance systems will have to change even further.

In the years to come, the nation-state will come under growing pressure from two different directions. One will be economic and ecological globalization, and the other will be natural resource management, environmental conservation and protection of quality of life. In order to deal with the first, the nation-state will increasingly have to give greater space to global governance systems – the World Trade Organization and global environmental treaties, for instance. To deal with the second, it will have to give greater space to local governance systems in which local democratic institutions are intensely involved in village and town governance. It is in this transformation of the governance systems that I see greater hope for those trade-offs to be adequately and consistently resolved, as required to ensure that global economic development does not leave a lot of people marginalized and uncared for, with irreversible damage to natural ecosystems.

## The role of civil society

A powerful civil society can play a very important role in smoothing transition in the governance systems of the world's nations. In the industrialized world, civil society has helped to ensure that governance systems pay attention to the effects of economic development on natural integrity. The emergence of the strong environmental movement in the 1960s and 1970s in Europe and North America showed that electoral democracy alone was not adequate to bring about the desired political responses to deal with environmental concerns. In other words, 'representative democracy' was not enough. The environmental movement challenged the idea that elected representatives, once elected, could do as they wished on behalf of the nation.

The environmental movement forced Western electoral democracies to make governance much more participatory, and indeed there has been a remarkable growth of the civil society in the West involved with environmental concerns – with innumerable citizens' groups forcing their leaders to make better trade-offs between environment and economic development. These groups today work at local, national, regional and global levels. Greenpeace is an environmental group started only in the 1970s but has today become a such a multinational behemoth that it is often jokingly pointed out that the sun never sets on the Greenpeace empire.

While civil society is quite strong in the Western world, it is only just beginning to grow in much of the developing world, especially now that electoral democracy is being embraced as a principle of governance by more and more nations. Civil society has become strong in some Southern countries. India, for instance, has a long tradition and history of citizens' groups, encouraged not least during the Freedom Movement by Mahatma Gandhi. Where civil society is relatively well-developed in the South, it has exhibited special strengths particularly in critiquing government policies and development plans, and in opposing development projects.

But even in these nations of the South, civil society remains weak in two important areas: analysing scientific and technical issues, crucial in the context of the assault that economic growth will make on natural ecosystems; and, in making policy interventions. Over time, if civil society is able only to oppose projects, and not to get policies changed appropriately, it stands the risk of discrediting and marginalizing itself.

Furthermore, the role of Southern civil society in terms of its engagement with emerging global economic and environmental governance still remains extremely marginal. As a result, many Southern environmental concerns, such as land degradation and desertification, the environmental rights and needs of the poor, are getting neglected in the global environmental agenda. Western environmental groups try to represent the interests of all humanity but remain caught in a highly conservationist agenda, which should not be surprising given the economic levels of the Western world. Even on a major environmental issue like climate change, there has been extremely limited intervention from Southern civil society. The concern about equitable sharing of the atmospheric space has been widely held but the ability of Southern groups to make effective interventions in the negotiating process has been extremely limited. As is inherent in the existing situation, national support for civil society remains low, and Southern environmental groups are not able to raise adequate resources domestically for these high-cost interventions. On the other hand, few Western donors provide resources on a sustained basis for such efforts.

It is important to recognize that in the emerging situation described above, if civil society is not strong, governments will be influenced more by the powerful special-interest groups, especially economic interest groups, and this influence will become ever stronger with further economic growth. It is not surprising that negotiations in the World Trade Organization have today become far more important than the negotiations for global environmental conservation, and, of course, there are no negotiations going on or even foreseen to deal with the problem of global marginalization.

## The role of small countries and NGOs

What role can small countries such as Norway, Sweden, Denmark or The Netherlands play in bringing a mega-global process into balance? An important one, I believe. Each small country has a small amount of money to influence the global process, and should use it for the maximum catalytic effect. Here are my suggestions on how to do this.

First, use aid funds for maximum political effectiveness in order to improve the governance systems of the globe and of the nations of the world. It sounds preposterous to ask a Western nation to intervene politically in the affairs of the nations of the world. But in a much more globalized world, it will not be as preposterous. Norwegians, like many Westerners, often love to point out that they don't want to impose economic development plans and programmes on developing countries through their development assistance programmes. But this is neither correct nor is there any need to be polite. In every possible way, from knowledge to technology, the West is determining and influencing the economic development of the South. A country like Norway should be frank and forthright and use its development assistance to bring about greater political democratization – at both national and global levels. Also, being a small nation,

Norway is not threatening and its role will be much more acceptable than say that of the more powerful nations like the USA or the UK, whose leaderships have often shown a lack of vision by trying to shape the world exclusively in their favour.

Within the international community, therefore, the smaller European nations should act like NGOs. In 1987, when Mrs Gro Harlem Brundtland, came to Delhi to present *Our Common Future* to the Indian government and NGOs, I had the privilege to co-chair the NGO segment of the proceedings with her. I welcomed Mrs Brundtland not as the Prime Minister of Norway but as the leader of one of the world's largest NGOs. This is because small countries like Norway, Sweden, Denmark and The Netherlands have often supported concerns of equity and sustainability far more than the economically more powerful nations. These countries must continue to play this role.

Small countries such as Norway should have specific programmes to support and strengthen the civil society of the South to improve national governance, and to participate in the development of global ecological and economic governance systems. Small donor countries should also fight for the creation of a global fund to empower the globally marginalized to deal with their 'ecological poverty'.

It might be useful for Norway, Denmark, Sweden and The Netherlands to study the role they have already played in the development of the civil society in the South. In the late 1970s, there was still very little acceptance of the role of civil society in determining development and governance. Around that time, I established the Centre for Science and Environment in New Delhi. Some of the earliest voices in India that I could hear then which were emphasizing the role of NGOs were coming from UN agencies. Within the UN, there was growing pressure from the smaller Western nations to open up the system to NGOs. I remember a senior Indian UN official telling me at that time, 'I can't understand these Dutch and Scandinavians. They keep telling us to involve NGOs all the time, almost as if governments are not important.' In the mid-1980s, it was Prime Minister Rajiv Gandhi who tried to open up the government to NGOs for the first time.

There has been a sea change in bureaucratic responses to NGOs since those days. The steady opening up of the UN system and the multilateral development banks to NGOs, including Southern NGOs, however limited their global role may be as yet, has also forced national governments into dialogue with their own civil society. The small Western democracies should continue to play this role as aggressively as possible.

# Index of people

Adams, Kath 41
Agarwal, Anil xiv, 45, 46, 143
Aina, Tade Akin 130
Almedal, Calle 55
Anderson, Robert xiii, 15, 19, 26, 32, 37, 38, 67, 71
Anzorena, Jorge 143
Ardila, Patricia 56
Arensberg, Walter 33
Arrossi, Silvina 142
Aspden, Liz x
Austin, John 41, 45
Aylward, Bruce 185

Ba, Awa 157
Barbier, Ed 70, 85, 114, 147, 173
Barbier, Joanne 173
Barnard, Geoff 56, 102, 147
Barnes, Jim 64
Bartlett, Sheridan 140
Bass, Steve 72, 85
Beddington, John 33, 41
Bicknell, Jane 142
Bie, Stein 159
Bijlmer, Joep 143
Bird, Roland 16
Bíró, Andras 53
Bishop, Josh 72, 185
Bjonness, Mie 149
Blitzer, Silvia 142
Boonyabancha, Somsook 143
Botero, Rodrigo 21
Brook, Karen 166
Brower, David 68
Brundtland, Gro Harlem 35, 66, 182, 234

Budelman, Arnold 162
Buren, Ariane van 98, 100
Burgess, Joanne 173, 184
Burgess, Peter 84
Burns, David 79

Cabannes, Yves 129
Cairncross, Sandy 130
Cameron, James 89
Carlile, Liz 56
Carmichael, Bill 53
Carter, Jimmy 98
Cattley-Carlson, Maggie 56
Caufield, Catherine 64
Chambers, Robert 111, 118, 153
Chauhan, Sumi 45
Chauveau, Jean-Pierre 162
Cheney, Barbara 45
Chirac, Jacques 163
Clark, William xiv, 12, 31, 32, 47, 66
Cockerell, Mike 68
Collins, Michael 185
Condamines, Charles 57
Conway, Gordon 33, 66, 183
Corea, Gamani 21, 22
Coulibaly, N'Golo 166
Craig, Ian 109
Craw, Jacquie 46
Critchley, Will 154
Cross, Nigel 56, 57

Dalal-Clayton, Barry 68, 198
Davila, Julio 142
de Lattre, Anne 159
de Silva, Don 46

Deane, James 52, 57
Defoer, Toon 162
Delville, Philippe Lavigne 162
Dembele, Babou 151
Desai, Nitin 67
Dewees, Peter 103
Diallo, Moulaye 159
Diallo, Sonja 157
Donovan, Deanna 81
Dubois, Olivier 15, 23, 24, 89
Dubos, René viii, 13, 23, 24, 126

Eckholm, Erik 46
Edwards, Mark 46
Etizioni, Amitai 218
Evans, Adrian 57
Evans, Julian 85

Falkener, Hugh 71
Fall, Marième 157
Foley, Gerald xvii, 45, 98, 100, 102
Foreman, Martin 56
Fuller, Buckminster 128

Gandhi, Indira 25
Gandhi, Rajiv 229
Ganjapan, Laxmi 109
Geldof, Bob 36, 67
Giessen, Ronald van der 79, 83
Goodland, Bob 35
Grant, Jim 56
Guèye, Bara 155
Gypmantasiri, Phrek 109

Haines, Ian 158
Hanna, Jill 68
Hanssen, Halle Jørn 54
Haq, Mahbub ul 21, 22, 226
Hardoy, Ana 142
Hardoy, Jorge 32, 33, 41, 66, 126,
    127, 132, 140, 142
Harrison, Paul 34
Hart, Roger 140
Hasan, Arif 143
Havelange, Francoise 57

Herzer, Hilda 142
Hesse, Ced 153
Hilhorst, Thea 162
Hinrichsen, Don 33, 35
Holdgate, Martin 90
Holmberg, Johan 54, 114, 157,
    184, 190
Horovitz, Richard 54
Howard, Bill 88
Hudson, John 88

Iglesias, Enrique 21

Jackson, Baroness *see* Ward, Barbara
Jackson, Robert 13
Jenden, Penny 36
Johnson, Brian 41, 64
Juma, Calestous 152

Kaimowitz, David 94
Kent, Tom 20
Kikula, Idris 197
Kimball, Lee 33
Kirkley, Leslie 31
Kotey, Nii-Ashie 87
Kummerfeld, Beth 56

Lamb, Rob 46
Lane, Charles 148, 149, 152
Leach, Gerry 33, 41, 66, 150
Leger, Ron 132, 143
Lembesis, Steve 54
Levy, Caren 140
Lewis, Christopher 98
Lieberherr, Francoise 143
Loevinsohn, Michael 114
Longbottom, Judy 165
Lorentze, Erling 93
Lorentzen, Erling 72, 210
Lovins, Amory 99

MacNeill, Jim 35, 65
Macrory, Richard 108
MacTaggert, David 60
Mahler, With Halfdan 56

had we opted for a soils convention instead of the CCD, an option which some are still pushing for. Many governments North and South share a global concern for addressing poverty, debt relief and HIV/AIDS, and creating more equitable trading systems. But these issues are being tackled elsewhere. Hence, the seats at the CCD are emptying fast with the audience moving to more attractive and up-to-date shows in town.

It has become clear that the future of drylands depends not just on drylands but on what happens elsewhere. Take West Africa, for example. The life chances of a Sahelian household hang upon the travails and successes of their migrant brothers and sisters, whether in the plantations of Côte d'Ivoire, selling CDs in the shadow of the Eiffel tower in Paris, or getting an education and a job in government or an NGO. It also depends on West African professionals arguing their case within the global institutions which set policy on financial flows, markets, prices, patents and trade. The Club du Sahel[13] and Comité Inter-Etat de Lutte contre la Secheresse au Sahel have clearly demonstrated the need to widen perspectives away from a narrow eye on the Sahel and broaden the vision to take in the West Africa region, and wider world of global opportunities. With more Cap Verdiens in New York than on the islands themselves, this is a perspective which marries more neatly with what local people themselves assess as their chances of making a decent livelihood.

## Soils hit the global agenda

The notoriously unglamorous world of soils suddenly became hot property in the mid-1990s. The World Bank launched its soil fertility initiative, and a rock-phosphate programme was developed by the International Fertilizer Development Center, International Centre for Research in Agroforestry and others. Ian Scoones and I had developed a proposal for work to examine how farmers actually manage the fertility of their land, and the importance of diversity between farmers, locations, and different kinds of fields and crops. This built neatly on Ian's work in Zimbabwe and Ethiopia, and on my interest from Mali fieldwork days in the negotiations between farmers and herders to exchange access to water for dung, the essential ingredient for a good harvest.[14] We were concerned to find some middle ground between the gung-ho approach of the chemical fertilizer brigade ('what we need is aerial spraying of rock phosphate across Africa') and the low-input, organic school who seemed to believe in the moral